Terence Beckett born 1944 in the historic Border
City of Carlisle, this is the authors second
book, this time covering his upbringing on the Botcherby
Estate during the forties, fifties and sixties.
Having previously worked as a scriptwriter
for the Dundee publisher, D C Thompson & Co.
He is married to Renee, with three children,
eight Grandchildren and one Great Grandson.
Now retired he enjoys writing poetry and verse.
A third tome is in production
hoping to be published in 2012.

"The Cannibal Mouse."

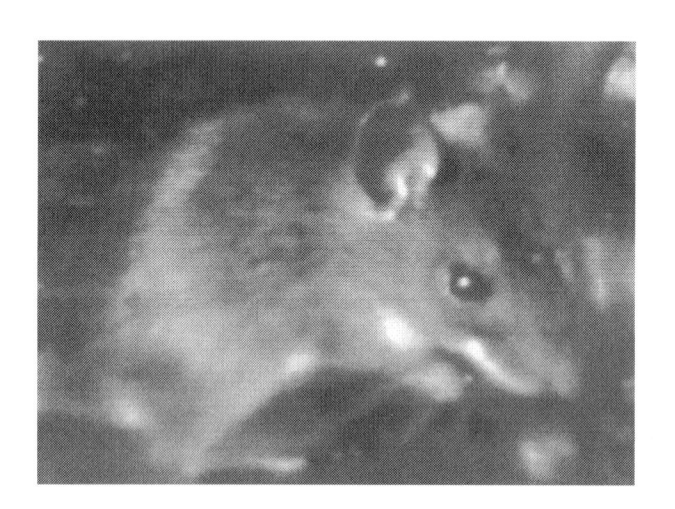

by
Terence Ted Beckett

Published by Terence Beckett 2011

Additional editing by Renee Beckett.

" Like riding a roller coaster."
Margaret Forster.

" Smacks of the authentic."
Melvyn Bragg

£ 8.99.

Copyright © 2010 Terence Beckett.
All rights reserved
ISBN 978-1-4709-5200-6

Contents.

Page 7. Luguvalium, an introduction.
      10. You can take the boy out of Botcherby. But!
      29. The Cannibal mouse of Norman St School.
      37. Have a drag, Go on, you'll enjoy it.
      41. Hooray, the Gasman's here.
      45. The Great Stanley Matthews affair.
      53. Look out, the Gypsy's are coming.
      57. Three rivers to cross.
      62. Dads flying Gnashers.
      70. Speech therapy ! Yea, Right.
      75. Apple blossom times.
      81. Working class hero's.
      87. Get some coal in mother.
      90. On the beach, Silloth , Glorious Silloth
      96. Moss side to Dracula's lair.
   106. Dining car capers.
   112. The Dreaded Garlands.
   118. In the shadow of Ben Braggie.
   122. King of Takama.
   135. Cocoa warriors.
   144. Bookies Bagman.
   148. Horses for courses.

Page 152. Four Joe's.
　　　158 Camp Botcherby.
　　　162. Harraby Sec Mod. (School roll, 1957-1958,　　Inc Staff.)
　　　191. Holy Moses supposes.
　　　196. Dance hall days.
　　　204. Campsite Passion. (AKA Dream on.)
　　　206. Smiles on the Golden mile.
　　　213. The Life Boys.
　　　217. Talent show Time.
　　　220. Grandmas mangle.
　　　226. Life's darkest day.
　　　230. Birthday Balloon.
　　　231. Beckfoot paradise.
　　　233. The day I met Melvyn Bragg.
　　　241. I had a dream.
　　　244. Easter, and here comes the Tally man.
　　　248. More super Hero's.
　　　253. Rose Castle Days.
　　　261. Wedding Bells over Eden.
　　　268. Botcherby Refreshed.
　　　272. WyWurry.
　　　273 The End. (For now.)

Dedicated to the memory of Philip James Beckett.
27/05/1967 to 29/06/2004.

Also by Terence Ted Beckett.

"Broken Stones"
A jumble of Verse and essays commenting on
Life's highs and low's,
Tragedy and Joy.
ISBN 978-1-4709-5222-8

All the names mentioned in this book have been taken from what is believed by me to be a reliable source and, every effort as been taken to ensure there correct spelling.

1   LUGUVALIUM. AN INTRODUCTION.

There has apparently been a settlement or community of sorts in the place we now call Carlisle, The Border City, virtually ever since man settled these Islands, surviving Ice age, Fire Famine and Flood. Much sought after, much fought after the fertile Solway plains resources back then made it a good place to be. Fine grass lands for grazing Sheep and Cattle, loam soils for the producing of crops and the seas bounty to boot. Well nothing has changed, it is still a great place to be. Still producing high quality breeds of sheep and cattle, Dairy and Beef, with crop production second to none. We have had our share of troubles but have always bounced back, what with Romans building forts and walls all over the place, blue faced Pict's flashing what was under their kilts, Vikings nicking our cows horns to put on there helmets, Scottish Pretenders, though I must say Bonnie Prince Charlie was a bit of a lad, then Oliver's Army, the Roundheads that is, not the song. The dreaded Reiver's helping themselves to what was left, talk about the Debatable lands, they were all at it. To see them now you would not think butter would melt in their mouths with their cute tourist attracting tartan clad Scots Border towns, traditions like riding the marches, and tossing the Caber, Just do not turn your back or they will be over here in their hoards nicking all they can carry. We have had it all thrown this way.
However, King Edward 1,old long shanks himself, liked it so much he even considered making it his capital City, it being nice and handy to pop over the Border and hammer the Scots, he did not seem to like them an awful lot. I expect the feeling was mutual. Unfortunately the marsh around Brugh by Sands where he made his final camp on the Solway Coast saw him off poor lad, in August 1307, all those bugs, flies and mysterious diseases, so that

did not happen. Shame really, would have been nice to see Queen Liz and Phil the Greek shopping down Botchergate on a Saturday, popping into one of the many charity shops for a second hand tiara or two, or in the Royal box at Brunton park, in their deckchair shirts cheering on the blues.
" One does support the lads, don't you know." chants our Liz. Phil abusing the referee. " Get yourself off to Specsaver's, you blind git, my wife and I think that was off side, don't you know." then turning to the club chairman." I don't understand that off side rule, its all Greek to me."

History recalls Botcherby first appearing in the records in the year eleven seventy, having missed being mentioned in the Doomsday book due to Carlisle being in the hands of our neighbours the Scots at the time of its creation, though we then were known by the name of "Bocharby". Due to this land being granted by William the second to a mercenary Flemish Gadgee Called Bocharby, in return for services rendered, no doubt numerous heads were separated from their bodies and much blood spilt to gain such favour. In return he was given the task of building a Castle , not the one we have now, to keep out the Scots and repopulate the area with English, only a partial success then, they are still here, I should know I married a Scotsman's daughter, and believe me what they say is true, as you will read in " Wedding bells over Eden."

Botcherby only became a part of the City Of Carlisle as late as nineteen twelve, the year my dad was born. (you will notice as we go on rather a lot of things occurred in this momentous year.)
At this time Botcherby was still very much a rural village surrounded by Farms, green fields and well stocked rivers, now of

course it has been absorbed into the City proper, with no less than four housing estates, two still partially council owned and two private. It still retains its Community spirit as you will see.

Still if its relative peace and quite you seek with easy access to both mountains and lakes, or a quick getaway to the Motorway north or south that floats your boat, this is the place to be…not that we are in any hurry to see the back of you, no no stay and spend your cash in the lakes villages or in the seaside resort's of Silloth and Allonby, then you can go, but mind you come back and see us.

Welcome to Luguvalium, the Border City, my City.

My home sweet home.

2   YOU CAN TAKE THE BOY OUT OF BOTCHERBY, BUT !

According to my Mam, the ever lovely Sally Gallefor, who should know because she was there, there being the front parlour room of number 235 Blackwell road, in Currock, I was born on a wet April afternoon, about four o'clock, it was a Thursday, the 20th day of an otherwise pleasantly sunny month. Trust me to bring the rain.
I was the second of eventually five children, the eldest and youngest being girls, Brenda Ann, Susan Jennifer, and Veronica Sandra, with my brother Brian John making up the numbers. Now for some reason my Mam could never quite explain my four siblings all had two names to my one. Whenever I queried this all I got was , "Well I liked the name Terence, could not really think of a second name to go with Terence, so you are stuck with it Terence!" I would like to think she wanted to bestow upon me the writing talents of a Terence Rattigan, or the good looks of a leading man, actor Terence Morgan, Thanks Mam, but so far it has not worked out that way. More like Terence the tractor if anything. Apparently the name Terence means Poet, so that's not too bad ,

better than being a slaughterer of innocents or son of the Devil, but only just. Apart from that there was nothing particularly significant about the day of my birth, other than I shared the date with Adolph Hitler, who still had a year of his nightmare reign to go, and Genghis Khan, nice man. Not that we were in anyway alike you understand, they had a taste for Invading other countries and destroying peoples lives where as I preferred a nice bit of cake, well, a lot of cake really which is why I was a little fat boy, and they were not, plus Hitler had a moustache, a really silly one, whereas I did not, otherwise not a lot between us really I suppose, depends on your point of view.

Currock then, or at least the bit I knew, being the aforementioned 235 Blackwell road, Grandma's house, more of which later, and 20 Ridley road, auntie Annie's home, the area boasted its fair share of amenities, all denominations catered for, C of E, Methodists and of course Catholics, with the mighty Father Begley, who struck terror into my Grandma and Aunties, causing my Granddad and Uncles to do a disappearing act when ever he seemed to be heading in their direction. With at least two Grocers, a chippie, Gents Barber, a Butchers and Chemist with later a bookies and ladies hairdresser. Now you have the choice of a Indian takeaway or a Chinese takeaway, all the others long disappeared.

I must have known it was going downhill so I up sticks and moved to the splendour of number 33 Botcherby Avenue at the tender age of two, carried all the way on my dads shoulders like a king surveying his realm. Travelling past Hammonds Pond, then by way of Lady Guildfords, through what we now refer to as old Harraby, up Durranhill road, still bounded by woods and green fields, no fields now, Harraby East having come into being in the late fifties. Botcherby was then a relatively new Council Estate, adjoining the small village of Botcherby proper, the Estate was made up of a mixture of two and three bed roomed red bricked Laing built council houses with front and rear gardens, some with bay windows making them appear, to a small boy at least, as being a bit Posher than the rest. Besides Botcherby avenue there is Merith avenue, Borland avenue, Ennerdale avenue and Holywell crescent. Durranhill road completed the estate with more bay windows than any other so was deemed even posher. However the really posh folk lived in either Wood street with its large country houses, one of which contained the Chief Constable and his family, later to become a home for delinquent boys, ironic or what, along with a couple of farms both of whom I believe belonged to the Bell family, who also owned the local butchers shop. Wood street would later become the home of the famous Carlisle Miser, Margery Jackson.

At the bottom of the hill just past St Andrews tiny Church was the Border Dairy from where our milk was delivered fresh daily by Mrs Robertson on an old pram chassis laden with milk crates. Becoming a local celebrity she carried out the service for at least sixty years or more barely missing a day, always cheery with bright red rosy cheeks. She always wore a brown overall with a blue striped apron, a head scarf tied beneath her chin, covered by an old grey raincoat which had seen better days if the weather was really bad. Her story was featured in later years on both Border Television and extensively in the Cumberland News.

Down Victoria road, turn right and there was Charlotte Terrace ,on the corner was Armstrong's Bakery, where on a weekend we would gather near closing time to buy stale cakes for a halfpenny, or if you were lucky we would get them for free. All the shops closed on Sundays and with no refrigeration, fresh food would not last until Monday so had to go. The shop is now a Bedding sales room. The old garage directly over from Armstrong's became a petrol station but that was destroyed in the floods of January the 9th 2005, never to recover, now six years later some homes on and

around Warwick road are still not suitable for occupation.
Victoria road is made up of Victorian and Georgian town houses. Some set back to accommodate large front garden's.
Feddon's Market gardens, just beyond the Magpie pub, now St Joseph's Court, made up most of one that side of the road, these nurseries along with the Rhubarb fields they cultivated behind the Coop dairy on Holywell Crescent, now also out of business, are covered by yet more housing, Scotby Gardens. Providing starter homes for those wishing to get on the ladder to home ownership .
On Durranhill road was the Coop store, built in 1933, the largest shop in the area, giving out the annual dividend, with most things wrapped in brown paper tied up neatly with string, an art in itself, such as sugar, flour, tea, biscuits. Later little blue bags appeared, then sticky tape, this was progress, still no fancy packaging then, or plastic or tinfoil, just brown paper, which your mother would keep neatly folded to be reused along with the string, nothing was wasted. Further along, past the big house was and still is the Florida Stores, going strong after all this time. The Coop Dairy on Hollywell crescent has also recently stopped trading.
However what I really missed about Currock was Hammonds pond, the boats, the ducks. Created in the nineteen twenties by local man Archie Hammond for the enjoyment of local boys and girls, they even had monkeys then, and a miniature railway which is still running. It was a wonderland, as long as you avoided the big boys who were just as liable to treat you to a swim in the lake, no charge, luckily it was not too deep and was much cleaner than it is now. However I had two girl cousins, Laa'l Irene Allen and her older sister Laa'l Sally Allen to look after me, tough as any boy, not to be messed with, phew, thank God.
They both bore the prefix Laa'l, so as to avoid confusion, they were smaller versions of my mam Sally and my Auntie Irene, mam's sister. Laa'l Irene in particular always seemed to have a

contingent of smaller persons following her about where ever she went, she just seemed to be a natural carer who everyone dumped their kids on, which was accepted with good grace, never a complaint, at least I do not think so. She would take us to the Salvation Army Hall on St Nicholas bridge to see the Lantern show. Shadows cast on a white wall with some salvation army man making animal shapes with his finger or cut out characters acting out some dare devil scene of adventure, usually giving a moral tale of good over taking evil, not like real life at all.. but at least we would get a glass of something and a couple of biscuits as recompense for our patience.

I recall my first visit to the Stanley Hall picture house, AKA the fleapit, on Botchergate with Laa'l Irene and the clan. I was too small to go really but a good old tantrum worked wonders and I got sixpence off Gran, anything to get me out of the house for some peace and quite. I think we saw Charlie Chaplin, something about a girl and a train,not too sure, followed by the obligatory B Western, could have been Roy Rogers or maybe Gene Autry, one of those anyway, both sang to their horses while playing guitar, yes there were funny cowboys around even before Brokeback mountain…yippee.

The Stanley is long gone, now being renovated by Macknights builders for the second time to become flats, for a short while it became a club then a dance hall for Rockers and Grebo's, but lacked support. Our Philip and his mate Andrew (Spud) Sinclair formed a rock band called Spellbinder winning the battle of the Bands competition here. I may be biased, but thought they were pretty good.

They went on to perform on CFM Radio and in the council funded Bands in the Park concerts which again died the death due to lack of support, regretfully a recurring theme in Carlisle, then we all complain about lack of entertainment in the City.

The Lonsdale Cinema, a recent victim of progress raised howls of protest at the thought of its demolition, calling for it to be transformed into a theatre, we had a theatre remember, plus the Sands could do with a little more support. My overriding memory of Her Majesty's theatre is of being a very small boy watching the Christmas Pantomime, whilst sitting high up in the front row of the Gods, holding on for dear life to the brass barrier in front of me convinced any moment I would be hurtling down to the dress circle, there to squash some white tied snob. That's the only time I recall being afraid of heights. I loved going to the theatre, paying my sixpence and walking up all those stairs, it did not matter that the carpets were worn and a death trap, the springs popping up through the tip up seats, snagging your pants, we loved it, nothing compared with real live entertainment, singers, jugglers and magicians, followed by the rib bursting comics. I did not know then but those were the death throws of variety, television was ringing the death knell. Who would have thought that little fourteen inch black and white tube would kill it all off.

Along from her Majesty's on Lowther street, just before the Ribble bus station was the Windsor Café where many a happy hour was spent drinking frothy coffee and feeding the juke box , one play for three pence or three for a tanner. Billy Fury, Tommy Steele, Adam Faith, Marty Wilde. When hungry the best Fish and chips could be found in Blackfriar's lane chippy with big Derek, always a queue there, later relocated to old Harraby when Tesco came to town and took over the old Central Hotel complete with the Dive bar. If you preferred some bacon, egg and chips or bangers and mash you headed for Bruccianis café on Scotch street now a Tobacconist. Later the Wimpey bar on the crescent became in vogue with its Amercican style Hot dogs, Burgers and skinny chips. preceding McDonalds by quite a way. But even that has been shoved out of the way by Pasta and Pizza palaces. Every

other outlet on Botchergate that is not a bar is a hot food carry out of some type or other. Sending for a carry out is the new preference to actually making some thing to eat, or dining out.
By the time the Beatles turned up we had grown out of Coffee bars and were heading for the pub. A pint was just as cheap as a frothy coffee we soon discovered, with a better effect.
The Blue Bell on Scotch Street, now a McDonalds fast food joint, being favourite because it had two billiard tables and no one enquired too closely about your age.
If I remember correctly it was Ninepence for a pint of mild and Elevenpence for bitter, with a pint of mixed for tenpence, old money of course, ten Regal cigarettes were one and a penny, or twenty for two bob with fish and chips for a shilling. You could have a wild night out for ten bob and still have change for the bus home. When I say a wild night out you have to remember the pubs all closed at ten and anyone coming home after eleven were dirty stop outs, held in great suspicion, especially the girls. With dad standing at the door waiting, God help her if she were seen coming up the street with a boy. The days of free love and sexual liberation were still to come, I must have missed that day somehow.
Plus of course the Blue Bell was nice and handy for the Market dance hall, more of which later, in " Dance Hall days ", everyone loved the Market Hall, only ten pence entry, best ten pence ever spent.
I do not seem to have any bad memories of growing up, not like some apparently. The papers and the Library are full of stories of tragic goings on in numerous peoples childhood, poor sods, my biggest problem was school, all that learning and stuff, well it was just not for me really, all that reading and writing, could not get to grips with that lot at all, nowadays everyone claims to be dyslexic , as good an excuse as any I suppose, but that one had not been invented when I was a lad so I could not use that , I just accepted

that I was more than a bit thick, but you did not need a GCE to be happy and I was, so there, stuff it.

That's not to say our life did not have its very real tragedy's, my sister Veronica was taken by Meningitis at the tender age of ten months, my brother Brian, taken ill at two years of age only to lose his hearing due to the side affects of Streptomycin, a form of penicillin, all responsibility of course denied by the hospital, litigation not a path available to the average person then. My sister Brenda lost her eldest son to a house fire whilst staying with friends, and my eldest son Philip died via suicide, God bless them both. So I think we had our share.

It was in the early part of 1952, England had a new young Queen in Elizabeth the Second and the austerity of the second world war was beginning slowly to fade, that Philip William Joseph Beckett, senior clerical officer at the 14th RAF maintenance unit chose to attend the open day at Norman Street School, to see what progress was been made by his six year old second eldest son Terence for whom he had hopes of high academic achievement. (I say second eldest son because unbeknown to me then I had another half brother living across town in Harraby, you never know the minute do you.)

Well, you cannot stop people dreaming can you ? Dad was born on the 18th January 1912, the year the Titanic sank, should have prepared him for disasters really, he left us on the 17th January 1974 the day before his 62nd birthday.

I can see him now, strolling into the classroom with his usual air of confidence, looking again as usual very smart in his suit and trilby hat worn at its normal rakish angle. He stood a mere five foot and half an inch tall, but insisted that half inch made all the difference, it was true, you could not miss him, always stood out in a crowd. Always wore a suit, not just special days like most of his contemporaries and that trilby, he loved that Trilby, always referred to it as his " Titfer," you know rhyming slang, Tit for tat, hat. Never off his head , he put it on when raising in the morning and took it off for bed, not that he was bald or anything, in fact his hair was always parted smartly just off centre as was the trend in dads day. Everyone just knew him as a very smart man. Also he was a very intelligent man my dad, well known and respected within the community of Botcherby, for then it was just that, a real community where people cared for and looked out for each other. He would often engage in letter writing for our neighbours when they had dealings with authority of any kind, like the tax man or Solicitors and such. Dad was educated to a high standard and knew how to compose a letter and what phrases and words to use in order to achieve the required affect, to gain the best result, much to the admiration of his peers. Regretfully I did not inherit this degree of scholarship as the poor man was about to discover alas.

  Upon entering the classroom he perused the many painted and pencil drawn pictures adorning the walls, some showing real artistic merit, some perhaps not so. Though you cannot knock matchstick men, look what it has done for that Lowry bloke. Mingling with the other parents, he smiled agreeably when eye contact was made. Brief words of greeting passing between folk, such as. " How do you do ?" or "Good evening." or " turned out nice again." . Poor Dad, being seduced into a false sense of security by the ambience. Making his way along the neat rows of tiny desks each one bearing a pretty little card with the relevant boy or girls name, again each one decorated with some nice design or picture, someone else must have done mine for me, because I could not write my name. Probable one of those clever little dicks from the private houses which bounded the school field.

He eventually arrived at his sons place of learning. Looking about him, he smiled once more as he raised the desk lid to further

examine the contents within, it only took the briefest of moments, then his face paled , trying not to look too conspicuous , quietly closing the lid he quickly moved away trying to space himself from what he had seen, a sort of panic raising in his breast, bile in his tightening throat, fear almost reminiscent of his time laying wounded on the beaches of Dunkirk before being rescued by a unit of the free French. There were school books in there alright, but nothing at all like any other he had seen before.
Upon opening one he had found not neat lines of script but large blotches reminiscent of Picassos blue period, some far Eastern like hieroglyphics along with lots of small blue fingerprints which covered every surface which were not already covered in crude outlines of match stalk men in mortal combat or undecipherable scribble. He moved swiftly around the classroom trying to appear all was fine, but not doing it all that well, his face ashen, breathing erratic.
" Are you alright." the young prim class teacher enquired, approaching him, with concern.
" Oh yes, I am fine. " he replied. " just a little warm in here don't you think.". then quickly as he could hopefully without arousing too much suspicion left the classroom, and the School vowing to himself never to return, a promise he truly kept.
With head bowed in deep reflection he left Norman street school. Crossing the cobblestone road barely noticing the Belisher beacon flashing its warning to traffic, fortunately there were few vehicles about on Greystone road with its red bricked terrace houses, common to Carlisle, heading for the bridge over the river Petterill, a temporary construction of old railway sleepers and steel girders, followed the clapboard fence enclosed footpath through Melbourne park, over slowly tinkling Tilbury beck with its abundance of Minnows and Sticklebacks, striding on up the slope of Botcherby avenue, ignoring his own house on the way, instead

progressing down and left onto Florida Mount, down Victoria road to his refuge. Within ten minutes or so he was sitting in his local, the Magpie Public house, supping a much needed cool dark pint of mild and Bitter, the sweat on his brow slowly evaporating in the pubs easy atmosphere after his hurried retreat from avoiding possibly disastrous, unforgettable embarrassment. Several refills of the soothing nectar later he felt able to make his way ponderously back up the hill on Victoria road to his Botcherby avenue three bed council house home. There with a display of great sadness he told his wife, my mother.
" Sally, I think our Terence is backward," and that she should not hold any great ambition for me, assuming she ever did.
God knows he was not far wrong.

 I clearly had issues with learning, reading was a mystery to me, writing, well I could not seem to control the pen, and each school book or paper put in front of me soon became yet another blue period Piccaso like scrawl, sums were no better, probably worse. Who needs to count, I never had anything to count anyway.
The only classes I liked a bit were drama and art, I used to love Morris dancing! yea ok…
I actually won first prize at the Carlisle festival of Arts, held in The Swanky Crown and Mitre Hotel Ballroom, for duologue with a lad called John Wetherall, Wonder what happened to him ? Are you out there John, lets know mate. John was one of the few at Harraby sec who never failed to wear his school blazer.
Fortunately ignorance is bliss and none of this bothered me until I was much older by which time it did not matter and my childhood is constructed of mainly happy memories anyway so why worry.
I did eventually become aware of the benefits of literacy, so that's alright then, innit !
Later in life I met up with an English teacher call Mr Omerod who

not only taught me to read, what an achievement, he so instilled in me a love of books I would read virtually one a day, it was like being reborn. Visiting Carlisle Lending Library two or three times a week to withdraw my allotted number of both four fiction and two non fiction tomes. I am still addicted to biographies, and find new hero's all the time. My debt to Mr Omerod is incalculable. Last time I saw him was when he worked as an announcer on Border Telly, wonder where he ended up. Its amazing how people who impact large on our lives just disappear. I wonder if they realise just what effect they have achieved.

I also twice won the student of the year award when I was sixteen and attending the local Technical College where I also gained two City and guilds certificate both with distinction, so there, something must have stuck in my grey porridge of a brain.
My Mam and Dad both attended the presentation evenings much to my delight and seemed very pleased, I suppose it went somewhere toward restoring Dads faith in his Gene pool.
Still why worry. Well he clearly did.
Despite being so fat I still managed to do alright at most field sports, except when they involved running cross country races which were pure torture, my belly wobbled so much it made me throw up my school dinner. At Norman Street I became captain of the football team, mainly because I was the only one with a football strip, my mother got it for me but from God knows where, it was a bright green top white shorts and green socks, I looked like a leprechaun, no boots though just plimsolls with the toes kicked out. Not that it mattered much, we never actually played anyone, just kicked about on Melbourne park. I cannot recall the teachers name who took sports, probably only did it for an excuse to get out of school and have a fag or some such. He was probably

as bored as we were, star students were few and far between for him to encourage. I never actually hated school, but struggle to find many good times. But one of those was the garden, Norman Street School had an extensive garden in which the pupils were encouraged to help out with the planting and caring for all types of vegetables , clearly something carried forward from the war years, when dig for England had a very real meaning. We all seem to love this part of school life, we would troop into the garden after being issued with smaller versions of spades ,fork and rakes etc.
our enthusiasm knew no bounds, and we all worked quite diligently and loved it when the crops began to show through the dark soil, growing to fruition. Potatoes, cabbages, broad beans, lettuces we grew them all, I do not recall what happened to all this fresh grown garden produce, probably ended up in the headmistresses Sunday lunch, I should not wonder.

The only down side that I recall was one day in the garden a boy uncovered a little field mouse's nest, which held six or more small pink babies ,eyes closed, wriggling at been discovered, totally defenceless. We all crowded around enchanted by the scene before us, some wanting to pick them up and hold them, others not quite so brave, girls squealing in mock terror. Then to our horror the teacher appeared alerted by our excitement and pushing us all to one side proceeded to beat the little creatures to death with his spade, calling them vermin and could not be allowed to breed in the garden. Some of the girls began to cry, while some of the braver boys protested at such perceived cruelty, I like to think I was one of the rebels. However what it did do was cement some of our beliefs that all teachers were bastards.
 This episode had some affect on me because I always found it difficult to kill any creature without exceptional reason. Though I have pulled the necks of chickens and rabbits and knocked fish on

the head, so maybe I am a bit of an hypocrite.
When I worked for John Reed the farmer, we would castrate piglets with an old razor blade, then rinse the copiously bleeding cut with diluted Dettol antiseptic, it must have stung something rotten, the poor beggars screamed like fury. Made my eyes water I can tell you. This was done to encourage growth by disturbing their hormone balance so bringing a better price at market. It was amazing just how quickly they seemed to recover from this ordeal, soon back to frolicking around with their siblings, scrabbling over mothers teats, seemingly non the worse. Still, I would not wish to put it to the test, no thanks.
We also took new born calves from their mothers and immediately put them in a darkened byre or loose box where they stayed alone for several weeks never seeing the sun let alone their mothers.
This was done to keep their flesh white and therefore saleable at a premium as veal. They would be fed daily on mums milk from a pail, we were the only other living being they met, poor beggars, probably thought we were its family. Then after a few short weeks were put in Hessian sacks to again avoid the sun, then taken off to market and the slaughter house.
If all those people sitting in there high class restaurants knew what was being done to satisfy their Desire for Haute de Cuisine dining they would throw up on their nice posh gowns, mans inhumanity to man pales to insignificance when compared to man treatment of the worlds animals.

Talking of John Reed, a man I both liked and respected, when I left the farm to go and work on the British Railways Restaurant Car service, a job organised for me by my Mam, I arrived at the interview which was held at the North British hotel in Glasgow, I was told the reference they had received from Mrs Reed in response to their request said I was an insolent and indolent youth,

I thought she was being kind never having heard these words before, that is until the man interviewing me explained them to me. It took me an awful long time to work out why she had said such things, after all she was an upright Church going women who only ever showed me kindness, I can only think she was jealous because I got on better with her old man than she did. Though, thinking about it I did drop then in it a bit leaving on such short notice out side the hiring. This was a two week period, held twice a year when farm workers could change jobs, gathering at various market places offering themselves for hire, good men being snapped up, the not so great being grudgingly hired on for a six month term agreed by an hand shake, though even then wages were not too great for either. But for all that I enjoyed my time at Moss Side , I learned to drive the tractors, an old Fargie and a huge blue Fordson major, plus I got to ride the bosses daughters pony, I used to use it to round up the milker's when they strayed into the Kale field or coming in for milking, which wound her up something rotten poor lass, not her fault I suppose I would not like it if some oyck took off on my horse. My mate Geoff came to see me one Sunday and had a go on the pony which kept throwing him off, how he did not break anything is a mystery. I thought it was totally hilarious.
But then I was a city boy out of my environment and unaware of country ways, but I was happy and never once homesick like some of my pals in similar situations. Old school mates Tommy Bell and Arnold Tickell both worked for farmers about two or three miles away so we would often meet up and cycle into Silloth for chips or to go the pictures. If it were not for my Mam wanting me home I may have stayed in farming, or some other country job, who knows. Tommy built a future with Carlisle Leisure at the Swimming baths, while Arnie went on to a successful military career.

A moment of shame that haunts me to this day occurred one blue summers day. I was slashing the dyke in John Reeds bottom field, which was bordered on one side by the Carlisle to Silloth Railway line. Each time a train went past I would wave frantically in hopes of being seen by some Botcherbyite or ex school friend or other.
" Ho, look there's that dickhead Terence Beckett in a field !" or something like that. Anyway getting back, while working I saw a young rabbit slowly moving along the dyke back, clearly not at its best. I stooped and picked it up, feeling its heart pounding in my hand.
It clearly was in trouble and no doubt soon to die.
With my new found country wisdom I felt the kindly thing to do was give it a quick, hopefully, pain free death. Taking its hind legs in one hand and its floppy ears in the other, I gave it a good yank, thinking to snap its thin neck giving the tiny animal instant relief. However, instead its ears parted from its head with a distinct pop. The shock caused me to drop the rabbit, which with a new found energy and no ears bounded through the dyke and away.
My heart sank, what had I done !. Poor sod , a lugless rabbit. Its survival even more dodgy now.
I still think of it now, fifty years on, God I must be a soft sod. Bunny probably ended up as lunch for some Fox cubs, nature has a way of sorting these things out, you know , survival of the fittest and all that stuff. Gulp..

Now I think on it another guilt trip that often pops into my mind, regards a local character I often came across in town, whether he was a day release patient from the Garlands Mental hospital or just some poor gormless sod who was put out each day by his family to get him out of the way I do not know. He was quite tall and very slim, always wore a flat cap, walking with a stoop he was another reminiscent of a Lowry figure, ie a matchstick man with a distinct droopy bottom lip. More often than not he was worse the wear for drink, shuffling along mumbling to himself, meandering along the pavement, never making eye contact with anyone, in a world of his own.

Though someone must have cared for him as he always wore a clean white shirt open at the neck, with clean polished shoes. Amazing the things you remember.

The day that comes to mind was probably a Saturday, because I was in town, when usually I would be at work on the restaurant cars, rarely venturing into Carlisle on a weekday.

Walking along Lowther street I got the need to pee, so headed for what was then the United Bus Station to take advantage of their bogs. Entering the Gents I noticed our friend standing by the toilet cubicles, but took little notice due to my need to point Percy at the porcelain.

It was only on my exiting the toilets that for some reason I looked down at our friends feet and saw an extensive pool of liquidised Poo, still very wet and still emerging from his trouser leg, Phew what a whiff, poor bugger, caught short within a few feet of sweet relief, talk about Mafekin. Looking up at his face I saw the very picture of desperation, silently begging help from somewhere or someone, my heart dropped to my stomach with real pity, but like all those around me just kept on walking and left the lad to his fate. I just hope someone, though I cannot imagine who, went to his aid, poor sod. What is it with me and tales of shit. Read on and all will be revealed.

Another interesting aside is that the professional criminal and serial killer Archibald Thomas Hall, aka Roy Fontaine, rented a small whitewashed cottage in the nearby village of Newton Arlosh whilst trying to avoid detection of the law, only a mile or to from Moss Side Farm. Unfortunately for him he trusted one of his

cohorts to dispose of the body of his latest victim, a women, Mary Coggles, one time prostitute, whom he had been having a relationship with and no longer wanted to continue, due I believe due to her nagging nature, I could be wrong of course but then it does sound like your average lady. Oops.
Poor girl was found just over the Scottish border laying half submerged in a stream, the job having been botched led to him going down and serving a life sentence, eventually dying in prison in his seventies. There you go, you just never know who you are living beside do you. Among his other four known victims were his employers Walter Scott Elliot and his wife Dorothy, for whom he acted as butler, so the butler did do it after all.

I do remember the last Carlisle man to hang for murder, in 1957 when I was thirteen years old, John Vickers done away with poor old Miss Jane Duckett, corner shop proprietor of Tait street. Now at the time I recall popular opinion saying the death was in fact an accident, with the aforementioned lady falling down the cellar steps causing her death, but of course had John Vickers not broke in to the shop in the first place she would not have had reason to fall, making manslaughter an option, so any way he was hung and that was that. Probably the most famous murderer in Cumbria's criminal history was the notorious Percy Topliss in 1920, an army deserter and petty thief who turned to murder while on the run, killing a taxi driver and shooting a policeman and a farmer in Scotland. He was eventually surrounded in Plumpton Churchyard and shot dead by local police marksmen. His various escapades have been made into a film on television and recorded in several books.
I went on to join the Restaurant Car staff of the Waverly Express, Edinburgh to London St Pancras, (aka the slow boat to china.)

And had two years of fun, though I was not always the one laughing. I met some crazy characters that I will never forget, never..

Besides the characters working on the dining cars I also got to meet many celebrities of the day, though most of the ones I met were all down to earth, and the age of "look at me I am a celebrity" had yet to dawn. They included, Cliff Richards, Marty Wilde, Billy Fury, among others. I would occasionally get to chat with Alfie Bass and Bill Fraser, better known as Bootsie and Snudge whilst waiting at St Pancras for the train to pull in. It was amazing how those famous people would get to know you through their use of the dining car and when they saw you on the platform would just saunter up and start a conversation. I suppose they needed company now and again just like everyone else.

Clearly travelling the country from top to bottom was not always a barrel of laughs. Having said that I have never had a problem talking to strangers, or even celebrities, must be something to do with discovering during my dining car days, that even the most famous people are just that, people, just as scared and vulnerable as the rest of us, sometimes more and with good reason.

3   THE CANNIBAL MOUSE OF NORMAN STREET SCHOOL.

It was while I was at Norman street school we had the saga of the cannibal mouse. Someone in their wisdom decided it would be a good idea to have a school pet and, after much deliberation by the teachers six small black and tan mice appeared, these were kept in a glass sided cage affair and once a week each class was given the task of looking after them. The boys of course were keen to handle the mice, while the girls giggled and screamed at the slightest reason.
The cage had to be cleaned, old food remnants removed and replaced with fresh along with fresh bedding and water. Everyone was very excited with our new little friends and each class took their responsibility very seriously.
Then summer holidays arrived, we all went off to enjoy the sunshine for the next six weeks or so. But not so the mice, they were left to their own devices, poor things. When we all returned to school, refreshed and ready to go it was not long until someone realised not all was well in the mouse dep't. look as we may we could only see one scrawny thin sad looking mouse. The cage was cleaned out and several pieces of mouse skin was detected along with the odd bit of shiny white bone, then it dawned, we had all gone on our merry way looking forward to the holidays without a thought as to who would feed the mice, so starving to death the poor beggars had resorted to cannibalism.

The surviving mouse was treated with great suspicion, for he must have eaten the last mouse being the last mouse standing, survival of the fittest, nobody wanted the poor chap and the next morning he had disappeared, probably facing execution for his crimes against mousedom, or perhaps he was taken to a better home where he lived a long and happy life, or did he go mad with recurring dreams of being eaten alive. Who can tell. We never bothered with pets after that, just as well really, who said teachers were clever !

We had a male teacher at Norman Street whose name I have long forgot, but what I do remember is that he had no time what's so ever for the boys in the class but the little girls were a different story. He would call them up to his desk and put his hand up their skirts and make them squeal. We did not understand about perverts in those distant days, but I am sure we had one here. I learned much later that he had took off with one of the lady teachers, God help her.
We had some boys at infant school from well off families, or at least a sight better off than we were, who would arrive each morning in their smart blazers and school ties, whilst I was a natural scruffy sod with my backside more often than not hanging out of my short trousers. These boys in the main were ok, but had one or two bully's in among them and, generally stuck together in a little gang. I use the word gang advisedly because that is what it was, and if they took a dislike to you life could be pretty rough. You were either in or you were not and I know which I wanted to be, but the choice was not mine and never offered.
Several kids suffered at their hands. They turned on me once or twice but fortunately I had some tough mates too, coming from Botcherby avenue did have its advantages after all.
There was a lad in our class called Leonard Winrow who was

always a little distant from the rest of us. He would keep himself to himself, but time has obliterated from my mind for what reason. His dad had the cobblers shop at the top of our street and from what I can recall was an ok bloke, but I was only seven or so at this time so cannot be sure of the detail, however what I do recall is that Leonard hung himself in his wardrobe, whether accidental or what
I never found out, god bless him. My first memory of a human tragedy. The family stayed there for a few years, Mr Winrow becoming a milkman then moved on to pastures new, I never saw any of them again.
We occasionally had boys and girls suddenly disappearing from class to learn later that they had died of some prevalent everyday disease, people still died from such things as Measles, Diphtheria and such like then. Unbelievably as it is now we lost several family and neighbours to tuberculosis. Amazingly life expectancy was a lot less in the fifties
Which is not that long ago ! My baby sister Veronica Sandra succumbed to meningitis at the age of only eight months or so as many kids still do to this day. Despite all the publicity given to this disease it still manages to confound diagnosis in even the most experienced of modernistic clinicians .
I was far too young to understand the tragedy that befell my Mam and Dad, they must have been inconsolable. Brenda my elder sister would have been around three years old and still talks of our lost girl to this day, so clearly even at that tender age had an understanding of what was occurring in the family, grief is contagious.
Brenda has since tracked down Sandra's grave which had got lost in the mist of time. Laying in a secluded area of Carlisle Cemetery with other infants lost to parents long ago, now flowers are freshly laid to show we still want to remember. I am sure she has forgiven

us for taking so long to be reunited once more.
Since Brenda identified Sandra's resting place several others have appeared to be rediscovered, flowers and other signs of fond remembrance have taken their brightly celebrated place among the overgrown shrubbery and trees.

Norman street school was a standard of its type, built at the beginning of the twentieth century in nineteen eight, at least that is the date displayed on some of the original cast iron guttering still in place to this day, being of red brick and slate with the most basic of adornment and the usual large windows. Inside there were glass fronted classrooms arranged around three sides with the central open area being used for morning assembly and various school activities, embracing the library and of course the obligatory stage for the enactment of Nativity plays and other traditional school entertainment's, including Christmas parties when all would bring along mothers creations, fairy cakes, sausage rolls and such, depending on the current rationing situation and the various families financial status, snobbery starts early in life.
Before I left the hall had to be put to use as an overspill classroom for the up and coming brood of war babies, they being the result of

absent fathers returning from overseas duty with armed forces and eager to resume normal relations with spouses.

With parquet flooring highly polished by the hundreds of infant bums shuffling about on it, no chairs in the hall then, the kids all sat on the floor. There was the obligatory piano for accompaniment to hymn and carol singing and of course school nativity plays and concerts.

The toilets where extremely basic across the school yard which seemed miles away in wintry weather. Rain lashing the open space. The urinal area was simply a depression in concrete running to a covered drain. This part was open to the skies, the afore mentioned rain doing its bit to aid flushing. The sit down toilets at least had a roof, but few actually used these except in dire emergency. Sitting on the bog left you defenceless against attack from all kinds of missiles being thrown over the low door, from water bombs to sticks and stones. In the winter your bottom just about froze to the pot, no nice warm wooden seat, just cold chipped porcelain, and shiny government property toilet paper which if you were not careful your finger could go through, yuck. During breaks, mid morning and afternoon no one was allowed in school, whether it be sun, showers, snow or sleet, we were often soaked to the skin, shivering, dripping puddles beneath our desks. The teacher on playground duty, akin to guards stewarding some deep south chain gang, would be inside looking out of a cosy window for misbehaving scallywags, bottoms to be later warmed by a swishing cane. Ever vigilant, usually with a cup of tea in one hand, blue smoked fag in the other. You were not always aware of these educators observing you until you transgressed then the sky caved in on you, when justly or no, buttocks warmed dramatically, girls as well as boys, which for some reason always seemed so much worse. But then, I remember an advert on Telly where a small boy said he did not like girls because " they whispered."

And they do, mainly into cupped hands held against another maidens ear. Queer how such an action could make you feel so inferior.

Apart from that already mentioned, I do not recall much in the way of bullying, though I am sure it occurred then as now. Gangs would form and if you were in you were ok ,but if not you could become a target. Bullying is a disease rampant and widespread, regardless of age or occupation, you never seem far away from a bully, whether physical or mental, its ever present in the cracks waiting to exploit the weakness in human nature.

I do remember one such gang who all wore little badges of a blue star, made from some early type of plastic, it was made up entirely of blazer boys form the private houses, whose dads were Insurance agents or ran their own business, one was a post master another made lemonade, all home owners, some ok some right gobshite snobs, not that I am bitter or anything you notice.

However it did not do at least a couple of these boys much good, two of them died young from heroin addiction, poor sods, they would not have realised just what they were getting into. No drug education, or examples to learn from then, knowledge coming all too late. Most of us had never heard of drugs of that sort, that horror was still to come.

Us council kids wore what we were given, some had no jackets at all, we quickly forget that poverty was very real for a few then. A couple of lads down our street had an alcoholic mother, working as a prostitute, a father who, always smartly dressed himself, appeared not to care and they often had no shoes never mind a posh blazer. I never got a blazer but I always had a warm coat, woolie jumper and boots. I loved those boots, making them spark much to mam's annoyance as this led to there prematurely wearing out. Never wanted shoes, boots were best.

The school has been upgraded and extended over the years, with temporary Portakabins being used for a while, Norman street will be a feature of Carlisle for a long while yet, on a recent visit to the Sands centre we watched a troupe of dancers giving it there all, having a great time, still going strong.

The walk from Botcherby to Norman street Infants went by way of Melbourne Park, following a raised footpath, boarded on both sides by a wooden fence. At the end of the path a small footbridge traversed the river Petterill, immediately on the other side a scrap yard, a fabulous wonderland for small boys willing to risk being chased by the irate owner and his ferocious dog.

Within the boundaries of the afore mentioned scrappy were all manner of strange and wonderful things, glass tubes perfect for peashooters, these often left a weird metallic taste in the mouth, the wonder is no one was poisoned, or maybe they were ?

A quick search would reveal pram wheel for bogeys, metal rods for swords, bamboo canes for fishing rods or bows and arrows. A fantasy world of amazing attraction.

My only ever broken bone came about due to some lads having a kick about with an old paint tin, seeing who could boot it the furthest or the highest, I was not really taking any notice until one of them shouted me over.

" Hi, Bucket." he called, "Bucket" being one of my numerous nick names, along with The "Reverend" and " Sir Thomas."

" come and see how far you can shift this old tin can ?."

Never being able to resist a challenge I immediately ran over and booted the can with all my might. The can barely moved but my foot crunched, hurting like hell, I had fell for one of the oldest trick in the book, the swine's had put a half building brick under the can while I had been distracted and wham ! I had kicked it with all my might. Three broken toes, tears streaming down my face. Off to the

Infirmary, who just wrapped my foot in a loose bandage.
" You cannot plaster broken toes." they told my Mam. " You just have to let them heal themselves."
Bastards, but when the pain faded I had the last laugh, three weeks off school, it was almost worth it.

On occasion boys would arrive home with strange stains on clothes, shoes etc, seeped in secretions which forbad description,, trousers often requiring repair due to contact with various jagged metals or glass,
Some lads even faced the disgrace of being frogmarched home by the local Bobby, much to embarrassment of fuming parents. Having the police at the door was not acceptable in those far off days.
But not even the fear of dog bites could stop the search for new and exciting objects to marvel at and display to less brave school pals who would gasp in awe at the marvellous discoveries of radio valves, bakelite creations of weird and mysterious design. The occasional bottle or can of mysterious liquid would hold chums spellbound, especially when poured on the school yard resulting in a fizzing bubbling cloud of smelly vapour, like I said
earlier, how no one died is a wonder. Health and safety was an issue yet to be conceived by Council geeks with nothing else to do to justify their inflated salaries.
Tragically the river Petterill would flood with amazing regularity, tempting young boys to test their courage crossing the turbulent brown waters, often resulting in the loss of a young life. The power of the floodwater catching out unwary souls is still to be learned. Raincoats and Wellington boots when caught by the flood waters can be a deadly trap, pulling the unwary to the bottom before you can save yourself.

4   HAVE A DRAG, YOU'LL ENJOY IT.

My first experience with smoking came when another boyhood friend called Ivor Charters and I bought a packet of domino cigarettes each, they were real cheapo jobs only four fags to a packet, well not even a packet really just a small paper bag. Which meant they were really dry and made you cough something rotten but we thought we were the bees knees and wanted to smoke them anyway. That night we set up my little canvas tent in my back garden and determined to spend our first ever night alone outdoors. Perfect cover for our delinquent intent, (no pun meant there.) or so we thought because we had just lit up our first fag and were puffing away like mad when we heard my dad approaching the tent. Panic stricken we quickly stubbed out the offending ciggies and lay prone pretending sleep. Dad stuck his head through the flaps and enquired how we were getting along, we answered all was fine, the air in the tent was blue with the remnants of fag smoke , but dad appeared oblivious to the fuggy fumes and after a moment or two returned to the house. Whether he was aware of our furtive smoking or just could not recognise the aroma through his own years of nicotine addiction I never did find out, but it did not stop us smoking the rest of the Dominos, even when it made us extremely very sick.

We would try anything for a smoke in those days, believing it made us hard and tough guys. We dried old tea dregs, grass, and dads old dog ends which he kept for hard times at the end of the month . Being a civil servant dad, most unusual for those days in the fifties and sixties, was paid monthly, so was always flush for the first two weeks or so of the month, but stony broke for the remainder. Time made him wise to this, so during the good times he smoked John players or Senior Service, making sure to keep all the dog ends for rollie's at the month end when he resorted to his Baccy tin, papers and fag rolling machine. Sadly, for Dad that is, I discovered his hiding place and his stash of dog ends kept disappearing. He probably knew why, but was not one for bother and liked a easy life, so my habit grew.

In the early sixties everyone except the most hardened smokers moved on to tipped fags, convinced this was going to save them from the dreaded lung cancer, which all now accepted was the price for a good smoke. Talk about rose coloured glasses. Still it has to be said, bad as it was for us, we all loved a fag. It was our refuge in times of trouble and God knows we all had some. A night in the pub in good company was all the more enjoyable for a smoke, say what you like it definitely raised the spirits and filled the cemetery, keeping the poor old grave digger in work. My elder brothers mate Donny Gordon, who lived in a corner bay windowed house on Durranhill Road held the prestigious position of fireman on the trains and was always good for a cadge of a fag, when asked he would produce with a flourish a packet of twenty Senior Service or perhaps Capstan, never refused. However due to the abandonment of steam Donny never got to be a main line driver, retraining as a bus driver with the Ribble Bus company. Still a nice bloke, still working at the Auctioneer Restaurant, always good for a chat.

I continued to afflict my body with tobacco for the next forty years, smoking everything from Wild Woodbine, woodbine tipped, Senior Service, John Players, Capstan, or even Capstan full strength, no wonder we coughed, occasionally when flush moving up to gold tipped Sobranie Black Russian, very cool to Camels, those dreadful French jobs which we received free while serving in the forces, these were confiscated by customs and passed on to us. I suspect they kept the good ones for themselves and left us to suffer, but anyway in did not stop us smoking them, we must have been daft or desperate, when you had a drink you would have smoked your Gran's old slippers. For special occasion's, Christmas or weddings, there were Hamlet or Castella cigars, but to be really cool you needed Café Crème cheroots, or if you could not quite afford them then liquorice papers for your rollies.

I only eventually gave up the weed due to ending up in intensive care with a supposed heart attack for the second time, only to discover later in was not my heart but my gall bladder causing the similar symptoms, I really did not want to stop and found it very difficult. I definitely was not one of your give up overnight bod's and feel no withdrawal symptoms , oh no, I did not give up without a fight. I spit out the dummy big style I did, then I made every ones life a misery with my moaning and complaining, how no one strangled me I will never know. God only knows how folk must suffer to give up hard drugs. Or maybe I am just a soft bairn. Though it turned out to be one of the very best decisions of my life. There is no doubt in my mind I would not have got this far had I continued smoking. My Dad died of throat cancer as did most of his Magpie mates, apparently the beer can cause throat cancer so combined with nicotine and tar from the smoking they were probably doomed for years through lack of education on the affects of these social habits. Lets face it every one smoked and if you did not you were considered an unsociable sod.

Ivor and I had other adventures when we were quite small, no more than four year old or so, We would wander off down Warwick Road, the main road from the East into the City, past the

Carlisle United Football ground, Brunton park. Inevitably due to our size some one would eventually stop us and ask were we were off to. People cared about that sort of thing then, now they would be too concerned whether they would be seen as some sort of pervert or something. We would then tell them we were lost and did not know where we lived or how to get there hoping to be taken in and given cakes or sweets to comfort us as would happen in Botcherby until our parents could be found and we returned intact.

However on this occasion that did not occur instead the police were summoned, arriving in their black limousine with police in large intimidating letters on the roof. For a moment we were stumped. So as all kids when not knowing what else to do we howled our eyes out. We felt the waves of sympathy flow over us and sensing an advantage took our chances, soon we were sitting in the back of the great big police car on our way to the main police station at Rickergate. We had a great time Ivor and I, not only did we have the thrill of being in the police station, but got lemonade and chocolate biscuits as well. Then not knowing how to deal with us we were handed over to the police women on the switch board who let us push in the leads when a light flashed indicating a call coming in, and pull them out again when the call ended, we were spoiled rotten.

This was such a success we tried once or twice more but were quickly sussed out and that adventure came to an end.

We got into all kinds of bother me and Ivor, but nothing serious or malicious. Just two little boys finding there way in the big wide world. Ivor was much more street wise than I ever was and I was inclined to follow his lead, we never got into any serious trouble but had some good laughs together. We eventually lost touch but I know he went on to be a HGV driver with his own rig, I can see him now head of his own convoy.

5   HOORAY, THE GASMANS HERE.

The Gasman would make his regular call to empty the penny coin meter, taking out the little cash tray that held the pennies he would pour them into an old navy blue army beret then sit at the kitchen table to count them, with a nice cup of tea provided by mam. Having noted the number of units used he would tally this up and bag the appropriate amount of pennies in little blue paper bags, then store them in his wooden Attache case, which after a number of house calls must have weighed a ton.
The remaining mass of pennies, called rebate, were then gathered up by mam and placed in little neat piles on the window sill, behind the curtain. This would always seem a strange practice to me as anyone looking through the window could not help but see them quite easily. I suppose this either proved the honesty of the people of Botcherby or else the naivety of my mother.
However, it was not external thievery she had to worry about so much, as that from within. The bus fare from Botcherby to the town hall on the big red Double Decker United bus was tuppence. You could either take the number Twenty Four which went down Victoria road before turning left onto Warwick Road over the river Petterill bridge by Carlisle steam laundry, later called the Red Rose, now a commercial Estate, then all the way up past the Carlisle United football ground, Brunton Park, past St Aidan's church, on up past the Lonsdale Cinema next door to the huge general post office before turning into Lowther street, then left again up bank street to the town hall. The number thirty went the same route but turned into Greystone road just before Brunton Park, This was a more circular and all together a more interesting route passing by our Norman street school hidden as it was behind the terraced houses of the said Greystone road, opposite Margaret

Creighton gardens, an estate built for the elderly (where my mam ended up,) right into Fusehill street, then left past the bowling green on Grey street, before joining the bottom of Botchergate, sight of the very first mainland postal Pillar box by the St Nicholas pub in 1853, then straight up past King street where my Mam was born, once a bustling area of two up, two down terraces with shared yards and lavatories, now all commercialised, on past the impressive Coop building to the grand Victorian edifice of the Railway station. Built in 1847 it was one of the first and most important stations in the north of England for a long time, designed by Sir William Tite, though now probably better known as the terminus for the Carlisle Settle line, with its devotion to the preservation of classic steam engines and trains. More recently it has achieved further fame due to its make over for the DIY giant Homebase and its national television advertising campaign.
On past Woolies, yet another lost landmark now B M Bargains, to Marks and Spencer's, once again ending at the Town Hall.
The Town Hall was a wonderland of big red Double Decker buses, all parked around the central island, home to Carlisle Cross and the public ablutions. Later in life this would be the congregating area on Friday and Saturday nights for the local Teddy boys.
Each bus carried its destination in large black lettering on the front, names to me being a new borne traveller, as romantic as any distant metropolis. Raffles, Currock, St Annes, Stanwix, Harraby, Denton Holme, then even further afield, places like Scotby, Wetheral and Brampton, wondrous places yet to be explored. The constant buzz of conversation and crowds all heading for parts unknown only helped to fill me with awe, I still love going on the bus, even just into town and back for the least excuse, sad or what.
So having been inflicted with the wanderlust I would take four pence from the irresistibly tempting pile and wander to the end of the avenue and strike out for town on the first bus to arrive. I never

got bored of looking out onto the world as it passed by, all those people where were they all going and what for, who lived in that house, what does that shop sell, old and young, all mysterious and up to something. I still try for the window seat when I can, but the gentleman in me usually gives way to others, soft sod.

Once while on my travels the bus pulled over to the side of the road by Margaret Creighton gardens and the driver leapt from his cab, looking up into the sky, shading his eyes with his hand, he stood rigid, the passengers wondering just what was occurring left their seats and joined him on the pavement. High up in the clear blue sky was a bright silver sphere, apparently motionless. It reminded me of those dirigibles the army used for practising parachute jumps in Bitts park in the late forties. However this was clearly no balloon, it showed no fins or basket, just a round shiny orb, what could it be , mystifying all gazing upward. Our friend the driver however, more concerned for his schedule than wonders of the universe, resumed his position in his cab and we were all soon on our way to town. Back on the bus was all silent, no one spoke or tried to explain what we had seen, very spooky.

I must have been very small when I first began heading out on this adventure as I can remember being questioned on more than one occasion by the clippie as to where my mam was and, did she know I was out on my own ?. Well, I clearly had innocent looking hazel eyes because my fairy stories were always taken for the truth. Either that or the United bus company only hired trusting souls to work on their buses.

When arriving in the town centre I did not go anywhere, but simply rejoined the queue for the next bus home again. Clearly the journey was the attraction not the arriving, and to some extent still is when travelling away on business or holiday. Mam must have been a poor accountant as I can never remember anyone querying how quickly the penny mountain shrunk.

On the other hand she was quite a laid back girl, so maybe knew all along what was occurring, but just let things happen so long as no real harm was done. I always believed my mam would have made a truly great hippie, being really a cool lady.
What I do know is the feeling of anticipation as the gasman made his way along the avenue, I could feel and hear those pennies jingling in my greedy little pockets already. What times the next bus !! Anyone got a penny for the gas. The day we went on to a quarterly account destroyed my Nomadic Joy.

6   THE GREAT STANLEY MATTHEWS AFFAIR.

It was the day of the 1953 FA cup final, Blackpool versus Bolton Wanderers, now remembered of course as the Matthews final, because it featured the most famous footballer of his day, Stanley , Later Sir Stanley Matthews.
Dad had recently pushed the boat out and purchased a fourteen inch Echo television, only the third on our street, so raising his social standing.
On the day all his mates, some new found, crushed into our living room, beer bottles in pockets to witness the final on the telly, still a novelty and in black and white, and more than likely the only way any of them would be able to follow the action as it played out live before them, travelling to see a final at Wembley was most definitely beyond there means. Never the less the enthusiasm was relentless, Much cheering heralded the confrontation when both teams entered the arena in the shadows of the mighty legendary twin towers. Dad sat like a monarch in the best chair, modestly accepting the admiration of the men around him. With the shrill of the whistle the match kicked off.
Meanwhile down at sandy bay, a small area of bank erosion filled with sand on the old course of the river Petteril, now straightened due to the flooding it caused, not to mention the many drowning of daring young lads.
Terence was hunting Lamprey with his spear made from an old dining fork tied to a bamboo cane when a shout came that a brown trout had been discovered hiding beneath a large waste pipe crossing the river. The boys all advanced in a predatory manner, each determined to be the one to catch the prize. Terence advanced

along the pipe, which was slippery and wet with years of algae and slime. Finally after more careful stalking, coming upon the trout lazily holding its position in the gently running water, he carefully took aim with his trusty spear, his tongue curled up over his top lip in fierce complete concentration, the trout moved forward to determine its chances of escape, Terence saw his chance and with a blood curdling shout lunged forward diving his mighty spear down toward the big brown shiny fish. At the same time his feet gave up their grip on the greasy pipe, hurling him into the water with a great splash and shout of indignation, he belly flopped into the shallow river landing with a squeal on to an old smashed bottle once containing velvety dark Guinness Stout. He missed the trout but did not miss the Guinness, life is cruel.

Stanley Matthews was flying down the wing leaving the Bolton defender floundering in his wake, he started to cut into the penalty box, when.!
" Dad," the quavering voice called. Dad looked around reluctant to take his eyes from the screen.
" Bloody hell, Terence ! " he exclaimed. " What have you been and done now ?".
Terence stood in the living room doorway, covered in blood, Nothing too serious thank God, not that you would know it, I must have looked like I had been through the mangle. Just lots of little nicks and cuts which bled copiously, with the odd deeper effort for good luck.
All the men in the room who had momentarily looked at the bloody scene quickly returned their attention to the small screen and Stanley Matthews. They had their priorities and young Terence was not one of them.
By the time dad had finished dressing the numerous cuts and grazes Terence looked for all the world like an Egyptian Mummy

pulled from one of the tombs in the valley of the kings, but worse than that Blackpool had scored and dad had missed the goal.
I did not take long to recover from my ordeal, for what it was, however I do not think my Dad felt quite the same somehow, it was his first live TV cup final and they did not have instant replays in those days so he had to wait to see the goal on the news later that evening, poor old Dad. Every year when cup final day arrives, you can bet your bottom dollar the commentator will mention the legendary Sir Stanley Matthews, and my Dad will mention missing the only goal due to the antics of his idiot son.
The fence surrounding Brunton Park, home to our local hero's Carlisle United, was constructed in places from sheets of corrugated iron, some of which being pre war, was in dire need of repair, especially where it touched the muddy ground, rusting away and so flimsy as to be easily pulled up enough for a young determined lad to get through, which we often did. All that was left to do was avoid the prowling stewards and you were in.
It only cost a tanner to get into the ground, that's two and a half new pence in modern parlance, but your sixpence could be put to better use, such as purchasing a hot steaming meat and potato pie from the Pioneer van, washed down with a cardboard cup of steaming Oxo, the only problem being it was often so hot you could hardly hold on to it, let alone drink the steaming stuff, Many a time we went home with a burnt tongue.
The crowds in the fifties were huge compared to today, though to be fair there was not the distractions or choices and going to the game was much more of a social affair, a time to meet old mates and comrades, catch up on what was happening elsewhere in the City. Families or workmates would group together forming alliances that lasted a lifetime. Extended families still looked out for each other, unlike today when relatives are barely aware of one another, Maggie Thatcher's statement, claiming there was no such

thing as society has proved correct, mainly due to her destructive policies.

Of course, the F A cup still being the big one, drew even greater crowds, cheering on the home club against mighty and minnow alike, while dreaming of drawing a first division club. In nineteen fifty Carlisle, managed by the one and only Bill Shankly, drew the mighty Arsenal away, holding them to a nil nil draw at Highbury, their home ground, a mighty feat in itself, before finally succumbing to defeat at home in front of a capacity crowd. The result being overshadowed by the gallant fight put up by the Blues. still talked about whenever FA Cup time comes around.

However a local derby with the likes of Workington Town was sufficient excuse to fill the ground to bursting. Health and safety rarely an issue, the crowd control basic, the passion beyond measure. Come on you Blues.

The greatest moment in the clubs history being the 1974 - 75 season when promotion was won to the first division, now the premier league, it only lasted a season, but what a splendid achievement. After three games Carlisle were top of the league, but the Gods of football decreed it not to be and by the time mid season arrived Carlisle's fate was all but sealed, relegation loomed large on the horizon.

It was during the Home game against the mighty Tottenham Hotspurs that a show of fair play occurred which you would be highly unlikely to see today. Martin Chiver's Tottenham's and England's centre forward of the day, lashed a ball at Carlisle goal which nestled firmly in the back of net. Virtually everyone in the ground felt it to be a good goal. However, amazingly Chivers approached the referee and pointed out that the ball had in fact gone in via the loose side netting, so was not a legitimate goal. The goal was subsequently disallowed and the game continued, the result being a one goal win for Carlisle. Say what you like, it was definitely a different set of values held by players in those times, where fair play mattered.

All those loyal supporters of so long ago would be aghast to learn that lowly CUFC, not only achieved four visits to Wembley in a cup final, an amazing feat in itself, but would twice be winners and the first team to play in a cup final at the majestic millennium stadium in Cardiff, a replacement setting while the new Wembley Stadium was being constructed.

My younger brother Brian was an excellent player as a lad and despite being deaf played a couple of trials for Carlisle United under the eye of the one and only Alan Ashman, probably our greatest manager. Unfortunately Brian's deafness proved to be too great a handicap and nothing ever came of it. There must have been literally hundreds of boys took trials at Brunton park over the years with a fraction getting anywhere. Some like Botcherby boy, Kevin Beattie went on to greatness with Bobby Robson and Ipswich Town, then achieving England glory. Others, Mortons Paul Simpson after a glittering career on the pitch returning to save United from the Battle ground of the Conference. Our own David Geddis one of the youngest ever to play in an FA cup final. Now Rory Delap storming the Premier league with Stoke, terrifying defences with his devastating long throw. The latest addition being my ex next door neighbour Grant Holt, climbing the dizzy heights with Norwich, the premier league new boys.

There are plenty names to conjure with, bringing with them each persons own particular favourite memories, the one and only Hughie McIlmoyle. My personal boyhood champion, Paddy Waters, don't ask me why, I think I just loved the name, sounded so great, his surname being pronounced "Watters". Alf Ackerman, top scorer. Manager and International player Ivor Broadis, all round Cricketer and United anchor man Chris Balderstone. Joe Laidlow, always managed to look slow but went like a train.

Record appearance holder, Hero Goalie Alan Ross. We could go on and on and still not do some one justice.

Anyway, back to the story. This was not to be my only calamity at sandy bay, a short while later on yet another sun soaked summers day I was watching the older boys swimming to and fro across the river, it seemed as wide as the English Channel to a little lad like me but was actually quite narrow. I took it into my head to try to walk across, god knows why, it just seemed the thing to do at the time, so off I went wading in. At first the water did not seem too deep and I pushed on confident of success, unfortunately the river deepens quite suddenly about half way across and I was very quickly in difficulties, one minute I was up to my waist in the cold swirling brown water and, the next I had disappeared below it and could not swim, I really do not recall if my life flashed before me, what little there was of it, but I do remember being terrified and convinced I was about to die, I can still feel the water being sucked into my lungs as I gasped for breath but found none. A blackness was closing over me. I was doomed.

Luckily for me a young girl, I never did find out who, was walking her dog on the far bank quickly realised my predicament, without hesitation she plunged in, I was saved.

I am told that I had turned a nice shade of blue, more Cambridge than Oxford, and with the help of some pals slapping me vigorously on the back, coughed up what seemed like half the Petterill. Some of my friends had already took off so as to be the first to break the news to my Mam that her son had drowned, so it was not long until she appeared with some of our neighbours, all convinced they were coming to collect my body. They very nearly were. Mam went ballistic, first holding me in her arms , then belting me around the ear she told me not to do that again, as if, frightening her like that. I blubbed like a baby, my heart pounded for ages after.

Funny though I did not feel any fear of water and was back at Sandy Bay the next day, but stayed on my side of the river until I learned to swim at the public baths, Mam made sure of that.
I still enjoy swimming to this day. Just to digress a moment however I did have another couple of bad experiences both in the sea, once in the Caribbean off the coast of Guyana in South America where I was stationed with the Army on internal security duties, I was swimming in the estuary of the Berbice river. The water there is extremely muddy due to the run off from the rain forest up country, and you literally cannot see anything beneath the surface. Well, I had been in the water for a short while when I decided that I had enough and began wading back to the shore, suddenly I was knocked off my feet by something very large swimming past me, I have never left the water so fast in my life, reminiscent of a cartoon character my legs churning up the water speeding to the shore . To say I was shocked is an understatement of the highest order. I was aware that sharks were plentiful in the area but had no knowledge of any attacks on swimmers or anything like that, in fact the young local boys went spear fishing along the waterfront and seemed to fear nothing, just me then ! God knows what it was and I suppose he ain't telling.
The other occasion was in the Med just off the rocky shore of San Antonio bay on the Island of Ibiza in the Spanish Balearics. I had learned to love snorkelling as you do, all the wonderful brightly coloured fish and corals. The water so clear it was like floating in space. I was quite carried away, both content and fascinated at the same moment when, the rubber mouth piece of my snorkel decided to detach itself from the breathing tube just as I inhaled deeply so as to gain depth, I quickly surfaced in an almighty panic coughing and spluttering, gasping for breath in fear of dear life. Fortunately a fishing boat was moored nearby and I hung on to its anchor rope

trying to regain my equilibrium. Needless to say I recovered in a short time then just carried on, but a bit more carefully this time. I still love the water and cannot resist its charms, having said that I am inclined to stay close to the shore, you never know what's going to happen next, and, well they do say things come in threes so that's my lot I hope. God willing.

7   LOOK OUT, THE GYPSYS ARE COMING !

Down the bottom of Botcherby Avenue was a track way leading to a disused landfill site, now part of the Metal Box open top factory where I would later be employed for two miserable years producing ring pull tops for coke cans, literally millions of the things.
There you could often see folk retrieving bits of scrap metal and stuff, which were either recycled ,to use the modern parlance, or carted of to the scrap man for cash. We spent many a happy day exploring the tip for treasure in the shape of pram wheels for bogeys and old jam jars to catch minnows ,sticklebacks and tadpoles, occasionally retrieving the odd item of value, but we were more interested in having fun really.

Other visitors to this track were the Romany's, real Gypsy's, not your modern day so called new age travellers. They would arrive in their gaily painted horse drawn Caravans which contained all their requirements for day to day life. At the back on a shelf would be a

double bed, under that was a large cupboard, decorated with flowers and such while at the side was the wood burning stove for winter warmth and cooking in bad weather. The rest
of the space was used up storing the necessities of life on the road, the rolled up thin mattresses for junior members of the family, though in mild weather they would prefer a tent or just crawl beneath the van. Most of the day to day cooking was done on an open fire, with a big black skillet and a large cast iron pot hanging from a metal tripod, just like in the story books.

The women never seemed to mind us kids, known to them as Gorgia, plonking ourselves down next to their kids and watching them, the mother would throw pieces of ham or rabbit on to the hot skillet to sear and then toss them into the huge pot over the fire along with all kinds of vegetables and big chunks of potatoes liberated from fields and gardens along the way. All the more surprising when you remember rationing was still on the go and meat still a luxury for the rest of us.

The big black pot would then bubble away sending up a cloud of steam and give out the most amazing aromas when sprinkled with fresh herbs collected en route from lanes and hedgerows. It smelled so good our belly's thought our throats had been cut. Regretfully we were never offered any of these delights so I cannot comment on their taste, but our mouths watered just the same, and the Romany kids looked the picture of health with their outdoor life and no school, lucky beggars. Although with hindsight maybe not so.

We often heard tales of them rolling hedgehogs in clay and baking them on the open fire but never actually witnessed this, though it is believed to be a generally accepted practice , nor the often told tale of when times were tough the odd rat would find its way into the pot.

I have no doubt their skills in living of the land were exceptional. We did not see a lot of the men who would be out and about collecting scrap metal, old batteries and the like. When they got some old copper wire or cables, rare commodities in post war Carlisle and elsewhere , they would build a fire ,place the scrap copper on a piece of old corrugated iron and burn off the covering collecting the melted copper in an old bucket or such like, apparently they got a better price this way and it was not so easy to trace where the cable etc had come from.
The Gypsy girls would call at the houses in the area selling lucky white heather, clothes pegs, bulrushes or even just a blessing. My mother always bought something because she was scared of being cursed, this being a common fear when the gypsy's called.. Occasionally she would have her palm read by one of the elder woman who claimed the gift of second sight. Whether it was genuine or not was not important the fear of the curse was sufficient to close the deal.
Silver crossed palm and all were satisfied, mam felt secure in her life and the Seer made a few bob. What in later life as a salesman I would call a "win win " situation. Even my Dad who had no time for these people took no chances and always found a good excuse to buy something inexpensive, he was a bit of a gambler my dad, but knew when to hedge his bets.
They were on the whole not entirely welcome in the area due to a reputation for retrieving anything not nailed down, which was probably not undeserved, but I was enthralled by them all the same. The romance of their lifestyle enthralled me as it had the world for centuries. It was just an illusion, I know now, in truth a hard existence, but who cares it's the wonder of it all that counts. By the time I became a teenager the Romany's had all but vanished, either absorbed into or driven from society, who preferred conformity to free spirits. Nothings changed.

Once travelling in the north of Scotland on a little used trail I came across a Romany family living in an arched tent structure of old pieces of canvas and rags, similar to modern temporary tunnel greenhouses, it was mid winter and bitterly cold, there must have been a dozen assorted adults and children, none of them seemed anywhere near clothed well enough to combat the chill, the kids barefooted looked like refugees on the television news. Any Ideas I had bore of the romantic life of Romany's left me that day.

I have read many books about other peoples adventures and travels, seeking new lives abroad, new starts, new challenges. Especially recently with so many folk heading abroad to the mountains of Spain etc, buying up small farms seeking self sufficiency and stress free living. Then making an even better living by writing about it all. Goat breeding, orange plantations and even olive farms. The only worry is how so many end up coming back home to blighty, strange that.

Since I was a boy like countless others, I have yearned for the excitement of living on a desert Island, fishing the clear blue waters, eating fruit fresh from the tree, drinking coconut milk.
 "sometimes I think the only nut around here is me," sailing the seven seas, discovering new and fabulous lands, well new to me at least. I did get as far as planning to go to Australia on an assisted passage, which would have found me working on a farm in that countries Red Centre. Needless to say it all fell through for one reason or another.

Still some things are just not meant to be and I did hear some years later that life on those out of the way farms was no picnic, in fact quite the reverse, some boys were being treated no better then slaves, with no or little pay and harsh conditions allowing no creature comfort. Phew, glad I missed out on that.

8   THREE RIVERS TO CROSS.

The rivers Petterill and Eden played large in our young lives. Carlisle's third river the Caldew was rarely explored being as it was on the other side of the City, though we did go fishing a couple of times down by Boustead's Grassing, past what was the Gas works with its huge tanks that raised and fell depending on there capacity. In the morning they were massive, full of town gas, landmarks viewed from all over town, ready to service cookers and boilers City wide, then gently lowered as the gas was consumed during the course of day, to be refilled at night when usage dropped dramatically. North sea gas put an end to their activities and you would not now know of its very existence. The entire site now flattened, a part of Carlisle history gone, along with the Crane makers Cowen Sheldon, most of the Metal box Company who produced the marvellous decorative biscuit tins, now very collectable and some bring hundreds of pounds at auction. Ferguson's Printers, major employers in Denton Holme along with Penguin confection and Kangol's, another obliterated site though still a world brand. I could go on all day, so much change in a single lifetime.

As well as swimming we fished with the proverbial bent pin and thread on a cane rod, sometimes actually catching a fish, dace normally or various fry seeking safety in the shallows, with the occasional eel. I hated eels they twisted around the line something rotten and it was all you could do to get rid of them being all slimy, how folk thought of them as a delicacy I do not know.

How we envied the big lads with their proper rods and reels, casting far into the stream looking to catching brown and rainbow trout mainly to take home for tea. Occasionally a Sea trout would make its way from the Solway to some ones frying pan. The weir at Holme Head bay was a favourite spot to watch the salmon leap, like silver spears through rushing white water, marvelling at their strength and power, determined to progress upstream to their ancient spawning sites in streams and tributary's, unless waylaid by the poachers gaffe.

Others, more interested in the fun of fishing camped on the bank seeking course fish, where quantity caught and held in keep nets to be weighed then freed later often out weighed quality.

Later in the season the more prosperous anglers would appear in their waders, standing in the middle of the river casting flies for salmon and sea trout. The Eden especially was always known as a great salmon river. Stocks now sadly depleted, with more fishermen than ever seeking to catch what limited stock there is, a common theme to all past Salmon courses.

A lot of our time was spent avoiding the water bailiff who took his roll most seriously, showing no mercy to those caught red handed. The water bailiff looking after the Eden and the Esk in our time was a bloke called Tom Brodie who had the uncanny knack of suddenly appearing on the river bank behind you, panicking loads of men and boys to dive into the river head first striking out for the far bank to evade capture. Even when you had a full ticket and were fishing perfectly legally the sight of him approaching still made the butterflies flutter in your tummy. He carried out his duties diligently for over thirty years I believe, when he eventually retired, his parting gift from his employers was to be allowed to keep the old company pushbike. Well, I don't think I would have bothered. Being a small boy did not excuse unlicensed angling and you could find yourself in juvenile court, or if you were lucky, nursing a thick ear, your catch confiscated, probably served up later for the bailiffs tea.

When you think back its hard to believe this type of activity could result in a criminal record, bringing with it shame on your family. My step brother Eric, caught riding his bike on the footpath in Melbourne park, was taken to magistrates court fined five shillings and even got his name reported in the Evening News, talk about zero tolerance . My best pal Geoff and another lad, were also caught cycling the same path and were also taken to magistrate court where Geoff only got fined two and six because he was the younger, the other lad got the usual five bob. We all thought life was much more simple then. Cor blimey mother.

We would feast on crab apples, usually followed by gut ache, and search the hedgerows for birds nests, strictly non political now, but accepted juvenile activity then, boys were encouraged to get involved in things like egg collecting, even the likes of Bill Oddie, much to his shame, admits to owning a birds egg collection which was thought to be morale building like joining the Boy Scouts or Boys Brigade. Talking of Boys Brigade, or Life boys, more of that later.

We would blow the eggs by piercing a hole in each end and blowing out the contents. Sometimes the appearance of a half grown chick would prick our conscience, but not for very long, well we were just kids after all.

Often we would come across the nests of Blackies, Dunnock, Thrush, Tits etc, whilst occasionally disturbing ground nesters like Lapwings, better known as Peewits, and Curlew. Conservation was not on the agenda then, so all was to a great degree fair game. Various wartime Airfields were scattered around Carlisle, some real, some bogus to confuse and mislead the marauding Boche into attacking wasteland and cardboard hangers. We were a Country low on actual arms so a little deception went a long way. The foundations of red bricked ruins were to be discovered in the long grass, well populated by wild birds, Hares and Rabbits. Skylark nests abounded, their elevated song clear as they flew into blue skies. Dragon flies, tadpoles and newts were all at home in the ponds, untouched by time. Too many old bricks set in ancient concrete for the plough to disturb, giving unintended sanctuary to natures residents.

People would still snare rabbits or shoot pigeons for the pot and collected wild fruits like brambles and berries from the hedgerows for jam or plate cakes. Mushrooming was a common activity along with crab appleing for making jam, preserves and all kinds of chutneys. Schools would organise outings to collect rose hips to sell to the local Chemist for the production of Rose Hip syrup. Herbs and wild foods were collected by the more discerning cooks to liven up bland ration meals.

At harvest time all would flock to the tattie picken field between Botcherby Avenue and the Little Sisters of the poor Nunnery, then join in hay making to gain a few bob and a bag of spuds or whatever to supplement our meagre diet.

The field we went to do the tattie picken was the site many years earlier of a flying circus which would visit occasionally and take people for joy rides, five bob a circuit of Botcherby, spotting your home from on high must have been amazing. Those old planes made of canvas and string, scary..

The more colour full small birds like Gold tits and Chaffinches were often caught to be traded or kept as pets, sold openly in the markets etc, where they were on a par with the likes of Budgies. Parakeets and other exotic birds not so generally available. Some even kept Jackdaws or Magpies which were exceptionally clever birds and could be taught tricks or to talk, often better than parrots, more obtainable and once well trained you did not even need a cage as they would stick around like homing pigeons.

Lots of folk bred pigeons, some for the pot some to race,

occasionally these becoming quite valuable as breeding stock, some still do, becoming worth thousands of pounds, but pigeon fanciers do not exist to the same extent. Lofts were a common site on allotments, mainly for some reason close to railway tracks, but also in back gardens. However bye laws, health and safety and public dislike of the rodents population attracted to pigeon feed droppings ,have all come to affect the sport. Others kept wild rabbits for meat which was still on ration, causing many a broken heart when a child's favourite bunny entered the oven.

9   DADS FLYING GNASHERS.

On beautiful summer days you just have to do something, get out of the house and make use of this glorious climate.
So one such day it was decided to head down to the river Eden in Rickerby park, just along from the war memorial suspension bridge.
Mam made up a picnic of hard boiled eggs, cheese sandwiches, a couple of packets of Smiths crisps, plain only then with the little blue paper twists of salt, no flavours, they were still to come, but luxury of luxuries a bag of broken biscuits purchased from Bank,s corner grocery and post office. I loved these bags of broken biscuits because they contained all my favourites, like custard creams, and if you were really lucky some chocolate digestives, heaven.
We made our way down Victoria road past the Magpie Pub where our Dad was carousing with his mates, onto Warwick road, past the football ground, turning right at Saint Aidan's Church, then right again on past the posh houses of St Aidan's Road with their gated driveways and shiny, freshly polished motor cars. Mainly Rovers, Singers and other British classics of the day.
We entered Rickerby park by the old Water Works gate, now a Municipal golf club house, then following the cinder path arrived at the suspension bridge. Now, Mam and my big sister Brenda were a bit wary of this bridge because it sometimes moved as you crossed it, not a lot, but just enough for you to sense it.
 Sometimes it made that funny butterfly feeling in your stomach. We lads of course would wait until we were half way across then deliberately jump up and down to make the bridge move and Mam

and Brenda panic and squeal, hurrying to get to the other side.
I could never resist stopping and putting my head through the bars of the steel structure searching the dark waters below for trout hanging against the current to snap up passing morsels such as May flies, midges etc, I dreamed of owning a proper fishing rod and landing these beauties, but than I would still need a licence or risk the water bailiffs hand on my collar.
The park spread out before us like a huge green quilt, dissected by the pattern cinder paths all leading to the magnificent Cenotaph, surrounded by stout railings, built to remember Carlisle's Brave war dead from two world wars, plus other senseless conflicts. Korea, Malaya, Aden, etc.
We chose a spot where the ground was level enough for Mam to lay the old bed spread she had brought for us to sit on, having first got rid of the thistles which seemed to grow in abundance along the bank, but far enough from the river to avoid splashes from her frolicking kids.
We were soon stripped off and wearing our swimming costumes, mine proudly bearing the red, yellow and green patches awarded for completing a breadth and a length, and two lengths of the public swimming baths, I was still trying for my mile patch, I got there eventually, but it was hard going.
On we ran into the water ,squealing as the cold nipped at out bare white skin. But nothing was going to stop us having our fun in the river, even occasionally stubbing our toes on the cobbled bottom or swallowing gob fulls of the stuff as we splashed around.
The better swimmers amongst us racing back and forth to the far bank, showing off. Games of tag and who could hold their breath the longest, were followed by terrifying the girls pulling them under water, then bravely rescuing them.
A short while later dad appeared, full of fun and bravado, no doubt induced by the several pints of beer he had consumed during

the two hours or so spent in the Magpie Pub, no all day drinking yet.
He soon persuaded me to part with my swimming trunks so he could wear them and join us in the river, I then had to make do with my underpants, very embarrassing. However we had a great time, being chased by dad who took on the roll of river monster, diving beneath the water and catching us by the leg scaring us and making me, Brian and Brenda rush for the shore in fear of our lives.

Then it happened, dad having once more been attempting to swim underwater to sneak upon us, raised up, and gaining a foothold lifted his head, then gave out with an enormous sneeze. We all stood and watched in stunned silence as his top set of false teeth left his mouth and in a great arc flew across the river, landing with a resounding plop several yards away. Stunned, poor old dads face was a picture of sheer disbelief and panic.
The hilarious laughter soon turned quiet however as it was realised poor old dad would be toothless until a new pair of dentures could be purchased which he could ill afford. No one was laughing now. The bank of the river by this time had attracted several other people intent on having a good day out, including several young fit lads who having witnessed dads predicament soon were in the water and a frantic search began, with bodies diving and splashing all around in total entropy.
Dad was devastated, convinced he had seen the last of his gnasher's which in all probability were right now being ground into the river bed by the numerous pounding feet of well meaning enthusiastic strangers.
The search went on for about a good hour or so, with more and more people being told the tale of the flying teeth and joining in. It was bedlam personified.

We had just about given up the cause and Mam was slowly and reluctantly packing our things ready for the miserable long trek homeward. Dad, who a short while ago had been in his element, now stood dejected by the waters edge, gutted, a sadder sight would have been hard to find.
Then ! amazingly a shout went up and a hand was raised , between its thumb and forefinger was grasped the illusive molars. Shebang ! The young man became an instant hero, with much back slapping and congratulating, a hero, with dad promising him all he could drink at the Magpie and more.
Mam, spread the blanket again and the picnic continued well into the evening, with dad staying firmly ensconced on the bank, slipping in and out of alcohol assisted unconsciousness . I can not recall him ever swimming again after that day, not too surprising considering his traumatic, most unwanted adventure.

Well, no one could believe the luck we had that day. Dad had almost cried with the relief of it all, while the rest of us teased him something rotten whenever the opportunity arose, which was more frequent than he appreciated. Still it gave us a day when the family were together, one we will not too soon forget.
We still went to the river over the years, swam and fished for tiddlers with a bent pin and and string on a piece of cane., or a jam jar on string, But dad never came again to the place of his nemesis, sticking to the Manor he new best, the good old Magpie. Poor old dad….
One Saturday night, when I was about five or six years old I was roused from my sleep by my dad clearly in the grip of yet more alcoholic joy, lifting me from my bed he proceeded to carry me down the stairs where, sitting me upon his knee, informed me that I had won the princely sum of two pounds in the Magpie Inn's weekly raffle.

Bemused, I held the two crisp oncer's in my hot little hands, whilst ignoring my mothers raised voice telling dad not to be so stupid, and to retrieve the said cash, but no he was adamant in his conviction, my name had been written by him on the raffle ticket stub, so it was only fair I received the lolly, I was overjoyed and determined not to part with my windfall, holding on tight to my money, ignoring my Mam's intervention I quickly bounded back up the dancers to my still warm bed. I slept the sleep of the fortunate, blissfully happy.

My next recollection is at the breakfast table next morning, dad in the early throws of a hangover being energetically reminded by mam just what had occurred the previous night, and the slow realisation of his loss of two quid.

Now to put things in perspective, two quid in 1950 was worth about fifty quid today, ie a lot of dosh to lose via an act of gross stupidity.

But as I have mentioned earlier dad was no ones mug and soon worked out a plan to retrieve his two crisp green one pound notes. On the table in front of me he laid with great exaggeration, two shiny new one shilling coins, (ten pence in today's money !) all bright and silvery, irresistible to a five year old, well who wanted two bits of grotty green paper when you could jangle two lovely silver shillings in your pocket. A deal was struck and all were happy, except later when I think about it I have a sneaky suspicion he also wangled a way of getting his two shillings back because I do not recall ever spending any of it !

I seem to be making my Dad out to be some sort of alcoholic, which is far from the truth really. He was first and foremost a family man, loving his kids and would do anything for us. It just seems most of my funniest memories involve some sort of drinking related incident.

Like the day he was trying to help his best mate who had had a severe skin full onto the bus, his mate however, so far out of it thought someone was trying to nick his wallet and poor old dad ended up with a huge black eye for his trouble, what a job he had explaining that to our Mam. Another time in the Magpie someone offered him a cheap leg of pork, probably nicked, dad always one for a bargain accepted without checking just what was on offer, as you do, then came staggering home with half a pig over his shoulder. Well, no one had a refrigerator then so it had to be quickly shared out with all and sundry, I doubt if he got paid by most so ended up well and truly out of pocket. Yet another black mark. Though I do remember dad saying I could have the tail and my sister could have the squeak.

One of Dads other pleasures on a Saturday or Sunday afternoon was to put our baby sister Susan into her pram and take her for a walk along through Scotby three fields, a walk popular with locals which presented no real obstacles as it meandered along beside Tilbury Beck, through as its name suggests, the three fields between Wood street with its lovely small church, and Scotby road, skirting the edge of Durranhill Army Barracks and back up Durranhill road. Of course you will not find it now, as with the camp it disappeared beneath yet another housing and industrial estate. Brenda and I would often accompany him on his sojourn having a great time searching the beck for stickle backs, newts and generally running amok, well me really I suppose, Brenda was a much more well behaved child and grown up, not one for running amok. But then, it is said still waters run deep so I will take a sabbatical on that one for now. What I remember most is the look of peace and contentment on dads face as he made his trek, he was clearly a man at peace with himself. Love to know what he

was thinking about ! Funny what stays in your mind. Innit !!
Now it's the grandkids we picnic with at the waters edge, skimming stones and looking for tiddler's. It is amazing the effect of a good day out in the sun has on everyone. I do not think lads get out and about as we did, running wild, instead when they are not on the computer or playing digital games, its
organised sanitized visits to show Farms or mini nature reserves to marvel at the Pigs, Goats, Ducks and Hens (Blimey.) or some sort of exotic animal such as Ostrich, llamas or Kangaroos along with the obligatory, ever watchful, Meerkat or two.
Love Meerkat's , don't you ? I suppose you must do going by the amount of them there are about. Hardly any wonder they are scarce in the wild, the little beggars are all in Cumbria being gawped at by us !. I wonder if eventually little African boys and girls will be taken to African farms to feed the baby Black faced ewes and Friesian cattle one day. Well !.

Many of the kids are in the attentive care of weekend dads, supported by grandparents, being spoilt rotten to make up for the desertion felt as a result of family break up and subsequent divorce. The day of the family appears to be over.
It cannot be easy being a part time parent, cramming all your love and affection into designated time slots, then being let down at the last moment because of some perceived insult or unwelcome comment. Despite the best efforts of well meaning carers, usually young idealistic women in overlarge coveralls and green Wellington's, these creatures never look that happy at being saved from extinction or the gruesome activities of the fur trade. Rare pygmy goats ungratefully head butting tiny tots who have just spent their pocket money at the entrance to buy bags of food in order to sustain their miserable little lives a bit longer, no gratitude those smelly little rarities.

Still, when all the wildlife has disappeared from the Earth, these will be our token appreciation to the hand of creation. Whether that be an all powerful God Head or Evolutionary genetic code, accidentally brought to our planet by some asteroid or other. Personally I adhere to the theory that we are the end result of some failed dire experiment by little green men, who even now are speeding as fast as they can to the far side of the galaxy in order to try and escape the eventual unavoidable Armageddon man will unleash upon himself in the name of some God or other, or maybe just for cash.

10   SPEECH THERAPY, YEA, RIGHT.

When Geoff Moses and I were around eight years old it was decided we required some form of speech therapy, still not sure just what for, though I am told that Aitches are still a mystery to me. This took place at the City Medical Centre in George Street right the middle of Carlisle, next to the old Maternity Hospital, where the Civic Centre now stands. The first time we attended, because it was quite some distance from Norman Street School, we were escorted by one of the staff. It constituted about a twenty five minute walk each way at a steady pace for our ages. However after that initial visit we were expected to make our own way. Well, you can imagine the many and varied distractions for two eight year olds on a journey like that, we were often very late, some times not arriving at all. The amazing thing is I cannot recall a single time that we were reprimanded over this, I can only assume no one was aware of our truancy, or more likely teacher was probably only too happy to be rid of us for an afternoon. I was most certainly not an attentive pupil, whilst I cannot speak for Geoff though, lets say I have my suspicions. Whatever the problem was with our speech, it either corrected itself or we still have it to this day.

I cannot in my wildest dreams imagine today eight year old kids being left to their own devices as we were in the nineteen fifties, travelling unaccompanied through the city streets, getting up to all kinds of things without it raising an eyebrow. Today it would at least call for an enquiry with the loss of jobs and possibly even prosecutions, blimey, the innocence of youth. Still on the whole I seemed to enjoy school, if not exactly enthralled.

Later the Council introduced School meals, which meant we did not have the dash home over Melbourne Park and back for our dinners. Instead we were led through the street crocodile fashion in neat little lines each holding the hand of a classmate. The

dining rooms were a little way from the school, next to the bridge at the entrance to the park and served both St Johns, and Brook Street schools as well as Norman street. We were in awe of the bigger boys from Brook Street who enjoyed a formidable reputation for being tough and always up for a scrap. We avoided them like the plague, though occasionally someone got picked on and bashed, usually for no other reason than to keep us little people in our place, I for one was happy to oblige, I could get into trouble without no ones help ,thank you very much.
Another introduction by the Council at this time was the school bus. It cost one penny and was always packed solid, some of the drivers were right miserable sods but some were plain daft, we would all sing, " Go wiggly waggly, Go wiggly waggly." and the driver would swing the bus back and forward over the road with kids falling all over the place in absolute hysterical laughter. No political correctness then, just daft folk having a great time.
I failed my eleven plus miserably, as expected, and went on to St Johns Junior School on Grey Street next to St James Church. one of the best things about St Johns was that it stood directly opposite the scrap mans yard, which we raided at every chance.
We would spend part of our afternoon playtime with our heads between the railings watching the various ragmen arriving at the scrap yard with their days collection, already sorted into rag types ,ie cotton, woollens, etc. with the occasional bit of old iron or copper. It must have been a some what lucrative trade as there seemed to be plenty folk doing it, (recently revived due to world shortages of base materials.) some just with push bikes others with horse and carts, and the really big time lads with a lorry.
One day a regular ragman turned up who had some sort of disability which not only made walking very difficult, but speaking also, we all felt sorry for this lad and would give a wave and an hello when ever he turned up.

Then one day he left his barrow loaded with sacks at the gate while he went inside for some reason, not a good idea, while he was away another ragman appeared whom none of us liked at all, he was clearly not a nice person looking for all the world like a Charles Dickens villain. While we watched on in disbelief this rogue began helping himself to the collection of the disabled lad and adding them to his own meagre load.. The swine !
He must have wondered what was going on because within seconds twenty or more eleven year olds were over the school railings and surrounding him,
" Thief, Thief." we all yelled at the top of our voices, trying to pull the sacks from him. We raised such a rumpus not only did the men from the scrap yard come out to see what was going on, but a local Bobby appeared from nowhere. We wasted no time informing everyone of what had occurred.
The rogue was made to return the stolen goods upon threat of a severe thumping from the scrap yard men and immediate arrest by the Bobby.
We were all very pleased with ourselves despite a telling off for being late back in class. The down side from this adventure was the fact that our friend , the rogue remembered our actions and we would often find ourselves being chased for dear life down some alley or other. But I do not think he was very successful, being a beer bellied drinking smoker chasing young fit boys.
One of the best known rag and bone men was a lad called Geordie Miller, he was full of fun and all the young kids would follow him all over the place, he was sometimes good for a scrounge of a fag too.
It was while I attended St Johns I received my first real taste of manic violence visited upon my person, the story goes like this.

While at St Johns in the mid fifties we had a brilliant male teacher, a young Canadian still training, seeming like just another lad really, he was always up for a laugh, and we all loved him for it, he was not like a real teacher at all, unlike the other staff who seemed perpetually miserable, though they may have had good reason with us kids running riot.
One day I decided to play a trick on him by putting some imitation dog Poo under his desk. We all waited for him to enter the classroom confident he would take it all in good heart. The door eventually opened and in stepped not our beloved teacher, who had called in sick that morning, (we subsequently discovered the young Canadians wife had died suddenly after a short Illness.) but the head mistress. She quickly spotted the fake dog Poo and demanded of the class who had put it there. It was a testament to the fear she induced when almost the entire class stood and pointed at me, thanks pals, I was doomed !
She dragged me to the front of the class and proceeded to knock seven bells out of me, she did not need a cane or strap, just her fists, the beating seemed to go on forever, I thought she was about to murder me, the blows raining down incessantly, punch after murderous punch. My pleas of innocents and regret gained me nothing, she was determined to have her pound of flesh, it was probably the feel of the hang mans noose around her throat that made sense prevail. Panting and sweating with her exertions she eventually dumped me back at my desk a whimpering sorry little boy. I carried the bumps and bruises for weeks afterwards.
It was no use complaining as I would attract no sympathy, teacher was always right in those days and my parents attitude reflected that. Were this assault, for assault it was, to take place today it would in all probability result in charges and a court appearance.. Or more likely retaliation from the pupil, who would then be the one in court.

In her defence, here I go again defending the indefensible, she must have been under quite some stress, what with the sudden death of the young wife and the strain of running such a school, I guess she just had enough and took it out on the first thing she could, me! Old bitch.
So that's me mentally scarred for life then ! No wonder I was so wary of older women .

11   APPLE BLOSSOM TIME.

Another of our pastimes in the summer months was raiding nearby orchards for apples, pears, plums, damsons, greengages and the like.
The local Nunnery, St Josephs, home to the Little Sisters of the Poor, always came in for special attention based on the theory boys in short trousers ran much faster than women in long skirts, not always exactly true, as many a red ear could testify, some of those Nuns could pack a punch, believe me. They rarely called the police, preferring more immediate Devine justice.
The other Nunnery on Scotby Road, our Lady and Jesus of the Sacred Heart, now Chapel Brow houses and flats, avoided much of our attention. Partly due to it being further a field and partly because the orchard was so much smaller, leaving you vulnerable to capture by fleet footed Angels.
The other thing was the incumbents, also described as vulnerable girls seeking protection of the church, however they looked more like a tough old bunch of middle aged women, the last thing you wanted was to feel their fury. Similar to the Garlands, more of which later, the majority of inmates (Sorry, Girls seeking the Church's protection !) were there simply because no one else wanted them, having been abandoned by families due to the shame of unwanted pregnancy, a common theme, or just had no one to care for them. Today they would be given Social Security payments, a council house and a boyfriend sneaking in when no one was looking.

The time that comes to mind in my orchard raiding career came one summers eve when the apples in the nunnery garden had been well harvested and the only really good fruit was high in the canopy. However we refused to give up and stumbled across a particularly heavy laden previously un-plundered specimen.

I quickly volunteered to climb the tree and throw down the apples, which I duly did, only occasionally glancing down to see my mates stuffing apples down jumpers and in bulging pockets.

After a while when looking down once more I could see the apples landing on the ground but no one was picking them up.

A bit mystified I made my way down, thinking everyone was loaded up and leaving I dropped down from my perch landing on my knees. My heart seemed to stop for directly in front of my nose were a huge pair of black boots, inside which were a pair of large feet belonging to a member of the local constabulary.

But worse was the black wet nose of a huge German Shepherd dog nudging against mine, a low growl coming from its throat, its hairs seemed to stand up on its heavy neck, for what seemed an eternity the dogs staring brown eyes were firmly fixed on mine. Then without a seconds thought to the consequences I was off like a sprinter out of the blocks. Surrounding the nunnery was a six foot red bricked wall, part of which can still be seen, which I cleared in a single bound, such being the incentive of being eaten by a big hairy dog, not bad for a short arsed fat lad.

There were other orchards nearby all bearing desirable fruit of one kind or another, none of which escaped our attention for very long, along with an abundance of things like peapods, strawberries, raspberries and blackberries, etc from the local allotments. We usually dined well, with just the occasional belly ache from eating too much to slow us down.

Occasionally boys would be had up for raiding Orchards, some being guests of her Majesty's Borstal system, but my luck held and I had a crime free childhood. well, officially at least. I often look back and count my blessings.

Some of my friends ended up on charges of one kind or another, but in the main we were just normal lads growing up post war with its rationing of sweets and stuff, so temptation was an ever present danger. Fortunately I was too scared of reprisals to steal anything of real value, unless I was absolutely certain of not being detected which I never was. Any way my mother would have murdered me for sure.

I suppose life was not all that bad in the nineteen fifties, just about everyone smoked in those days and the local pub was still the hub of the community, especially on weekends, though no one had much when it came to cash, but everybody seemed to know how to enjoy themselves regardless. The adults were determined to put the austerity of the war years behind them and get some hard earned pleasure out of life. Sing songs in the Magpie Inn at a weekend, and bowls on summer days, with darts, dominoes and football teams, life could be good for most.
No drugs then, very little street crime, when thefts or suchlike did happen neighbours pulled together to find the culprits, then either handed out their own brand of justice or passed the villains over to the police. The thing was everyone knew everyone else, and you did not shit on your own doorstep. Strangers stood out like new pins and while neighbourhood watch was a far off innovation, it already existed without saying. Another thing, there was a lot of rough tough diamonds in Botcherby, so you crossed them at your own peril.
We still had street traders and what have you coming around then, such as street singers looking for a spare copper or two, Tinkers seeking pots and pans to mend, knife sharpeners with their mobile grind wheels, Hurdy Gurdy men playing weird tunes on their mobile Organ like instruments which no one could recognise, and

of course Rag and Bone men with their brightly coloured balloons tempting the kids to bring out their Mam's and Dad's old ,or some times not so old coats and stuff in order to have one of those wonderful balloons. This transaction would often be followed by an irate parent running after the rag man to recover their one and only top coat, occasionally ending in threatened if not actual violence, the rest of the neighbourhood looking on in great amusement. Days were hardly ever dull for long. Now the rag and bone men are making a comeback, I could hardly believe my ears the other day when the call, " Rag, Bone.." rang out in our street, two blokes in an old truck loaded to the gunnels with washing machines, fridges and all kinds of stuff calling out for scrap, clearly money to be made again, what goes round comes around apparently.

Horse and carts were still very much the order of the day. Still in use by various tradesmen and street vendors. The old men and woman would rush out with their shovels when ever a horse did its business, collecting the manure for their rhubarb and vegetable plots, organic gardening is nothing new.
The horse has now made an amazing come back ,with more horses around now than at the turn of the 19th century. Its true you see them everywhere.
Most folk grew fruit and vegetables of some kind, even if it were just some rhubarb and a few potatoes. Some had planted fruit trees in wartime when things were in short supply or even non existent. My dad was never a keen gardener, mainly because he had to work long hours like most folk, then often have to walk home from the 14th RAF maintenance unit where he was employed as a Civil Servant, away over the other side of the City, past what is now Kingstown trading estate, one time Aerodrome, a good five mile slog at the end of a hard day.

Though as he grew older and working conditions improved giving him more free time he took a real interest in cultivating flowers, he even got a garden shed where he would disappear with his paper for some peace and quiet from his noisy and expanding family.
It was while laying the concrete foundations for the aforementioned shed that we dug up an old first world war rifle, an old top loader, probably 303 calibre which was covered in rust, well past any use. Dad reckoned it must have been buried by a deserter from the horror of the trenches in France and Belgium. There would not have been any houses here then most likely just fields or possibly woodland, Botcherby still being a small remote outpost of Carlisle. I wanted to believe it had been used by a bank robber or a secret agent plying his devious trade. Anyway dad would not let me keep it and got rid of it somehow. It was never mentioned again.
We also dug from the shed foundations an object made from some type of twisted metal strands , formed to a horse shoe shape with roundel endings, my Uncle Brian and I pondered on this strange item for some time, unable to deduce what on earth it could be. Dad, eventually getting fed up of waiting for his shed to be completed took the thing from me and threw it over the hedge into the council Nursery behind,
" there." he said, " it's gone for ever now get on with the job in hand."
It was soon forgotten until many years later, watching an Archaeological programme on the telly, one of the diggers produced something very like what we had found under the shed. He told us it was a Torc, a form of jewellery from Celtic times made usually from strands of twisted gold and worn around the neck by both men and women, now worth a small Kings ransom. When I told dad about it he told me not to be so daft and that it was more likely a bit of old spring mattress. Still, I do wonder

from time to time, did the old git throw away a fortune !!
Right, back to the deserter, poor man was probably scared out of his wits. At the time he would have suffered all kinds of punishment for showing cowardice, including summary execution. Time has taught us just what horrors were being experienced by these men, most just boys, in their local pals regiments, so named due to recruitment taking place on a Village, Town or workplace basis. Entire communities lost all their men folk at a stroke , going over the top together, dying together. They went joyfully to serve King and Country, singing as they went, unknowing often to certain death, millions never coming home, a generation lost, then bugger me if we did not try to do it all again just twenty one years later.
Glad I missed that lot, where these men stroke boys found their courage astounds me, hardly a home in the land was spared. God rest their souls.

12   WORKING CLASS HEROES.

It is with enormous affection I remember our neighbours on Botcherby Avenue. Two gentlemen I held in some awe were Mr Harrison, who lived three doors down from us and was the driver of the ash cart which travelled the streets weekly collecting the general household rubbish, which in those days was in the main made up of ashes from the coal fires we all used before gas and electricity were in general use. There being very little other rubbish as then everything that could be recycled was. Not because of our being environmentally aware as we are now out of necessity, but because nothing was wasted due to our having very little to waste anyway, newspaper was required to light the fire, etc and cardboard always came in handy. There were no plastic bottles or plastic carrier bags, they would arrive thirty or so years later in abundance.

Mr Harrison would sit in his cab like the master of operations, which indeed he was with his crew scurrying around him like drones around the queen bee, emptying the heavy bins of ash into the cart. Now and then Mr Harrison would leave his seat of power to check the load was being distributed correctly and no space was being wasted. When he was satisfied the cart was fully loaded ,off he would go, with his minions clinging on to the sides like limpets, to the land fill site, to give it its politically correct name, or as we knew it, the ash dump where later after all the ash men had gone home for the day people would congregate looking among the rubbish for any usable or saleable items.

Even in those relatively hard times it could be surprising just what some folk would discard such as rags or scrap iron, etc, it could all be taken to sell to the local rag and bone merchants. Old Jam jars would get you a halfpenny each, lemonade or beer bottles up to two penny each. Wood for the fire or to repair a fence or shed, even odd bits of furniture which could be put to some use.

Our immediate next door neighbours were Mr and Mrs Lightfoot, fabulous people, as kind and generous as it was possibly to be, and even better, Mr Lightfoot was an express train driver, not a common local driver, but mainline. I thought he was a local hero and he was well respected in the avenue, on a par with the doctor or our teacher or whatever. Mrs Lightfoot was a lovely woman , not at all common but very ladylike, correct and polite, but not at all snobbish, more down to earth, but correct. Her only son Donald became a Knight of the Realm for services to radio in Rhodesia, wow!!. When he came home on his infrequent visits he always came laden with presents, like bows and arrows or spears. Can you imagine that, real bows and arrows and real native spears.

Mam told me once how poor Mrs Lightfoot was brought down to earth, the Lightfoot's had an outside toilet, unlike us posh Beckett's whose toilet was at least in a sort of porch way. One day feeling the need the poor women went to the loo, sat down to do as you do, when the toilet bowl disintegrated beneath her, God what a shock she must have got. Mam, alerted by her shouts for help rushed around and rescued the unfortunate women from the wreckage, her knickers still around her ankles. Luckily no real harm was done other than a loss of face and a slightly scratched bottom. Not funny I know but then….

Naturally I thought Donald a great hero, a great white hunter, leading the Safari across the vast African savannah , rifle slung nonchalantly over his shoulder protecting the ladies from ferocious wild beasts, then hacking his way through endless jungle, discovering lost mines laden with gold and jewels.

In fact he was a broadcaster on the local radio, hardly ever left the town, preferring the cool of a good bar. Still he did get a knighthood, so clearly did something right.

Mrs Lightfoot's daughter Dorothy also did well, she went on to marry another Sir, a military man of great rank. I don't suppose many in Botcherby have a similar claim to fame as that.
A chap called Geoff Twentyman who played football for the mighty Liverpool amongst others, married the girl who lived in the house opposite ours.
It was Mrs Lightfoot who cared for me when I was sent home from school poorly with what turned out to be a burst appendix. I ended up in the City General hospital to have the necessary surgery, to this day I can remember dreaming of being chased by a bunch of Nazis through the wards, with their square helmets, swastika flags, and high kicking marching, must have been the effects of the gas, I was terrified and still have recurring nightmares to this day. Only now its Lions and Tigers that pursue me, sometimes crocodiles, never puppies or anyone nice, just hope they do not catch me !. Blimey that's a worry, is it an omen, so if they catch me I am done for, oh dear !
Just down the street from us lived a guy called Joe Winthrop, he was a big bloke, even to us kids. He had two cauliflower ears and a broken nose the reward for years spent as a professional heavy weight boxer. My dad reckoned he could have been a "contender" to use that well worn word in the pugilist society. Dad said with the right management and the odd break he could have been big time, the fact that he had two cauliflower ears proved that a lot of punches missed their target due to Joes superior skill in ring craft. Still like many others Joe missed out, dad said he was taken advantage of by less than scrupulous managers, just like Marlon Brando, in " On the waterfront." He could have been a contender, but always had a smile , whenever you went to his door you could be sure of a welcome. What a nice man. Another local hero.

Others who I doubt if I shall ever forget include the Monks, Fosters, Ivison's, Cowen's, Underwood's, Boustead's, Lennon's, (No relation to John I don't think.) Scaif's. Mr Scaife senior and his two sons must have been great readers, always walking back from the Library with arms full of tomes.The John's, Skinners, Banum's, old Mr Banum had a model Spitfire on his sideboard which I coveted greatly and could not resist picking up whenever I had the opportunity. Mrs winter, Gordon's. Mr Gordon had the most amazing rock garden, I could not pass it without stopping to admire it, strange boy. The Stell's, Ridleys, Carrigans, Mrs Adams and her penny to view television, first on the street. The Gardeners, Bells, Wilson's, (Good old wacker.) Joe Rowley the grocer, later moving to Brampton were he went into the early house insulations business, global warming was just becoming an issue.
Mr and Mrs Banks in the post office, I was scared stiff of them, dunno why, they just looked so stern whenever I entered.
Mr Parr the greengrocer, the Grice Brothers at the Croft, Charlie, Bill and Dave with Cousin Theo. The Redpath's, diamonds all.
I cannot recall anyone really nasty on Botcherby, but then there must have been, struggling to think who. Mates included lads like, Willie Wilson, Brian and Trevor Redpath, Peter Gill, Brian Cowen, his younger brother John Cowen, who died young of a broken neck falling down some stairs, bless him, such a nice lad. Having said that the first time I came across John some kids I knew claimed he had pinched their sweets, so not knowing who he was I thumped him on the nose causing it to bleed profusely, needless to say the poor lad had not done anything just been picked upon as he was quite vulnerable due to his slight build and quiet nature. Something else to feel guilty about. Ronnie Brown and Dennis Snelgar who I shared basic training with at Fulwood Barracks in Preston, Ronnie went on to survive an ambush in Aden where several of our pals died. John Lapping, always good for a laugh,

Laurie Johnston, Tommy Bell. Alan Wilson who partnered me in a couple of talents shows, which we won, naturally. Keith Wilson, Derek Skinner, Anthony Carrigan, John Underwood a great pal. David Ridley, Harry Winthrope, Gordon Heap, Leslie Hayes, Les lived in one of the old private houses at the bottom of Victoria Road, therefore qualified as a posh. Peter Farish. So many smashing people, can't say a bad word about any of them, just a cool lot altogether. The girls included Jennifer Ivison, Jennifer Ridley, Pamela Monk, Irene John, Irene Bell, Eileen Skinner, the Adamthwaite's, Julie and Olwyn, Olwyn Banum my sister Brenda's pal, June Harrison whose dad drove the ash cart, one of my hero's. Down the hill lived Brian and Winnie Nelson, She was a well known local character, working as a waitress in Binns restauarant, her son went on to be a councillor for Botcherby Ward. If I have not mentioned you, sorry, will try better, next time.Last but not least of my hero's was Tommy Styles, my sister Brenda's boyfriend, he was always dead smart in suits he helped design himself, with folded back cuffs and other unusual features, he always looked like Mr Cool. Rock on Tommy.

Despite rationing still being on the go, I do not recall exactly starving to death, as some from this period would have you believe. I do remember well however every other Friday, this was sugar ration day, or as we knew it, sweetie day.

Not a lot to choose from for sure but those gobstoppers and liquorice sticks found an eager bunch of customers and kept us quite for some time, well you try sucking a great gobstopper and chatting at the same time, not easy I can tell you, though some could achieve it, even if understanding them was a bit difficult with all that drool coming from their own gobs.

When mam took us to the City picture house in Carlisle City centre, she would take us into Marks and Spencer's where she would buy my sister and I a jelly each, normally used to make a

pudding they were an excellent substitute when no other confectionery was to be had. No popcorn or grab bags of goodies, but mam would on the odd occasion produce some home made toffee, no questions asked where the sugar, severely rationed, had come from. It was extremely brittle, like eating sweetened broken glass, but went down eventually improving the occasion no end. One of the prevalent problems of course was nits, we all got them, you could not avoid them, playing at School or in the street we all mingled and if one became infected so did we all, embarrassing for parents but of no consequence to us kids. Dad would sit for hours combing through our hair detecting and cracking louse eggs, each time he would call out, " That's another bugger bit the dust. "
You could distinctly hear a click as the nit succumbed to the tweezer action of his thumb nails. Then with our heads bent over that days Daily Mirror he would give our locks a good combing, catching the little horrors remains as they dropped. Nothing has really changed, nit combs and shampoo still hold there own on the Chemists shelves, some things refuse to go. The nit Nurse, still a feature in school, and if she heads your way, O'God the shame of it. Every so often a medical team would turn up and we would be paraded in front of them so they could shine a little torch into our eyes or worse shove a wooden spatula into our mouths to hold our tongues while they looked down our throats, causing many to retch and nearly bring back breakfast. We were all inoculated for Measles, Diphtheria, Tuberculosis, etc. those huge needles, terrifying, it was all you could do not to pee yourself with fear. There were so many deadly disease's about then, we do not realise how lucky we were.
In later years the school would assist the local health authority by getting students to distribute leaflets advertising the awareness of mobile mass X Ray units in the vicinity and encouraging people to take advantage of them. So aiding the reduction in T B etc.

13   GET SOME COAL IN MOTHER.

My earliest memory of my mother is of us sitting on the top deck of a United double Decker bus going along London road in Carlisle, toward old Harraby, New Harraby still green fields, yet to be constructed. Where we were going or for what reason I do not know, however what I do remember most is that the seats, far from the luxurious upholstered ones we enjoy today, were made of wooden slats, much the same as a the type found in public parks etc. Why this has imprinted itself on my brain I do not know, unless they were so hard they imprinted themselves on my infant bottom.
I also seem to recall mother pointing out the old tram sheds, what significance they held for me has been lost in the mists of time, as the last tram completed its final journey some ten years previously. What I do remember though, is sometime later being pushed across town in my pram to visit a coal merchant who, spookily, had his premises behind the afore mentioned tram sheds. Having arrived at the coal yard I had to vacate my pram to make way for a bag of coal, which mam then pushed back across town to our house with me hanging on to the side, no doubt howling all the way at the indignity of it, I was not a forgiving child.
I can only assume we had no cash the day the coalman called on his round, not in itself an unusual occurrence, which would then explain our journey when funds improved . Strange what sticks in your mind.
Those days like most others in our neighbourhood. We were never that well off but mother always made sure we kids never suffered, usually to her and dads detriment.
My dad never trusted the coalman and when times improved and we could afford the coal delivered dad always stood by and counted in the sacks dropped in the coal house. He claimed if you

did not watch them they would jump on the coal pile so it sounded as though they were delivering more than they actually were. Clearly somewhere along the line dad had had an unfortunate experience with a darkened face character. I think the lesson must have sunk in because I still have a distrust for coalmen. If you are a coalman . Sorry! (Dunno why I am saying sorry, we have Gas.)

Because we had no electric light in our coalhouse the afore mentioned place was black as pitch, Dad had the unfortunate habit of lighting a piece of old newspaper to illuminate his way to collect a shovel of fuel for the living room fire.
One such evening we were all sitting around the radio listening to some unmissable show of the day when mam happened to mention she could smell smoke. Dad looked at the fire inquisitively, then satisfied nothing was amiss there, got down on one knee looking up the flue checking that the chimney was not alight, all seemed well and no one thought any more about it .
A short while later our Brenda went to visit the loo, which was positioned outside the back door directly opposite the coalhouse. Suddenly we were all startled by an ear piercing scream and en masse rushed outside to find the reason for our Brenda's distress, oh my God, the coalhouse was well ablaze. Like the fires of hell it glowed and showered sparks, better than bonfire night. For a moment no none moved rooted in shock at the sight before us. Then dad came to his senses, luckily a few buckets of water later and things were under control again, soon we were washing our blackened hands and faces relieved that we still had a house to live in.
A week or two later an electric light was installed by one of dads mates, along with one in the outside toilet. We all thought it was great and so posh, not many in the street had an illuminated bog. The day of the newspaper fiery torch was done.

There was no cash for the luxury of toilet rolls, instead we had to cut the old newspapers in squares and string them together to be hung on an nail behind the toilet door. We must have all had black bums from the printers ink.

Though we had no spare cash for luxuries we still always had a Sunday lunch made up of roast meat of some kind, with Bisto gravy salts, served with the obligatory roast and boiled potatoes, cabbage, or turnip, but always tinned peas. Also for some reason we always, or at least it seems to me, to have roast leg of lamb.

 I know we lived in a part of the world famous for its Lakeland bred black faced ewes, a breed of sheep able to survive virtually unaided on the winter fells, until brought down to the valleys to lamb in early spring, but surely other meats were available at comparable prices. I suppose she and Dad liked lamb, so that was that. Never a week went by without mutton hotpot, chopped belly mutton with onions and carrots topped with thinly sliced potatoes and baked until brown and crispy, luscious. The only thing was, this was the cheapest cut of mutton and very greasy which when hot was nectar, but when it went cold and served a second time the grease set like candle wax , losing some of its appeal. Once in a blue moon a chicken would turn up, roasted with sage and onion stuffing, the smell always brought back memories of Christmas, Santa Claus and sleigh bells.

We were never in any danger of starving, my little plump body bore witness to that, but things like tripe in onions and vinegar did not go down quite so easily.

14   ON THE BEACH, SILLOTH, GLORIOUS SILLOTH.

Another early memory is of my first day trip to West Silloth, the trip out on the train was as far as I can remember my first train journey. (Little was I to know, the first of many.)
The thick black electric power lines ran adjacent to the track on telegraph type poles and dad convinced Brenda and I that they were actually pipes taking lemonade and beer to Silloth. We would believe all he told us in those days. On another occasion he told Brenda not to swallow the bubble gum she was chewing or her floating ribs would stick together, no sooner had he said it but she went and swallowed the gum. Realising what she had done she howled her eyes out, it took dad ages to convince her that he was only kidding.
When we arrived in Silloth we had to follow a sandy track past the then working dock with its ships from Russia and Canada, bringing their cargo of wheat to Carr's Flour Mill. Dotted among them were the shrimp boats manned by local fishermen where you could buy a poke of fresh boiled shrimps for a few pence, incidentally the mill is one of the few things still around and functioning, supplying flour to local bakeries and biscuit makers. I worked there briefly as a security guard in the seventies, it was hard work patrolling at night in the gloom, continually having to climb narrow metal stairs and ladders, up and down. Must have been worse in the days when wheat had to be lugged up to the silos. The Mill itself was apparently powered by a rare form of giant steam engine called a " Carel", which was featured in later years on TV by Fred Dibnah. Jonathon Dodgson Carr, immortalised of course by Carlisle born author Margaret Foster, apparently walked from Kendal, the then County Town of Westmorland to seek his fortune in Carlisle, using

the mill, opened in circa 1836 to provide the flour for his water biscuits manufactured in his Bridge street bakery in Caldewgate. The bakery is still there of course, but now much larger, part of a world wide Conglomerate. However its reputation for producing high class biscuits remains intact. Almost everyone in Carlisle has either worked there or has a relative who worked there, including my Mam and all her sisters, plus several surviving family members. My brother in law Alan Stewart being employed there for over thirty years, mostly on permanent nightshift, meeting his wife Audrey, my wife's twin sister there, it's a world of its own... Back to Silloth, then.

Many of the Silloth lads were not too keen on all these sailors from exotic parts landing in their town, convinced they were going to steal their women folk, some of whom were quite happy to have kisses stolen by a romantic seafarer, well they do say all the nice girls love a sailor, don't they, thereby causing lots of punch ups at pub chucking out time. I do not recall anyone being to seriously hurt, but jealousy is a powerful motive to do harm to a rival in loves game so who knows what wounds real or implied were inflicted. Many of these sailors carried knives as a habit in foreign ports, so it was not always wise to confront them.

Silloth had its own cop shop then and needed it in the season when the population increased by ten fold or more, with young lads out to prove their manhood in front of admiring young girls. Risking life and limb diving into the sea of breakwaters or into the docks off the Dock gates, very dodgy, still letting off steam and testing strength or courage is all part of growing up, even if some never quite did.

Having disembarked from the train we would cut across the end of the tracks then would skirt around the golf club slipping between a wall built of old upright railway sleepers to the sand dunes.

As we made our way for the first time I recall we were passed by several large trucks full of sand, I became alarmed that they were taking the beach away before we could get there and once again howled like a good'en. I seem to remember crying quite a lot as a kid. Well I need not have worried because we had a great day, paddling, building sandcastles, eating sand encrusted sandwiches while Mam drank tea from one of the few tea bars scattered about the dunes, now long since gone, so much we recall.

Dad would adjourn to the nearby pub, the Cumberland, until two o'clock closing time when he would reappear full of the joys of spring, a short while later to fall asleep with his white hanky over his face, fluttering as he snored. Brenda and I would try to bury him in the in the sun warmed sand, but the sand just kept sliding off his beer filled belly as he breathed in deep sleep, causing us to give up and return to the more productive task of sandcastle building, or crab hunting in the occasional rock pool, not that we would pick them up, we were far too scared of being nipped by those sharp little pinchers. Better sticking to paddling and what have you.

Dad always said if you could see the Isle of Mann from the beach it was probably going to rain, if you could not see the Isle of Mann from the beach it was probably raining. Everybody loved Silloth, it was the place to be on summers days, it seemed all of Carlisle decamped there. It would be jam packed and of course we all knew each other as entire streets emptied and trudged down to the Railway station where more often than not extra carriages or sometimes entire trains had to be put on to cope with the virtual evacuation of entire areas of Carlisle. The old carriages with no corridors would be locked by the guard to stop us kids messing about going from carriage to carriage as we recognised school mates or neighbours. The train would stop at every hamlet or village en route, Burgh by sands, Kirkbride, Drumbrugh, Skimberness, you name it, it seemed like every cow shed had a platform attached to it. By the time we got to our destination the train was at a crawl with the little puffer engine struggling to cope with the strain. The only real problem being no corridor or toilet so if you needed a pee you either took a risk and jumped out to relieve your self in the bushes by one of the halts or if you were tall enough peed out of the window on the move, God help anyone leaning out of the next window along, desperate times call for desperate measures. Girls just had to suffer.

We kids of course thought Silloth was pure heaven. As we got older we would go camping in the sea grass covered sand dunes, much to the annoyance of the police and dock security men who appeared convinced we were some kind of pirates or buccaneers set to raid the boats in the nearby dock. They would invariably move us on but as soon as it got to dusk we were back, cooking meals of tinned baked beans in our Mams second best saucepan, which we had sneaked into our packs, on open fires of drift wood, of which there was always lots. We often wondered if the wood came from sunken ships lost far out at sea, maybe victims of a U boat attack or a sea monster. More likely just bad luck as a huge wave engulfed them or trawls snagged on the bottom causing boats to capsize suddenly before evasive action could be taken. Fishing Boats are still lost today along with the lives of men and boys from nearby towns like Maryport, Whitehaven or Workington, and on the other side of the Solway, Annan, Kirkcudbright and Portpatrick. The Isle of Mann also bore its share of sea borne tragedy. During the second world war the Isle of Mann was a virtual prison camp, holding Italian and German nationals, some of whom had either been resident in Great Britain for many years. (Italian Ice Cream parlours were a common site), some were even born here. However the Government of the day felt no chances could be taken so off they were shipped, fear of fifth columnists embedded in our minds by an aggressive press.

If the weather was not too good we would adjourn to the penny arcade, between the promenade and the town green, which always seemed to cost a lot more than a penny. But the lights and music were intoxicating, usually hits by stars of the day, " The penny arcade," by Roy Orbison repeated constantly, being an obvious selection in later days. But when we were young it would be the strange high pitched voice of country and western singer, Slim Whitman, " Jezebel" and the deep voice of Frankie Lane, or "Crying" by my favourite of that time ‚Johnnie Ray. What about the unforgettable first number one by Elvis, " Heartbreak Hotel." followed by "Blue Suede Shoes", or " Love Letters In The Sand" by Pat Boone, who was very famous in his day, giving the up and coming Elvis Presley a run for his money, as well as being a great grandson of the western pioneer, Daniel Boone. Strange the things that stick in your mind.

Now Silloth is a bit of a ghost town, even on hot summer days the visitor numbers are not that great unless something special is occurring, But we still make the occasional trip out reviving old and happy memories. Later we would often spend a week there on Stanwix field with its mix of caravans and wooden chalets. We stayed in a converted railway carriage called the " Dandy", it had three bedrooms plus a kitchen and large living space, far better than a cramped old caravan, we felt quite posh when folk stopped on passing and stared our way, clearly jealous. We would have spent the rest of our lives there if we could. The beach was literally two minutes away and the site sported a clubhouse with entertainment of sorts, Punch and Judy for the kids and local singers etc, for mams and dads. Some would get up and dance, the shy young girls having to be cajoled by the braver of the lads. I would imagine many a lifetime bond was struck on Stanwix Field, or in the dunes beyond. The beer was more expensive than the Cumberland pub so dad was not always all that keen to stay too long. Just out side the gates was a fish and chip shop which is still there today, opposite a small council estate with all the houses painted white which fascinated me, something about seaside chippies that make them taste special.

Stanwix Holiday Park, to give it its modern title, is still there, still in the hands of the Stanwix family, though now it sports a large swimming pool, bowling alley and a fabulous show bar, with both a national and international cliental. Highly recommended.

The town sported its share of novelty and rock shops to explore, business being brisk for the short season before returning to a steady trickle the rest of the year. Whilst its heyday has long gone, the way of most coastal holiday locations, people still are inclined to head there when the sun shows itself, but the train line went with Beeching in the sixties, so it's by car we appear now, some days you cannot get parked , others the wind is so strong you cannot get out of the car, But never mind, we still have fun.

15   MOSS SIDE TO DRACULAS LAIR.

When I worked for John Reed of Moss side , near Newton Arlosh, I would cycle into Silloth most nights with my then mates from schooldays, Tommy Bell and Arnie Tickell, both working on nearby farms, two smashing lads. Years later after having lost contact I met up with Arnie in what was then British Guiana in South America both serving with the Army on internal security duty, small world.
We were three working farm boys, so were very fit and thought nothing of cycling for miles. I would sometimes bike home to Botcherby and back of an evening in all weathers, a round trip of about forty miles and still get up at five or six in the morning for milking.
In winter I would often find a fox loitering in the main byre keeping warm, if John Reed had known he was there it would have been curtains for Mr Fox ,dead certain. But I like to think we had an understanding Mr Fox and I, I did not bother him and he did not bother me, so we remained friends of a sort.
The milking parlour was always lovely and warm regardless of conditions outside. The cows generated a huge amount of heat, and manure !, which all had to be shovelled up and taken to the midden each and every morning. It did not surprise me when years later I heard of the affect cows gases, such as methane, were having on the ozone layer, they were just eating shitting machines, with a side product of milk.
Tommy, Arnie and I loved going to the cinema in Silloth, followed by a plate of chips at Trespardeens Chippy. We were far too young to drink and getting served in a pub back then was nigh on

impossible, not that we missed it, we were easy pleased.
There was a keen young bobby based in Abbeytown who had very little to keep him occupied so he used to hide himself somewhere along the Silloth road hoping to catch cyclists not using their lights, sad bugger. We would look out for him and if spotted would deliberately turn our lights out then cycle past him as fast as we could peddle, he never caught us, we could hear him puffing and panting behind us, but he had no chance, our head start saw to that. Even more frustrating for him was the fact he knew fine well who we were and would question us when he got the chance trying to trick us into admitting it was us he had chased, what a plonker !

There were occasional dances in Newton Arlosh village hall, a standard tiny red bricked building common to most villages around. Bands there were always the likes of Jimmy Shand, or one of his many clones, with Country or Highland fiddle music, the choice being regulated by the local elders, no pop or rock, no fear. The younger members of the village population would sit on the side lines, wishing to be somewhere else, only dancing when pulled onto the floor by Granny's and Granddad's, causing faces to blush with embarrassment, then sitting again at first opportunity. You had to go to such as the Market Hall in Carlisle for up to date Rock "n" Roll as seen by these kids on top of the pops, there all the top bands of the day appeared. Roll on Dance Hall Days.

The very first time I got the worse for drink, however was while I was working for John Reed. A new lad I had met who was working on a farm in Abbeytown, a Geordie again whose name I cannot remember though God knows I should because he talked me into cycling in to Wigton for a night out. John Reed had cautioned me against going into Wigton with tales of thuggery and violence, but I knew better and off we went.

It was not a long cycle ride, and I had travelled it many times before but always in daylight and only passing through, so we soon arrived in the town. There for the first time in my life we went into a pub, I think it was the Lion and the Lamb, or possibly the Kings Head, do not ask me which one. I had only ever drank shandy before and should have stuck to them now.

We quickly downed two pints of mild beer and I was flying. It was all I could do to put one foot in front of the other, completely unable to walk straight I could hardly talk, what a state.

We left the pub and made our way to a local coffee bar which was down a short lane off the main street. This was very popular locally and frequented mainly by kids our age. It was packed full of local lads and lasses talking and singing along to the juke box blaring out tunes of the day, such as Gene Vincent and Eddie Cochran, but the rest was a blur.

We eventually got to order a coffee each then I decided I must pee, as you do, so I stumbled my way to the bogs which were situated in the foyer. I remember still being very unsteady on my feet and seemed to bump into several people en route.

Eventually arriving in the toilet I stood in the first stall and began to relieve myself whilst leaning against the wall to keep a steady aim. I became aware of someone talking to me but was unable to understand what was being said, not that it mattered.

I came around some time later, God knows how long, laying in the toilet one foot in the open stone urinal. I was covered in blood and my back was soaked in pee from the wet floor. I struggled to my feet slipping sliding as though I was on ice. I faintly recollect several lads in black Crombie type coats with white shirts and black slim Jim type ties standing around me. I had met some of the local hard men who had taken a severe dislike to me and appeared to be suggesting I leave town, bit like a cowboy film, I took their advice.

It was explained to me later, as I cycled back to the farm, by my so called Geordie friend, who I soon realised had abandoned me to my fate, that I had inadvertently knocked over the coffee of one of the girlfriends of the local tough guy, which honour stated had to be sorted. Just how tough you have to be to get together with your mates and batter some totally defenceless young lad the worse for drink I do not know. I hope these bastards read this and realise just what cowards they really are.
No one saw fit to help me, even the local bobby's turned there backs on me, well I was a stranger so it did not matter, who wants to spend half the night filling in reports which will go nowhere. John Reeds warning echoed in my ear all too late, and I still had to cycle the five miles or so back to the farm.
I must have got back ok because when I was called to work at the usual six o'clock I rose to see a blood soaked pillow and sheets, if Mrs Reed did not yet have a good reason to dislike me, she had one now. All I got all day was ," I told you so." and " No, you cannot have time off to go to the Doctors, tough luck." and
 " I had better get these stains out or it is coming out of your pay." Oh, Happy days.
When I went home at the weekend I called into the Cumberland Infirmary to be told my nose had been broken and the duty Doctor just gave it an almighty tug to straighten it, causing me to yelp and yet more blood to flow.
" Just give it a little tug down now and again. " He advised. " and you will never know it was damaged." He was right, you would never know it had been damaged, my beauty preserved to this day.

It was years before I set a foot in Wigton again, and still do not like the place very much. Though having said that it is much the same as any other small town now, all its character been tore out, most of the old town long demolished and replaced with the same old modern housing or supermarkets. The main street has lost all the small individual shops, bakers , greengrocers, shoe repairs, etc. replaced with Building Society offices, Estate agents and national chains selling exactly the same products in every town or City in the country. Even the long established cattle auction has shrunk. The only main employer being British Sidac or whatever it is called now, a huge factory upon which the town depends for virtually all its employment.

I met Melvyn Bragg, one of the towns few famous names, now Lord Bragg of Wigton many years later in Silloth, but that comes later, except to say a more contradictory figure from those in the aforementioned incident you could not wish to meet. Sometime later when I recalled this incident to him he admitted the town did at one time have a problem with pointless violence on its streets. A theme common almost everywhere now.

My next experience of over indulgence was even worse if that's possible. Now I am sure that you have heard of projectile vomiting, well here's a tale of projectile shitting. For those easily upset look away now.
While I was working on the restaurant cars the powers that be decided to send me, along with a dozen or so others on a course to the British Rail Catering College New Lodge near Windsor, under the world famous British Chef, Arthur Hope, an extremely prestigious man in his day within high cuisine circles.
The course was a three month residential affair, all male and all either teenagers or early twenties, a recipe for trouble of which there was plenty one way or another, mainly drink related.
New Lodge was used for some pretty sumptuous affairs and had its own bar which the students were allowed to use on an evening.
The night in question a couple of my new mates and I were

experimenting with a mixture of Guinness and Newcastle brown ale, the effect on me was devastating, once again I experienced the wobbly leg syndrome.

I have never taken LSD but would imagine the outcome to be similar. Pretty soon I began to feel rather ill and rushed upstairs to the toilet outside our dormitory, making it to the bog I put my head over the toilet bowl just as a jet stream of ale exploded from my throat, unfortunately and unbelievably a similar explosion let go from my backside. Stunned I felt the hot liquid shit run down my legs, dear God, what to do, for a moment I was paralysed with panic, there seemed to be shit everywhere, some how I struggled free from my incredibly soiled trousers and leaving a trail of brown liquid dung behind me fell into the shower, clothes and all, thank the lord for showers. Struggling to come to terms with this disaster I cleaned myself and my clothes, which included my one and only suit and best shirt. I then had to set to cleaning the entire toilet and shower area, you would not believe how shit can spread it was everywhere. My so called friends took turns to come and view my ordeal, but no offer of assistance was forthcoming. They all just thought it too hilarious for words. Swine's.

To be honest I would have done the same should the horror have befallen one of them. Obviously I never managed to live this incident down during my remaining period at New Lodge and in time everyone from the tutors to the cleaning staff became aware of my indignity, taking advantage to further humiliate me at every chance.

I did not touch a drink again for some time after this, but eventually took up the baton once again and still managed to make a fool of myself over and over again, but avoided crapping my trousers, thank Christ.

I came close to killing myself at New Lodge due to my own stupidity.
The Lodge was a one time country house in quite extensive grounds. It was very large or at least looked that way to me and my fellow students, used to council housing. At each of the four corners of the Lodge stood a large tower, the top of which could be reached via a spiral staircase. The first time I decided to explore one of these towers, which incidentally were strictly out of bounds, upon reaching the top I tentatively looked over the side of the mock battlements, common to grand houses like this, I saw a ring of gargoyles fixed to the walls just below, wanting a closer look I lent over, with a bit of a stretch I found I could easily rest my weight on the nearest Gargoyle, stretching out as far as I dare to improve my view, To my extreme terror the Gargoyle came away from the wall and crashed to the ground far below. I began to slip forward unable to find any purchase with my flailing arms I managed to hook my legs around the decorative battlements, I was convinced that I was about to die a horrible death when to my intense relief a mate who had followed me to the tower wanting to know what I was up to arrived on the scene, seeing my predicament he quickly hauled me back. My heart was pounding at a thousand a minute, I was scared out of my wits. I could have kissed him, but managed to restrain myself, do not want give anyone the wrong impression do we.
So if I have nine lives, already having used one up by nearly drowning, things needed to improve. I reckon that one or two more have been used up in various accidents since then so I need to keep counting.

Talking of those bleeding towers, on another night one of the other lads got paralytic on the evil drink so it was decided to carry him still on his mattress from his dormitory to the top of one of the towers and leave him there overnight. It took several of us forever to get him up there, he weighed a ton, but he slept like the preverbal baby, never wakening once despite the struggle we had going around and around the staircase.

Any way we eventually managed to succeed in our mission. It was with much satisfaction, not to mention broken backs, we left him to his fate, poor sod.

He reappeared early next morning cold and wet, it was November and it had rained during the night. For some reason he was not at all happy and threatened us all with blue murder, luckily he was not the bravest of souls so failed to carry through with his threat. Unfortunately when word got out what we had done all hell broke loose, we were lucky not to be sent home, along with our P45's. The health and safety officer reckoned had our victim got up for a pee in the night and went over the parapet no one would be laughing, but we did, every time the poor bloke walked in the room, what an evil bunch we were.

Near to the Lodge was the village of Fifield, where Mr Teezy Weezy TV hairdresser and friend to the stars lived, I was assured on more than one occasion that several other TV personalities lived round about but I never saw any of them.

Directly opposite the Lodge however stood Bray church, long since abandoned by the clergy it was used as a set for Christopher Lee and co in Gothic Dracula and Werewolf movies, plus other various Hammer horror flicks. We were determined to see what was in there and eventually gained access through a side door, some of our talents stretching beyond the kitchen. It was just as you have seen on the pictures, covered in dust, with giant cobwebs hanging down, it was spooky I can tell you, we expected Frankenstein or a Wolf man to appear at any minute.

But it still had all the accoutrements associated with a country Church, an Alter complete with candlesticks, and a large lectern with a big old Bible on it, all over looked by a large crucifix of a very sad looking Jesus, though I suppose he did not have a lot to laugh about did he. Then along come us lot and the film people to desecrate his home.

The times I have sat in our local fleapit in terror of Vampires and ghouls, never thought I would end up in their lair, good job they are not real… or are they.

We generally had a good time at New Lodge, I was not a good attentive student but I suppose something must have penetrated even my thick skull.

I spent a bit of time in nearby Windsor which was a nice place to wander, also Eton just across the bridge, with all those schoolboy Toff's scurrying about in their top hats and tails and the older ones punting on the Thames with their girls, picnic baskets stowed away in the stern. It must have been glorious on golden summer days, but this was November so I did not envy them quite so badly.

You just would not believe how some folk live if you did not see it with your own eyes, I really thought it only happened in my old William books. The ruling classes, God bless us every one, as a certain young Dickens character stated, more than once.

I never got to view inside Windsor Castle, could not afford the entrance fee, our wages were not great, so we were perpetually hard up. However there were quite a number of second hand bookshops which fascinated me for hours on end, some were a virtual Aladdin's cave of adventurous and captivating tomes. I have always had a love of books, since learning how to decipher the written word at a late stage in life compared to most.

So with deep pockets and little, or more often, no cash, there was no way of procuring said tempting delights, other than holding your nerve until the shopkeeper turned away, all too trusting those Booksellers with the likes of me around. Not that I have a habit of stealing you understand, I just could not stand all those rich kids getting what I could not have, and besides they were all second hand, its not like they were new or anything is it. My mother would have murdered me if she ever knew, God bless her.

Like every good country house New Lodge had its spectre. The local legend was that a headless horseman, yes, that's right, a headless horseman, roamed the dark lanes around the Lodge, and while I never encountered him, thank goodness, sometimes when wandering back from the local village ale house in the pitch black of night, no street lights here, any sudden or unknown noise would cause us to quicken our pace, whilst looking nervously over our shoulders until safe inside the welcoming warmth of our dormitory.. The locals of course insisted the legend horseman to be real enough. I never actually met anyone who had seen him but spoke to several who claimed to know someone ,who definitely knew someone, who was definitely related to someone, who had seen the horseman and lived to tell the tale, but whose hair had turned grey overnight, yea, I know, you have heard it all before, but its true, honest !!
The actual great house that was New Lodge also had its own White Lady legend, said to roam the corridors at full moon. Now, it would seem that there are a lot of these White Ladies about because Rose Castle which is featured later in this tale also has a fabled White Lady legend, I thought I saw her once watching me from a second floor window whilst I was hanging washing out in the Bishops private garden, don't tell him by the way, not supposed to do that ! When I looked back she had gone, maybe she had wanted me to wash her white shroud, must be getting a bit soiled by now. Despite being at New Lodge so long and making so many new friends I do not recall a single name, they came from, Derby, Wolverhampton, Edinburgh and London. How come I remember that yet not a single name..

16   DINING CAR CAPERS.

Eventually I returned to my job on the restaurant cars and my boss Frankie Moffat, AKA killiecrankie. Frank had a huge influence on me, despite his many faults, mainly due to his alcoholism, I worshipped him. Whilst he was always drinking he hardly ever was seen to eat anything. He often had little patience with other folk and the fact he had the biggest nose I have ever seen then or since did not help. Seeing him people would stare and could not resist mentioning. " You must have the biggest snozzle I have ever seen." followed more often than not by severe violence.

We had a real bond, which I do not think I had with anyone before or since who seemed to really care for me like Frankie apart from my future wife Renee.
There were times when Frankie fussed over me like a mother hen. When we lodged in Kentish town hostel he felt the need to protect me from the rough and tumble of life away from home, even though this was nothing new to me, his life experience saw the dangers in everything. Some boys could be bullied or worse taken advantage of by unscrupulous men, homosexuality was still something of a mystery to me. I do not mean to cast aspersions on the gay community, we had lots of gay waiters on the restaurant cars and never met a nasty word or deed from any of them, in fact quite the opposite they also mothered me, ensuring I was neat and tidy at all times and did not go unshaven or unwashed.
I know however of others not so lucky, who met the dark side of life in all its cruelty. Fortunately such occurrences were far and few between and my memories are extremely happy ones.
The Kentish Town hostel offered good clean basic accommodation for a small outlay and attached to it was an excellent Railwaymen's club where many a good sing song could be had.

There was no animosity, except for Franks nose, despite blokes being from all over the British Isles, Irish, Scots, Welsh and other nationalities such as Indians, Checks, Poles, we had them all.
One of the meanest tricks we got up to was to identify which of the stations on our route had won the best kept station of the year award. A much coveted title especially by the smaller stations who would create the most spectacular floral displays along pristine platforms, all scrubbed and freshly painted with not a thing out of place.
We on the other hand were just plain Evil. We would collect all our used tea bags, coffee grains, egg shells and used napkins etc in large black dustbins and as we approached the nominated winner of the small station trophy at speeds of up to one hundred miles an hour would lower the carriage windows and pour out the bins contents, timing it so as to cause the maximum effect, the litter would spread the entire length of the platform causing the most possible mess.
Amazingly and to some extent disappointingly we never heard of any repercussions of our dastardly deeds, the poor sods must have known what was going to happen from previous victims, sorry I mean previous winners. Perhaps in some perverse way they accepted it as a backhanded compliment, well it does take all kinds.
Every morning when staying in the Kentish town hostel I would awake to the clanking sound in the next cubicle of Frankie opening his two bottles of beer for his liquid starter without which he would not be able to function. Later we would leave the hostel along with the rest of the crew and head for a greasy spoon café just along the road where we would indulge in a breakfast of strong black tea and bacon rolls dripping with fat. Why we should do this when we could have had as many bacon butties as we

could wish for free in the dining car I do not know. It always amazes me how the same food can taste so much better in different environments. I must have eaten bacon rolls in a hundred other places, roadside burger vans, Macdonald's and numerous cafes but none came near to matching the offerings of that little greasy spoon in old Kentish town. Once we had been sated we made our way down to the Restaurant car in the nearby marshalling yard where the days work would begin.

I however would be sent by bus to Saint Pancras station to collect the days rations.
This bus journey was an adventure in itself, the people of London were nothing at all like Carlisle folk, for a start they were all colours and creeds, (we had very few of these at home,) all standing silently, patiently, never saying a word. No good mornings or idle chatter like the bus stop at the bottom of Botcherby avenue where queues invited gossip, obtaining the latest news or scandal.. All these Kentish town characters, like out of some Arabian story, were waiting to be transported to places mysterious, while the pavements behind were a torrent of non stop human activity. White city folk in their dark suits and bowler hats, west Indian women wearing brightly coloured scarves tied about their heads, orange clad Hari Krishna boys, bare foot even in winter. It was like an everyday early morning Carnival.
Arriving at the station I would claim a large barrow and load it with the inevitable sack of potatoes for me to peel by hand, plus the meat, fish and vegetables, all to be prepared for lunch. No tinned or frozen food allowed, along with crates of beer, such as Blue Bass and Guinness . All of course meticulously recorded and God help me if anything was missing or short.

I would then make my way to the relative platform from which our train the "Waverly Express" would depart.
Whilst sitting on my heavily leaden trolley I would get celebrities of the day come over to talk to me, unlike today they were not always being chased by dickheads with cameras. I learned that show business could be a lonely existence. Being regular travellers they would know my face from the restaurant car, among others I met regularly were Bootsie and Snudge, aka Alfie Bass and Bill Frazier. They looked just the same as they appeared on telly, Alfie would be so untidy whilst Bill was like a tailors dummy.
At other times we would hide pop stars in our changing room to avoid marauding girl fans, we had Cliff Richard, Marty Wilde, Billy Fury. Poor lads were sometimes a bit worried. By far the strangest yet most remarkable man was a famous tipster called Ras Prince Monolulu, all dressed up like an African king carrying a shield and spear, wearing colourful clothes, with a Head dress of feathers and animal skins shouting out his trade mark slogan.
" I gotta Horse, I gotta horse. "
He was without a doubt the most famous Blackman in England at that time due to tipping the outsider called Spion Kop to win the Derby, which it did at one hundred to six making him and several others quite wealthy, at least for a while. I later discovered his real name was actually Peter Carl Mackay a west Indian, who died believe it or not in the Middlesex Hospital having choked on a Black Magic chocolate given to him by a visiting journalist. You could not make that up.
Often we would have stars and celebrities come to the kitchen to thank Frankie for their meal, he took it all in his stride, he had met lots of top people, sportsmen, like the Italian heavyweight boxing champion Primo Canera. World Champion, 1906-1967 and the great Henry Cooper, who died whilst this tome was being written in 2011. God bless him.

Politicians such as Harold Wilson and Edward Heath. You had to be quite someone to impress our Frankie. I dread to think what would have been said if Maggie Thatcher ever turned up in the dining car.

Regretfully now and again Frankie's affliction would take hold of him and he would go off at a tangent when no one could talk sense into him, it was not always wise to try. He would wander off down the train until he found one of his many regulars who he got on with and that would be that, for regardless of his drunkeness everyone loved him, what a strange man he was, some days the kitchen was like a meeting room so many folk wanted to say hello. It would then be left up to me to put out the dinner menu. I would panic but always managed to get by. When you are travelling along at speeds of up to one hundred miles an hour you have little choice. Plus Frankie trained me well, it was as though he knew there would be times when he would not be around.

The Restaurant car conductor as he was called, similar to a Head waiter / manager, was George Robertson, a vastly experienced restaurant man, he was the boss no one would cross.

He was the proverbial hard but fair type, when I carried out the kitchen duty in Franks absence he made sure I got an extra share of the tips which we all relied on to subsidise our meagre wage, especially the married members of the team. One time however I recall he decided I was cutting the peel off the potatoes too thick, can you credit it, then deducted some tips because , he declared, I was undermining his profits, what bastards people can be when they try. That day my share of the tips was a paltry two bob bit, clearly making a point, so I took the pet as well and left it deliberately on the hot plate. Lets see him pick that up.

One of the lads I worked with on the trains invited me to his home in Edinburgh for his Eighteenth birthday party. His name was John Monroe, he lived in a typical Edinburgh tenement block. The apartment was very small but cosy, as I recall, very warm. The furniture was clearly made with this type of home in mind, tables that folded away and beds built into the walls, with an old cast iron stove complete with bread oven in the main living room. The style of the place was distinctly alien to someone brought up in a three bed Council house, all being on one level with no wasted space. Johns devoted Catholic family were very kind and gave me a warm welcome. During the course of the evening everyone took there turn to get up and entertain us, I remember John sang a lovely rendition of Ava Maria, bringing tears to the eyes of his mum and young sister Mary. Its amazing how some people can have such nice singing voices, I do envy them. I used to know the words to every song of the day when I was a teenager, but could not sing a note, much to some folks annoyance. However it had been a very long day and by the time the party was over I was shattered, partly of course due to the several cans of heavy beer I had consumed so once again I let myself down by visiting the toilet and falling asleep on the pot , its true , you cannot take me anywhere. Somehow poor John sorted me out and next morning I was clearly forgiven my misdemeanour . I was given a guided tour of the City, visiting the Heart of Midlothian, St Giles Cathedral, then scanning the roof tops via the camera Obscura, fabulous.

This family were clearly and rightly proud of their homeland. However I did note that I was never invited back, Wonder why !

THE DREADED GARLANDS.

When we were kids the name Garlands put the fear of Christ up us, it was only over the field from Harraby School, but was avoided like the plague. Thoughts of the local mental asylum conjured up visions of drooling maniacs roaming the grounds bloodily dismembering anyone foolish enough to enter. The name would be whispered by such as aunts and grannies for fear of calling down who knows what dreadful affliction with its attendant shame. Having a relation in there was worse than being in prison.
I suppose the hospital did have its share of dangerous individuals, but the most by far were just sad sick men and women in dire need of care and attention.
I was employed at the Garlands, originally the Cumberland and Westmorland lunatic asylum, built in 1862, better known locally as the Garlands mental hospital, as a cook for two years in the early sixties. The majority of this time was spent working at the new facility called, the " Clinic," this part of the hospital was ultra modern compared with the remainder of the complex. All was new and light with spacious communal areas for patients, furnished with comfortable armchairs, colour televisions, with bright floral curtains and cushions, just like home.

The main hospital however, despite the best efforts of dedicated staff members remained, in appearance at least, like a cross between a Victorian workhouse and a dumping ground for societies unwanted misfits and embarrassments. The most of these unfortunates were undoubtedly in the correct place, but many were there simply to get them out of the way of incapable or uncaring families. Victims of prejudice and double standards.
Many a young girl fallen to unwanted pregnancy found her way here , some to stay for a life time because they simply were not

wanted elsewhere, young lads too young for prison and thought to be of no further use to society suffered a similar fate.

There were some wards which carried high security status due to the unpredictability of the patients, violence still a major factor which often required draconian measures to control.

Overcrowding added to the problems and discomfort of the hospitals inhabitants. Beds were packed together, a row down each side of the ward with often a third down the centre, giving barely leg room enough to pass between them. The nights could be full of horrors we are fortunate not to know of. How staff and inmates coped day after day with those basic, almost inhuman conditions retaining their dignity and good humour is to say the least amazing. One of the problems faced by the dedicated Nursing staff was a mixture of patient incontinence and many inmates having a mental age way below normal, accidents in bed or ward were only to be expected and then quickly dealt with, however those committed out side were only discovered when some unfortunate stood in it. So patients were taught when having dropped a load somewhere they should stick a feather or a twig in it making the turd a bit more obvious and less prone to the squelchy shoe syndrome. Food was produced in the large Victorian style kitchen with its high ceiling and skylights adorned with moss and greenery growing in abundance, like the proverbial hanging gardens with coloured blooms, living decoration, encouraged by the sub tropical conditions of warmth with steam clouds generated by huge vats of boiling potatoes and cabbage day after day , summer and winter. The menus in the main were set for the week by the catering officer. These being restricted by the large numbers involved and the confinements of budget. Very little changed as the main diet consisted of minced beef, mashed or boiled potatoes, and cabbage, all cooked in huge commercial steam heated pans. Breakfast was made up of porridge or cereal for the most part, with the occasional luxury of scrambled or boiled egg, again all cooked by steam power generated by the Hospitals own coal fired boiler house. Special diets were provided for those requiring them but it was not always apparent just what the difference was.

I am sure every effort was made to brighten and vary meals but lack of imagination, time and work space complicated issues to a great degree. Of course the patients were not the only ones to become Institutionalised. Some of the staff were a bit weird to say the least, they said the longer you worked there the more like the patients you became.

Many of the inmates were allowed to work within the confines of the hospital buildings and grounds. Gardening, growing fresh vegetables for use in the kitchens, there was also a small farm, a butchers and a bake house producing fresh baked bread daily, along with pies and cakes. they even made a splendid wedding cake for mine and Renee's wedding. . At special times such as Christmas mince pies and puddings were made in abundance and birthdays cakes produced to mark special days, staff often going to great lengths to ensure these times were not passed without celebration.

Not all of the carers hearts were in the job, it can't have been an easy environment in which to spend your working life. But, having said that a great many were devoted to the well being of their charges, going the extra mile to improve an otherwise wasted life. There was also a part time hairdressers, tailors and of course a Church, now converted to modern homes and renamed Worthington place in honour of the designer Thomas Worthington. (1826 - 1909.) the entire site has now disappeared virtually, reborn as a new modern housing estate, like so many other Carlisle landmarks.

The head cook at the clinic was a Scot from Bonny Bridge near Aberdeen called Jimmy Lamb, he ran the kitchen with the same up to date policies as the rest of the Clinics management team. Menus were far more adventurous within the rations supplied. We were encouraged to include more interesting and appetising dishes to the daily meals, much to the appreciation of both staff and patients alike, often creating meals to a particular patients liking, hopefully aiding recovery and brightening their day. The main patient type where those suffering various types of depression, so any sign of caring helped, even if it just aided appetite.

The hospital butcher Jimmy Mulholland, was a regular visitor to our staff room, enjoying the open and friendly atmosphere the clinic provided. What a lad he was, mad as a hatter, always laughing and joking with loads of tall tales to tell.
He married one of the nurses called Arlene Little who had been a pupil at Harraby Secondary while I was also there. She was in a higher stream than me and my thick mates, so did not really know me. She and Jimmy left the Garlands to run a very successful butchers shop on the outskirts of the City in the village of Great Orton. Regretfully neither survives, but are certain never to be forgotten by family and friends. Jimmy's son carries on his dads business, doing very nicely.
It was Jimmy Mulholland, charge nurse Joe Feddon and Jimmy Lamb among others who waylaid me on the eve of my wedding to Renee, offering to buy me a one way ticket to Ireland so avoiding life long servitude and when I refused the swine's black boot polished me from head to toe, and I mean ever where, from the hair on my head to the soles of my feet, including any personal areas in between. It took a mighty long shower and bath to restore me to virgin whiteness for my nuptials not mention the damage done to

my other wedding tackle. None of these lads are still here and the world is poorer for their loss.

I eventually left the job at the Garlands also, only to return some five years later after being demobbed from the army. Before leaving however I took revenge on the catering supervisor for some perceived slight or other, now long forgotten. I covered every keyhole in the place with a strip of the new almost invisible sticky sello tape. Not having the best of eye sight apparently he struggled to realise what was afoot, and had to send for a joiner to obtain entry. Fortunately my five year absence gave him time to mellow and no grudge followed, or at least I was not aware of one, but maybe I just did not know of it !!
To say I was astonished at the changes brought about in the Hospital during my time away would be an understatement. The advances in the care and treatment of the mentally ill, especially in pharmaceuticals were just amazing. Patients who I would not have gone within fifty feet of before, now approached me, embracing me, welcoming me back with great smiles of recognition, having been saved from the dark depths to which they had previously been cast, apparently, or so I had thought, without hope. It took quite a while for this new found familiarity to sink in, but was most acceptable for all that. The advantages did not stop there. Due to the large numbers of patients being released back into the community because of the changes brought about by the effects of a simple pill changing their lives, wards were now much roomier, with the quality of life for those left behind being improved beyond measure. The stigma of incarceration still hung in the air and would take much more than a mere pill to dissolve.

We all have heard stories of men and women convinced they belong to the Monarchy, well one such lad at the hospital was of a

similar state of mind, each morning as part of his ward duties he would arrive at the kitchen counter to announce,
" It has happened, the Queen and Charlie have been arrested."
apparently for impersonating our friend, and were, at the very moment Incarcerated in the Tower of London, any minute now the Prime Minister would arrive at the Garlands to escort him to Buckingham Palace and
" Place me on the throne of England."
 We of course would all be found positions in the Royal kitchens and would want for nothing, the Corgis were going to Battersea dogs home. This news would be received with much cheering and bowing, then next morning would be repeated over again, well, whose to say his claim was not valid, after all there are those who have challenged the House of Windsor. One day, one day..

However I did not linger for long in my second stint at the Garlands. Whilst there were still many nice and characterful folk there the comradeship and ambience I had known was gone forever.
I felt I did not belong.

18   IN THE SHADOW OF BEN BRAGGIE.

Between leaving the Garlands for the first time and joining the Army, I worked for a brief time at the aptly named Sutherland Arms Hotel, an old coaching Inn, most attractively presented, with about twelve to fourteen letting rooms, a restaurant and a pleasant ambience in the lovely village of Golspie, in the glorious County of Sutherland, to the north of Scotland.
It was a one street affair like so many villages, with its basic amenities and shops, a couple of Pubs and half a dozen fancy goods emporiums for the visitors, a links golf course running along the shoreline. The scenery needless to say was magnificent, rugged and heather strewn, glowing purple with the odd diamonesque sparkling Burn making its way down the mountain, the mighty Ben Braggie, not quite the edifice of Ben Nevis, but beautiful just the same, casting its shadow down on the village , as immortalised in the ballad of the "Shadow of Ben Braggie."
The Scots, like the Irish have a song about everything and the good folk of Golspie were not going to be denied theirs.
 My stay was all too brief, I cannot even recall any of the names of the people who worked at the hotel. Renee and I were accommodated in a wee But and Ben at the rear of the building, as it says, it was comprised of two rooms, a small bedroom and a modest kitchen cum sitting room divided by the small addition of a toilet and bathroom. It was very cold, having only a small coal fire which also heated the water, never raising the temperature higher than tepid at best. Sparsely furnished with an ancient suite of sorts and threadbare carpets and curtains it was not really what you could call a home from home. There was a large front garden which sloped down to the road and we did set to trying to create a vegetable patch, but the ground was like concrete, not ever having

been worked before, nothing would take despite Renee's green fingers. So we settled for a few chickens in a small outhouse at the rear, hoping eventually to get ourselves a pig to breed from, whilst just along the road toward John O Groat's was Dunrobin Castle, home to the Dukes of Sutherland, and occasional retreat of H M the Queen and Phil the Greek. It was a very imposing structure , glistening white turrets just like something out of a fairy tale. The Royal cars were a familiar sight passing through Golspie and as such raised no great interest.

One day while standing in the small hotel car park having a quick drag on my Benson and Hedges tipped, the Royal car came sweeping down the highway, they are wonderful vehicles which just seem to glide along effortlessly. It was a bright sunny day and the car in question had a large Perspex dome like affair, so the crowd could better see the Royals I suppose. No escort or outriders, her Maj clearly felt quite safe here. Anyway, there was not another soul in sight and to my amazement the two Highnesses were going at it hammer and tong. Phil the Greek was getting a right earful, the Royal digit was getting a good wagging under his sneck. God only knows what he had done, but lets be fair, he knows how to get into trouble with no help from anyone. They both briefly looked in my direction but clearly decided I did not justify the courtesy of the Royal wave and got back to their bickering. It was just like watching my Mam and Dad Barneying over some perceived slight or other, amazing. I had never thought of the Royals as being normal before, just goes to show.
A short while after arriving in Golspie Renee collapsed while waiting for a bus to town. While a fellow passenger attended to her I rushed back to the Hotel for a glass of water, in my panic I returned with not cool refreshing aqua, but hot water, what a dorc. Later the local doctor arrived to see her, well, I could not believe

my eyes, talk about a wild highlander, he had a long grey beard and wore the kilt, with a Tam o' Shanter on his head. No exaggeration, Honest !.
He proceeded to examine my wife , whilst I kept a close watch, well you never can tell. After a short while he announced my wife to be pregnant, something which delighted us both, however his next announcement did not leave me quite so pleased. He then strongly advised Renee to avoid contact with her husband until such time as the Bairn arrived, we had only been married six weeks! and worse still, she took him at his word, that was that, no more romance for seven and a half months. I have been suspicious of hairy doctors ever since. If Doctor " Dangerous" Brian Scroggie of Saint Paul's practise should ever read this, you are excused Brian, you I liked.

Renee hated Golspie from the start. Partially due I am sure to the fact of her having fallen pregnant with our Daughter Karen not long before arriving there, hormones probably. Is that not the usual excuse !   She was soon headed back home to Carlisle, with her big sister Dorothy and her husband Tony, who had made the car journey from Carlisle to collect her. Followed by myself a short while later, I however had to make my own way home.
The people of the village were very nice in the main, but the odd one or two made it clear I did not belong, again.. that's life. We are not all perfect, my dream of a life in the country with my hens and pigs were dashed, not for the first time and certainly not the last.
One time whilst walking on Ben Braggie I had a surreal experience, I suddenly felt a wave of warm air waft over me, creating a sense of security and deep calm. Then I heard a voice, it was indistinct but somehow I knew it to be God addressing me, at the time I well understood what was being said, but almost

immediately it was lost. This was not the first time I had such a state of grace. Several times in my early youth I went through the same experience, causing me to believe I was destined for some religious career, however I must have failed the test as no such thing occurred. Except the time spent with Father Pepping at St Andrews who seemed to understand better than I what was occurring, strange, he was a real kindly man, a Saint if ever there was one, or so I thought at least.

On another occasion while walking the lower slopes of the mountain I came across what I took to be the ruins of a small cottage, the roof being partially collapsed and one wall completely gone, but on drawing near realised it housed a local family, one of whom, a lady of about forty, worked at the Sutherland Arms as a kitchen help. The place was a wreck yet was home to these folk, who despite all, looked clean and tidy. Welcoming me in I was offered a cup of tea which I could not bring myself to accept seeing their plight.

This was 1964, I could not believe people lived like this in a civilised Country. However I went on to see real poverty in South America and the West Indies which destroyed any ideas of Godly intervention saving mankind. These poor folk in northern Scotland were rich in comparison, whilst we were Kings.

I still treasure my memories of Golspie, fleeting as they were. Another time it may have been different, who knows.

19   KING OF TAKAMA.

Upon returning to Carlisle I worked for a short while at the Silver Grill Restaurant on English street, a very grand place, with silver service and waiters in tails being the norm, nothing quite like that in the city nowadays more the pity. The décor was regal to say the least though the kitchens, whilst producing marvellous cuisine, was a little behind the times with regard to hygiene, health and safety, though no one got harmed, more through luck than anything else. The head Chef was old school and crossing him could be severely hazardous to your well being. All kinds of cooking equipment was inclined to take flight across the kitchen when he became upset. Like most Chefs he liked a drink, so as the day progressed the danger increased. It was common practice for Cooks and Chefs to be plied with ale, to restore lost liquid and vital minerals sweated out in the kitchens heat. I have never investigated the statistics, but it would not surprise me to discover a higher rate of alcoholism within the catering industry than just about any other.
It was while working at the Silver Grill that I decided to join the Army, not one of my better decisions in hindsight, but there you go, what's done is done. Having said that I did have some great times and saw some of the world, mainly South America and West Cumberland, yea, that's right, Bootle, just along the road from Millom, every ones dream posting, Christ , you join the Army to see the world and end up fifty miles down the bloody road.
After basic training at Fulwood Barracks in Deepdale, Preston, where I never did achieve the level of bullshit that my comrades gained, my boots never shone like glass nor my brasses reflect the

light, I just could not get there despite all the time spent trying.
I was top in weapons training, so killing people was not going to be a problem, but looking smart whilst doing that was not going to happen. We were sent to join the Regiment, the Kings own Royal Border, the Local Border Regiment having amalgamated with the Kings own Royal regiment.
More Government cuts, nothings new !!

They were then based in British Guiana, I should really have listened more carefully to our Geography teacher, Mr Thackery, because I thought we were headed to Africa, when our destination was actually South America. Thicko or what.
Guyana or British Guiana as it was then known was one of the last remnants of an already defunked British Empire. The ruling party there was the Peoples National Congress, with Prime Minister Forbes Burnham. The socialist Cheddi Bharat Jagan, was the peoples choice, funnily enough my dad was a supporter of his, strange man, but he was not wanted by the British, so was militarily deposed and Burnham, a much more acceptable anti communist alternative, given the job. We were there to keep the peace.
I had not been long in the country when some guy tried to get rid of Forbes Burnham by taking a pot shot at him, not the last to do so I might add. The would be assassin made off into the bush rapidly followed in hot pursuit by me and ten other keen and Gungo squaddie's from Cumberland. Needless to say we did not catch or even come close to catching him, we were merely a diversion, encouraging the poor sap to run into a trap further up river. He was never heard of after that, just quietly disappeared.
However we had a great adventure, we were made welcome where ever we turned up, in riverside villages of palm leafed huts, housing diminutive families of the indigenous population of

Amerindians, or Diamond and Gold towns scattered through the bush. Gold and Diamond mining was and probable is still a huge business in that country. Amazingly, one of the methods used to collect diamonds from the middle of river's where they were washed, accumulating over the years, by tropical rains in the hills, was to anchor a log raft in the centre of the current, tie a rope around the waist of a young boy, then weigh him down with a huge rock, then throw him in the fast running water, he would rapidly sink to the bottom ,scooping up a bucket of mud. The men on the raft would quickly pull him to the surface where the mud would be sifted to find the diamonds, if any. Then the operation would be repeated until the boy was exhausted and another youngster was volunteered for duty. The kids seemed to love it and had no fear or perhaps no awareness of the dangers.

Not like us big tough Squaddies who were scared out of our wits by tales of giant Alligators and swarms of man eating Pirhana. Nonsense I know now, but looking into that brown swirling water you would believe anything the locals told you.

No one was allowed to take any Gold or Diamonds directly from the bush other than through Government licensed agents who patrolled the Rivers in their magnificent powerful boats, buying up all to be had.

While many of the prospectors had spent years away from home, made fortunes time over, then spent their hard gotten gains on drink, gambling or prostitutes in the gold camps where a bottle of beer cost ten and twenty times that in the towns, and a night with a women would leave you broke. There was not a huge amount of crime, jungle law was brutal and swift, but who was to know when someone did not come back. The prospectors, having blown their wad, being left with not even enough to buy a new shovel would then have to beg a stake of an agent to go back and start again. These men would often spend months alone in the dangerous jungle never getting enough cash to go back home without losing face. Dying alone of some fever or other, their bones never to be found. On our return we took a couple of old timers back with us to Georgetown, I doubt they were as old as they looked, walking skeletons, but were unlikely to survive another season in the bush hunting diamonds.

Regretfully it was while in that fabulous country the powers that be in the form of the Adjutant, discovered my catering qualifications and without any warning transferred me from ten platoon C company, where I was very happy, to the kitchens. Well, when I say kitchens, what I actually meant was a grass roofed shed, with no walls, ten million flies and the most basic, highly flammable petrol fired range you could ever encounter. This was it, welcome to Takama training camp, like something out of the bridge on the river Kwai, the squaddies spent a maximum of four weeks jungle training in this rattle snake infested pleasure dome, I was there for five months.
Officially the only person in the Infantry Regiments allowed to grow a beard is the Pioneer troop Sergeant. While I was the only cook in camp, worked seven days a week, and slept in a lean to behind the cookhouse where each evening the flies would vacate the pleasure of the kitchen, and emigrate to my bunk to keep me company in the long dark nights. I possessed the only living mosquito net in town, which buzzed violently when I turned over in the night. The Officers must have been a little concerned for my mental health as I sometimes did not shave for days at a time without rebuke. The younger members of the camp would sometimes stare at me in disbelief, you could smell the fear they must have had images of Vietnam vets on wacky baccy, going berserk to the strain of the Nineteen twelve overture, slaughtering all before them, and this was the man who was feeding them.

As far as I am aware no one actually died of food poisoning, but I bet there were some close calls. The holes in the ground which passed for latrines never seemed to take too long to fill.

Once when a certain platoon, having done their tour, were preparing to return to what civilisation there was, the decision was taken by their gung ho Company Commander that they should do a forced march through the bush rather than take the easy option of going downstream on the local ferry as was the custom. The ferry usually took about forty eight hours, the march was estimated to take about a week. Don't you just love the Officer class.

On arrival in Georgetown a full seven days later, about fifty percent of those lads needed medical treatment for various tropical diseases, and all were eaten alive by leeches and mozzies.

Some developed leg ulcers which eventually caused their demob. Several years later I met up with one of them, he had been the company clerk in headquarter company, we met again in Castle Street by the Cathedral, he was still crippled, still going back and forward to Newcastle for treatment, and no! he never got a pay off or a pension.

Before they even set off, one bright spark had given a local Amerindian a packet of fags for his spear, something we all were inclined to do for souvenirs. On receipt of their cigs they would smoke them all one after another until they were finished, coughing like good uns. The loss of the spear etc, was not a problem they just loped off into the nearest jungle to emerge a short while later with a new one. The soldier in question was practising throwing the damn thing when he skewered a lad through the shoulder. God it must have hurt, but he must have been a tough little sod because the Medic simply cut it off at each end with a serrated knife, he then had to put up with that until they could get an Army Air corps helicopter to Medi Vac him out later that evening. He spent the day walking around the camp smiling at

everyone, showing off his predicament.
All the nuts are not locked up.
Often during the night some of the cattle belonging to the local Gauchos, South American version of cowboys, would wander into the kitchen attracted by God knows what, can't have been the food. So I would lob in thunder flashes to scare them away, many a panicking sprog sentry, thinking the Cubans were attacking, called stand to, ruining every ones night sleep and coming close to shooting each other.
On one occasion one of the cattle ended up getting shot and killed, no names mentioned, causing a panic as to who was going to have to pay for its loss. The solution came with the suggestion that the latrines were due to be filled in and moved elsewhere, condemning the poor cow to a shitty grave. I wanted to relieve it of a few steaks first, but was advised by the Company Commander not to push my luck. I don't think he all together liked me very much.
He, the Company Commander, had just returned to the regiment after a year with the Elite American Rangers and clearly thought he was son of Audie Murphy, (Americas most decorated soldier of the second world war, and later star of many Cowboy movies, for the less enlightened.) He, the Major, would sneak about the camp at night trying to catch the sentries by surprise. One or two marra's wanted to surprise him with a bayonet up his arse. You could hear him coming a mile off, like an elephant crashing through the bush.
One night I was on stag, (Guard Duty) with a mad Scouser who had been trying to work his ticket for months, seeing his opportunity to reduce the officer class by one dick head, whilst getting out of the Army by reason of insanity, it was all I could do to stop him putting a round into the Barm pot.
After five horrendous months I was sent to Battalion HQ situated in the old Mariners Club in the Capital city of Georgetown, a

much nicer civilised posting altogether. We slept in lovely clean sheets every night in a fresh almost, fly free environment. This was due to the Medical orderly going around most days with his favourite toy, a sort of ray gun that spewed out noxious fumes killing every living thing in range, it was petrol based with additional DDT, a bit like agent orange that the yanks were so fond of, remember that stuff, lots of Vietnamese do. Then one day the bloody thing exploded in a ball of flame. Not only did he come close to wiping out the entire Headquarter Company, but made himself bald in an instant. Still no one died, not even the flies who returned from their vacation all the better for it, in fact they were Buzzing !!

It was about four o'clock in the afternoon on a pleasant blue skied Saturday, the city was winding down for the weekend and all was quite. The moment only broken when Radio Guyana crackled into life to announce the gift of several millions dollars to the people of Guyana from the American government to fund the construction of Guyana's first proper road connecting the capital to its second city, previously only reachable by boat, New Amsterdam.
There followed a few seconds of silence prior to the John F Kennedy library and the American consulate disappearing in a loud ear splitting explosion. Some people are just never happy.
In the paper next morning the lady librarian who had vacated the building merely seconds before the event, said. " I never suspected a thing." She was now unemployed.

Amazingly, while on patrol one time up river passed the afore mentioned New Amsterdam, we were put on alert due to a report of flying saucers having landed. (No kidding, Honest.)
I had not had an interest in UFO's up to this point, we all found the stories were quite scary for a while and the newspapers were

full of reports and so called photos of several UFO's on the banks of the Esquibo river. Silver disc's just like in the movies, which is what they probably were. By the time we got there all was quite. They might have waited ! Still, they put the willies up someone enough to have the British Army on stand by.
Can you imagine that, me in the war of the worlds.

Our job in British Guiana was to prevent Fidel Castro and Che Guevara from running arms into the country, so preventing the threat of Communist revolution spreading throughout the continent. We never saw much in the way of action, Che was off exploiting his talents elsewhere at the time, mainly in Africa, so we were not even on the correct continent, and for all his talk, Fidel did not like to leave his own fireside. There was the occasional incident when boats tried to land arms on deserted beaches. One story going around was about a young Second Lieutenant being captured and raped by some interlopers, but it could have just been propaganda to scare us, if it was, it worked !!
Che eventually took up arms again, not in Guyana but in Bolivia where he came to an untimely end on the second of September in 1967 near the village of Palmerito in the south east of that country, at the hands of that corrupt government and the much relieved CIA.
I was barely aware of who Doctor Ernsto "Che" Guevara was, at that time, but like so many other romantics beheld him as a hero later in life and still do. No matter what, he was a man of great principle and courage, dying for a cause he passionately believed in.
Upon returning to the UK we were stationed in the picturesque village of Honiton, in Devon, where Renee and our daughter karen joined me in married quarters, which were in fact mobile homes fashioned from Portakabin's. They were great, with a nice kitchen,

bathroom and spacious living room, two bedrooms, not very large but did the job, and so we spent a wonderful year or so there.

It was while stationed at Honiton that Renee's twin sister Audrey arrived for a visit, staying for two weeks, enjoying the Devon sunshine. One morning, nearing the end of the first week of her stay we heard a commotion, which turned out to be Audrey dashing for the bathroom, arriving, thank God, just in time to vomit violently down the toilet, it was only after she had flushed away the contents of her stomach that she realised her false teeth were no longer attached to her gums. She had flushed them away as well. The poor girl was mortified.

We put our heads together to attempt to work out the reason for her sudden predicament, but none was forthcoming. No strange foods had been consumed, no surfeit of alcohol been drunk, nothing at all could be blamed. It was only when Audrey's daughter Alison appeared on the scene approx eight months later that all became clear. Alison is now in her forties, how time flies! and Audrey is happily married to Alan Stewart, they have a second daughter Emma. Alan originally a HGV Engineer, gave up that trade due to back problems and went to be night shift manager at Carr's biscuit factory for over thirty years. They still live in Cargo village on the outskirts of the City. We have spent many happy holidays together in a private Villa on the Canarian Island of Lanzarote.

The other great memory regarding Honiton Camp was the night I arrived home to our portakabin well the worse for drink, much to the annoyance of Renee unfortunately. Stripped off for bed stark naked I sat on a dining chair next to the large picture window which took up a large portion of the front of the kabin.

There I instantly fell into a deep drunken sleep. As I said Renee was not at all amused at my antics so before going to her bed she opened the curtains of the aforementioned window, so next morning around six am I awoke to an audience of several dozen squaddie's all admiring my meat and two veg. Revenge had been well and truly taken.

It was again while at Honiton that the horror of Abervan occurred. When those huge dark coal slag heaps slithered down engulfing the local School and houses around about in black ooze. Condemning dozens of innocent lives to a dreadful close.
I volunteered to go but was spared the horror those soldiers endured pulling tiny boys and girls from cold dark tombs. Their little faces blackened causing further heartache to already distraught parents. A couple of platoons and the medical squadron were rapidly dispatched to assist the rescue. Many a young lad was haunted by nightmares for weeks and months after such a dastardly experience.
Another horror of a different kind occurred while I was working in the Sergeants mess, a young soldier working as a waiter, lost his baby daughter. At first it was all a bit of a mystery just what had happened, then unbelievably the baby's mother was arrested and charged with the babies murder. It made all the national papers at the time. Apparently they were living in privately rented accommodation on the out skirts of Honiton, a small flat in an old farm building, the entrance to which was by way of some old concrete stairs.
The Police claimed, supported by the evidence of this young squaddie, that the wife had thrown the baby down the stairs in temper, killing the poor soul outright. We were all stunned and showered the poor lad with sympathy and support. However, a couple of weeks later the police appeared in the mess without warning and arrested our young friend, charging him with the babies murder. Confusion reigned. It turned out he had done the dirty deed and framed his wife, who by all accounts was not the brightest, he got five years, probably only did a couple, rotten little

shit. Goes to show you just don't know whats going to happen next.

Then I made my next mistake regarding the Army. I was still employed in the kitchens with little hope of an early return to the platoon, so I felt if I was to remain as a cook then I may as well reap the benefits and transferred to the Catering Corps, where after a brief stint training in Aldershot I was sent on attachment to the Royal artillery in the West Cumberland village of Bootle. A smashing place in itself where the few lads stationed there were treated far better than your average posting, with private rooms and waitress service in the mess, amazing.
It was while here I lost my thumb to some weird infection, I spent some time in the West Cumberland Hospital at Hensingham, where a short while later my first son Philip would put in an appearance. While on the ward there I met an old West Cumberland miner called Sid. A couple of years earlier Sid had stood on a rusty old nail while down the pit, being an old school type of character he had simply pulled it out and carried on working, not like now, no accident report or visit to A and E, no sir. But that was not the end of it by a long way, Sid's wound became Gangrenous resulting in the loss of his foot, which would have been bad enough except the gangrene kept coming back, he then lost his lower leg, followed by his thigh, now there was no where else to go, Sid was going to die. As I lay in my bed I moaned and groaned about the bloody pain in the remains of my thumb, Sid offered companionship and sympathy, made me feel a right burke, he waiting to meet his maker and I with a sore thumb. He enthralled me with tales of the mines he worked and the tragedy's that befell the West Cumberland mining community, the loss of fathers, sons and children as young as seven in the Pit's. I was sorry to have to leave

him to his fate. I have lost his surname in the passage of time, but his ever smiling face will stay with me forever. It was common practice in west Cumberland to name their kids , Tom, Sid or Joe, not Thomas, Sidney or Joseph, nowadays this is taken for granted , but was peculiar to the west of the County then.
There are several monuments to lost Pitmen down west, they make for emotional reading, reminders of a lost age, not necessarily a better one. King coal had a lot to answer for, with many children paying the price.

Once again we were put in married quarters an excellent three bed semi number 5 Hycemoor Way, roughly half way between the Station and Eskmeals ranges. We were very happy here for the next two years or so, it being a small but close community of service families and civilians alike. While here Renee gave birth to our eldest son Philip James again at Hensingham Hospital, Whitehaven. A small, if pebbly beach was only two minutes away where many a happy hour was spent. However, as was pointed out on more than one occasion by Philip, Sellafield Nuclear power station was a mere mile or so up the coast, so God only knows what substances we were paddling and swimming in.
We made many friends and the time flew by before our being posted to Tidworth in Hampshire, attached to the 14th field ambulance unit. We did not like it there at all, a concrete desert, mile after mile of grey houses each a copy of the one before.
The only Jungle being of the Urban variety. No lakes ,mountains or streams there. But it was shortly after that I was given compassionate discharge due to Renee being taken ill. On reflection I would have preferred to stay in the Army, just not at Tidworth, no disrespect to the citizens of that town.
My error, as I mentioned earlier was in leaving the regiment who went on to gain honours in both Aden and Northern Ireland, and

while they suffered casualties in both campaigns, with several of my old friends and school mates, such as Ronnie Brown and Arnie Tickell, even the Company Sergeant Major, known as "the Slab" copped one. Despite several Carlisle and Cumbrian lads lost or wounded, the Regiment gained great Esteem.
I was so jealous, still regretting that move to this day. Well done boys!

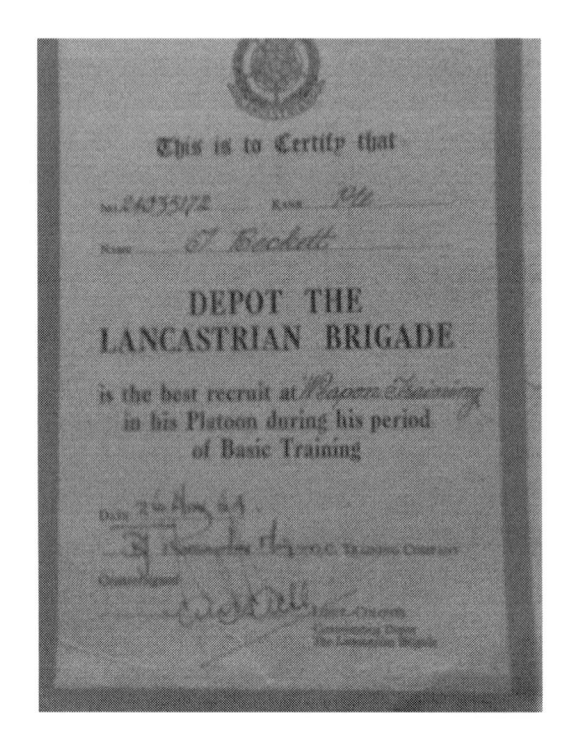

Best recruit weapon training, quickest killer in town !

20   COCOA WARRIORS.

Every year there was the Botcherby Carnival to be enjoyed, with a magical colourful parade around all the streets made up of the Carnival Queen, a most sought after and coveted position, her numerous attendants, none of the girls wanted to be left out of course, all wearing the dresses mothers had spent weeks on end making from whatever material they could get their hands on. Parachute silk and other mysterious bits of cloth would be procured by hook or by crook by under pressure dads and uncles. The Carnival queen would be seated on her throne with a huge smile on her face, her train trimmed in sparkling tinsel from last years Christmas tree. Her attendant girls arranged around her, equally attired in sparkly uniforms, resplendent on a brewers dray or flat trailer borrowed from work especially for the day by one of the dads, usually when his daughter was involved, preferably Queen . This was then decorated to the highest degree by the matriarchs of the community, drawn by the coal mans horse all done up with coloured ribbons, bows and paper flowers, etc.
A wonderful sight, bringing great cheer all round. All was led by a local band, more often than not the salvation army, proudly marching for God. Behind them would walk the committee, all dignified and proud, some in military uniforms, de-mothballed for the occasion, or bearing Civilian chains and badges of rank, Aldermen and suchlike. Then would come the Carnival queen followed by her guard of honour, the Brownies, Cubs ,Scouts, Boys Brigade and Girl Guides, etc. Bringing up the rear was the fancy dress parade, cowboys ,spacemen, witches, chimney sweeps, you name it, they were probably there. Some ingenious, others not so, but all lovingly prepared and worn with a smile of achievement. Unfortunately, this particular year my sister Brenda and I were

suffering from a bout of impetigo, so mam, quite rightly had banned us from taking part, due to the contagious aspect of the condition. We were heart broken, but determined to be there in the procession. We did everything we could to persuade mam to let us enter, we begged ,pleaded, cried, attempted blackmail and made the poor women's life a misery, slowly but surely between us we wore her down. Then a plan was formed.

She had insisted we could not go in the fancy dress because all and sundry would see our spots so being immediately aware of our illness, we pointed out if no one could see our spots they would be none the wiser. That's where the tin of cocoa powder came into the story. We went as cannibals, covered from head to foot in a coating of deep brown cocoa powder with large canes for spears, tea towel turbans, partly wrapped in old sheets, only the whites of our eyes showing.. Come the day and mams heart was in her mouth, but we were not a bit bothered and had a great time, even winning a third place prize for novelty. A bit of cheek will get you anywhere.

Afterwards we all went to the carnival party in the School hall, with lots of sandwiches, plate cake, buns and sponge cakes made by the ladies of the commitee, with custard and jelly for afters. It was brilliant. That night as we soaked in the bath we were in heaven, not to mention the biggest cup of cocoa in the world..
We entered every carnival for years after that but none so memorable, or so nerve wracking for our mam.

We believed some weird stuff when we were young, if we should see an ambulance we would mutter, " Hold your collar, never swallow until you see a four legged animal." out of fear of catching the fever, what ever it was. When we were teenagers and discovering girls, if a girl looked normal but had fattish legs we reckoned it was because she was having loads of sex ! Wishful thinking, and when they refused to go out with you, then they were clearly Lesbians, whatever a Lesbian was !

Botcherby School was many things to many people, besides a School it was a youth club, dance hall and used by the locals as a meeting place for whist drives, beetle drives, you name it ,it probably happened. Now it is the focal point of the community still. Here you can learn to speak German, or knit, perhaps you want to do some line dancing or take up water colour painting, maybe even play carpet bowls, it is all happening here along with good old bingo, and yes there is still the youth club, apparently.

Botcherby has its place in the history of the English - Scottish Border disputes. It became known as " Botcherby " around 1170, prior to which it was named " Bochardby." taken from the name of a Flemish mercenary in the service of King William 11, who ordered him to construct a castle to keep out the marauding Scots and repopulate the area with sympathetic English. There you go bet you never knew that then. Clearly our Flemish friend was not entirely successful as the Scots, either in the form of Rievers or Invaders just kept on coming right up to the late nineteenth century, with Botcherby being within the boundaries of the Border area known as the Disputed lands coming in for its fair share of attention from sometimes blue faced marauders in kilts and no knickers nicking our sheep and cattle.
In the nineteen fifties we still were terrorised.
Every year when Glasgow holiday week came around all those merry Scots passed through Carlisle in their droves on there way to Blackpool or Butlin's holiday camps , there was no M6 motorway then so anything or anyone travelling north or south had to pass through the centre of poor old Carlisle. The shopkeepers along the main streets such as Botchergate would board up their windows as

protection against the odd flying beer bottle or two. Then a week later they would have to do it all again for the return journey. They certainly seemed to know how to have a good time those mad Jocks in their kiss me quick hats and singing patriotic songs , often at our English expense. I would say those Lancashire breweries must have had to work overtime to satisfy the thirst built up over fifty one weeks of working and saving to experience one joyous week of extravagance beneath Blackpool's legendary Tower. They would dance the night away in the Tower ballroom and probably turned a few landladies hairs grey before the week was up. No doubt there would be a mini baby boom nine months later, alcohol having helped lower a few otherwise stout defences.
Many a wedding bell would ring before the next Glasgow holiday week and the boarding up once more of Carlisle's shop windows.

Meanwhile, back to Botcherby. At the bottom of Wood street stands the lovely Saint Andrews church, built as a missionary church to service the needs of several local villages before being swallowed up by the encroaching Botcherby housing estate and now trapped completely by the new ring road and even more new housing. When I was about there were at least three working farms and two Market gardens, plus the Corporation nurseries directly behind Botcherby Ave. There the flowers for the public parks and gardens were grown in profusion to brighten up the City centre and improve the lot of its citizens. These greenhouses and nursery beds were well protected by high fences of barbed wire and such, so rarely suffered the attention of marauding yobs, actually I was totally unaware of their existence for a long time, so well were they hidden from prying eyes. Durranhill housing estate now covers what was Durranhill army camp, populated mainly buy national service conscripts, killing time until they could all go home. When you passed by the barracks they would lean out of the window and enquire loudly if we had any sisters, if so would they like to come and play with them, it took a while for some of us to work out just what they were on about. But we did, eventually.

Many English regiments were based here at one time or another including of course our own Border Regiment which was instrumental in bringing my own dear dad to Carlisle along with many other Scousers. The reason for this or so I understand it was that at the outbreak of the second world war in Cities across the country men rushed to sign for their local regiments, these of course filled there quota's fairly quickly and despite introducing second, third and forth battalions were still well over subscribed so the poor lads not wanted by them found themselves being attached to such less well filled Regiments like the Borders. Consequently lots of Carlisle boys and girls of my generation find themselves half scouser, which may explain the ground swell of support in the area for Liverpool F C.

Another connection with Merseyside of course is the great " Bill Shankly," one time Carlisle United F C player and manager who went on to legendary status with his beloved Liverpool .

Dad was in the regular army for about twelve years prior to the out break of war when due to his reserve obligation he was recalled to the Colours. He was posted to the Border Regiment then stationed at Carlisle Castle. While there he met our mother who was working as a barmaid in the Irish Gate Tavern just along from the Castle gate, now long disappeared beneath the dual carriage way of the ring road, Castle Way. He swears it was love at first sight and often said our mother was the most beautiful girl he had ever seen, but then he would wouldn't he or mother would have bashed him.

Mothers name was Sarah Gallefor but of course she got Sally. After being born and spending her youth on King Street off Botchergate, the family moved to the council houses of Currock. More later.

Dads story went, that in around nineteen twenty nine or so, rather that take the path of his siblings, some eight brothers and sisters, and enter College life, as desired by his mother and Father, who owned several grocery emporiums in and around Liverpool so therefore could afford the expense, higher education being still the provenance of the well to do. He chose instead to run away from home and enlist into the Kings Regiment of Infantry, steadily rising through the ranks to the position of colour Sergeant. Seeing service in north Wales, where the locals refused to speak any English in the company of squaddies, then Ireland where they were even less popular. He was not an ideal soldier, being reduced in rank for some misdeed or other on more than on occasion.

He claims one of his proudest moments was during a camp inspection by the commanding officer. The words, " Corporal Beckett is a bastard ," were found written in large black lettering on the newly white washed ablution block, causing the Commandant to say, " well, at least one of my NCO's must be doing his job right !".

He also spent several years as a Pseudo teacher, many recruits being illiterate, he taught those who wished to improve themselves to at least write their own name and read written orders. After twelve years he was demobbed, but was soon back in the khaki courtesy of Adolph Hitler and his marauding mob.

Mam and dad were married just before he went of with the British Expeditionary Force to Belgium having been recalled to the colours as a reservist. Not long after arriving in Belgium, having barely crossed the French border, dad was on the receiving end of a Nazi bullet. He swears that his unit were out numbered and severely out gunned by the advancing Jerry, which was probably an understatement . They were in the process of carrying out a strategic withdrawal from hastily prepared defensive positions, ie running like holy hell across an open field for dear life, when one

of the dastardly Hun shot him up the bottom. Allowing dad to later claim to be the only man in Carlisle with two arse holes.
He was rescued by a unit of the free French who carted him all the way back to Dunkirk, then disregarding there own safety, got him aboard a ship back to Blighty and an Edinburgh hospital where he spent the next three months or so before once more being demobbed back to his wife in Carlisle, and it was there he spent the remainder of his days.. He would never have a bad word said of the French, not like some. Hardly surprising really when you read of the horrors of that evacuation, despite the claim of a glorious achievement.
Another of dads problems were his bunions, an affliction he shared with my wife Renee. Renee's are one on each foot just below the big toe, causing a slight deformity of the alignment of the rest of her toes. However she is too chicken to get them sorted having heard such horrific tales of crippling pain.
Dads were also on the side of his foot but also on each heel. He blamed the boots he was issued in the Army, claiming they were always too small. As he got older he would cut circles out of the side of his shoes to allow the bunion to poke through, then cut a slice from the heel to do the same there, finally using an old lace to hold the leather together so as not to actually lose his shoe. He put up with this for years poor man, in rainy weather his feet were permanently soaked.
Once fully recovered he was given a job as a clerical officer at the RAF fourteenth maintenance unit at Kingstown, on the northern side of the city outskirts. The opposite side to were we lived. Mam and dad first lived with my grandparents, this did not suit my dad at all, so when I was about two years old we moved to our council house home in Botcherby avenue where he spent the remainder of his days, dying of throat cancer at the age of…sixty one years and

three hundred and sixty four days, just one day before his sixty second birthday, so failing to qualify for his works pension by just one day, also denying my mother her rights to claim a share of dads work pension, do not ask me why, I do not have a clue, but sounded very dodgy. A couple of years after dad died mam moved across the avenue to a two bed roomed house which suited her better before eventually moving to Margaret Creighton Gardens where she too eventually passed away.

Botcherby like most neighbourhoods in those post war days was quite self sufficient when it came to shops, we had the Silver Grill Bakery, a Butcher, belonging I believe to Bells farmers, a Grocer, run by the another of my hero's, Joe Rowley and his glamorous wife. (So glamorous I fail to recall her name). The Greengrocer, Mr Parr, Cobbler, Mr Winrow, a Gents Barber, the Post office and general store run by Mr and Mrs Banks. The Fish and Chip shop, and Grice's croft who provided fresh produce such as lettuce tomatoes, etc. Just along the road was a Cooperative store and Florida stores, in between which stood an old Mansion house, where it was commonly believed the Carlisle Miser Margery Jackson lived, (1722-1812.). However I am assured by my friend Geoff, she actually ended up in Wood street, and if Geoff says so I for one believe him. She would wear the same old clothes for years despite owning large chunks of the city, then died with in excess of one and a half million pounds under her proverbial pillow, the Church and of course the Magpie pub also, eventually, when they were finally legalised in the late fifties, a Bookies, owned by Mr Downey. I do believe my mother and father were his best customers and helped to make him very rich, eventually opening several other shops around the City. They both loved horse racing with a passion right up to their dying day. They literally placed their last bets the day before they passed away. My dad died a good while before mam so she probably laid out the most cash.

Her non de plume was Sally B and was eventually known to every bookmaker in the City. You could ask them if they knew Mrs Beckett and they would have to think about it, but mention Sally B and their eyes would light up in recognition. A few days before she succumbed I visited mam who told me she was not at all well and could not leave the house to get her bits and pieces from the corner store, so off I went to get them for her, a sliced loaf, some tinned peas and a small jar of coffee or some such. We sat and chatted for a while , mainly about the struggle she had to pay her day to day bills and how the Labour party had let her generation down, but she still cursed the Tories to high heaven and Mrs Thatcher in particular. Eventually I had to go on my way back to work and said my goodbyes with a promise to return soon, seeing how she was not well enough to go out.

Later the same afternoon as I made my way down Botchergate in the City centre, I espied my poor sick mother leaving Corals the bookies , she then strolled up the street to the nearest bus stop where she could catch her regular bus home.

After her bus had departed I entered the aforementioned bookies and enquired as to whether my mother had been in today, " I do not know." the lady behind the counter claimed. " Who is your mother anyway?"

" Mrs Beckett." I replied. " O, I do not know that name at all dear." she said. " You may know her as Sally B ." I ventured.

"OH ,of course." she replied with a knowing smile. " You should have said that in the first place, yes Sally was in a little while ago, I made her a nice cup of tea while she studied the form pages, lovely Lady Sally, we have known her for years." Say no more.

22   BOOKIES BAGMAN.

  My dad used to occasionally help out a local bookie who worked the hound trails, dad would act as bookies Bagman, record the bets, work out the odds and what have you, no pocket calculators then, just swift mental arithmetic, but normally the bookmaker who incidentally was also the local window cleaner, strange combination of trades but whatever turned you on, he would take care of the cash, keeping it close to him in his little brown leather bag. One day however after a particularly good day at the trails, fate intervened and the bookie had to go off somewhere on an urgent errand, the reason escapes me why but no matter, off he went on his merry way leaving dad in charge of the brown bag and its contents of that days takings. Well, not only had it been an extremely busy and financially rewarding day but a very hot thirst inducing one as well, so it was only right that dad stopped off at the Magpie pub on his way home treating himself to a thirst quenching pint or two, or three. To cut the story short it came to pass that dad got into convivial company, with the crack flowing along with the ale. Dad being a man who always stood his corner had soon finished what little cash of his own he had on him, and not wanting to be a party pooper and cut short the session he felt it only right that the bookie should not begrudge him a loan from the cash bag, seems fair enough, he thought, after all he had slaved all day in the heat and such. So the session continued on apace, all were having a great time and dad was particularly generous when someone said they were a bit short and unable to honour their commitment to the buying of a round, he told them not to be concerned as he would cover their predicament so ensuring they all had a great time. Happy days.
The next morning, being Sunday dad was late up, and only roused when he heard the rapping of the heavy knocker on the front door,

struggling into his trousers, still wearing his shirt from the day before, he stumbled down the stairs, pulling open the front door to see who the hell was calling at this time on a Sunday.
There before him stood the bookie, smiling.
" I have come for my bag, Bill. "
" The bag.?" dad replied, whilst trying to engage his brain through the pain of his hangover.
" That's right, Bill, the cash bag ,I left it with you to look after," leaning forward, suspicion building, he continued. " you do not look too well Bill, I hope nothing has happened,"
" no, no, " dad stuttered. His face paling further as realisation dawned,
"Christ !" he thought, "where's the bag."
It did not take him long to find it, stuck down behind the sofa where he distinctly remembered putting it for safe keeping the night before. Not a lot of point really because there was hardly anything worth stealing in it, most of its previous contents were now resting in the till of the Magpie, all safe and sound.
Now if this had been in Chicago or Las Vegas dad would have been entombed in a block of concrete holding up a bridge or a flyover, but lucky for him in was the nineteen fifties in Carlisle and fortunately the bookie was not connected to the mafia or even the Kray twins so dad survived.
Needless to say his days as a Bookies Bagman were done . I have no idea if he repaid the money, highly unlikely as he was permanently broke, but life went on, the bookie even carried on cleaning our windows, I am not sure if he put the price up.
There were a lot of nice people in Botcherby.

Hound trailing is clearly an acquired taste mainly pursued by country folk I think, certainly not one I have subscribed to. Basically what occurs is early in the morning, or perhaps the evening before, weather dependent, some bloke sets out with a bag of aniseed tied around his waist on a length of rope, he then proceeds to drag the aniseed over fells, fields, dykes and moor land for literally miles, five if it's a pups race, ten or more if its seniors. through yellow flowering Gorse, purple heather and fresh sparkling mountain streams, crossing ploughed land and plush meadow. Covering miles and miles. Apparently the scent of the aniseed drives the hounds to distraction and is totally irresistible. When finally released by their manic owners the mutts take of in a baying howling scene of mayhem, like the hounds of hell fleeing Hades in a cheap horror film, unfortunately not always or even rarely in the same direction. Some hounds go missing for days or even weeks, some are never seen again, one or two could be side tracked by the aroma of a passing red brushed fox, or a long eared mountain hare, while still others roam the darkening fells for eternity, to be glimpsed only by the occasional shepherd tending his flock as the mystery hound disappears over a rising crest or plunge into a ragged deep cleft in the rocks. The haunting baying of a forever lost hound jangles the nerves, quickening the senses with its doomed call, some just get lost.

When travelling tight country roads it is not unusual to come across ten, twenty or more cars, battered land rovers, bright new top of the range four wheel drives, etc parked haphazardly along the dyke back leaving you if you are lucky the absolute minimum of room in which to pass them. There will be men and women dressed in their wax jackets and flat caps standing on roofs, bonnets, gateposts scanning the horizon through their high powered binoculars, searching for the prize hound or just the one carrying their money. Then in a frantic race they would be off in convoy to the next favourite viewing point to go through the same excited routine, until a champion was declared. Then back to some kind of normality until the next mad escapade.

The winner, being of course the first dog home, to be greeted rapturously by its demented owner. Always supposing of course that there is no challenge, for it has been known believe it or not for dogs to be ringed, where a similar looking hound joins the race in an advanced position, so gaining an unfair advantage, or maybe the favourite has been slipped a mickey finn curtailing its performance, it has even been known for a bitch in heat be used to distract hounds with other delights in mind. It then only remains for the winning owners to shoulder his laurels and liberally pat the dog, the betting fraternity go on to collect their winnings or mourn their losses, mainly the latter. But is has to be said great fun seems to had by all, even some times the hounds. The rules and regulations governing the sport were formalised in 1906 at the founding of the Hound trailing association, which continues to function to this day, without my assistance.

22   HORSES FOR COURSES.

 My Mam and Dad were both very charitable people, every week, without fail, they donated a slice of their earnings to the Bookies support fund, never failing to ensure the Bookies welfare and sustenance. They could not bare the thought of those poor bookies going short, or at least that's the way it seemed to me a devoted anti Gambler, (except for the lottery of course.) To this day the thought of backing a horse with my hard earned cash brings me out in a cold sweat. Something to do with my inability to stand losing money.
Dad and Mam on the other hand were near fanatical horse racing fans, barely a day would go by without a flutter, usually horses, occasionally the hounds, nothing too heavy. Mam never quite lost the housekeeping, though you always knew when Dad had a bad day, he could not afford to go to the Magpie and would sit watching telly with a face like a smacked arse. They both knew their limitations thank God, not like some who would lose all and sod the consequences. To be fair they did derive huge pleasure from the Gee Gee's and it was never begrudged, we kids never suffered as I recall, as I said earlier my childhood memories are full of joy.
My parents loved Carlisle race day and when funds allowed would dress up like royalty and head for Durdar Race course. Mam would look amazing in her finery and with his trilby dad looked like a film star. They both read the racing pages from back to front and had a knowledge of runners and riders second to none. I doubt if they ever had a really bad loss, too canny for that, but did have the odd biggish win when we all benefited with ice cream and lemonade. The good days well outweighed the bad.
My uncle Brian, my mams youngest brother was even worse, he

possessed every form book going and according to my dad could tell you where a horse had its last shit but could not back a winner. Brian was a lovely fellow everyone loved him because he was the baby of the family and always had a ready smile for all. Sadly he died fairly young, never really recovering from a stroke, spending his last years in a nursing home on Wigton Road. Mother used to visit him every week without fail even though it broke her heart to do so. When he died the Gallefor name seems to have gone with him, people always used to refer to him as the last of the Gallefor's.

One of my mothers several other brothers was my Uncle Harold, a professional soldier, with almost thirty years service under his belt. He achieved the rank of Colour Sergeant before eventually retiring back home to Carlisle. Each Regiment had a group of Colour or what otherwise was known as staff sergeants whose historical roll was to care for, and if need be protect to the death the Regiments colours, these being the Regiments flags, from loss to a potential enemy on the battle field. Something regarded as worse than death. The latter days of his military career were spent with the Junior Leaders Regiment. This troop of young soldiers was set up in the early nineteen fifties to select and train young boys as potential future None Commissioned Officer', IE, Corporals, Sergeants, etc. He was without a doubt my most favourite uncle, always smiling and cheerful. My Dad on the other hand never seemed altogether that keen on Harold, not that I was aware of any reason for ill feeling, other than Harold was a Gallefor and dad always told me stories that helped justify his undercurrent of dislike for the Gallefor men at least .

Apparently among other things, when Mam and Dad were lodging with Mam's parents, at mealtime he would always get the smallest portion of what was going, the other men, my Grandad and various uncles would invariably get two chops to my dad's one, or two

Yorkshire puddings to dad's one, this despite dad being the main breadwinner in the family.

He was always convinced that the Gallefor clan did not like him so you can see how the resentment would build up. There was also the question of religion which caused no end of bother, Mam was a Catholic and dad a Protestant. Apparently the local Priest approved of the marriage as long as dad agreed to bring us kids up as Catholics , which he was more than willing to do for the sake of a happy home life for my mother himself and us kids. However, you just knew there was going to be a however. Between my sister Brenda being Christened and my arrival a new Priest arrived on the scene the self righteous father Begly, he proceeded to renege on the deal, he denied my mother access to his Church while she was married to a protestant, which broke my Mam's heart and resulted in the rest of us becoming Church of England.

The Gallefors were all terrified of this priest, as were most of his so called flock. They would literally hide whenever they saw him approaching in their direction. And if he knocked on the door my Grandma and Aunties would all but faint in panic, the men folk would disappear either up the stair or out the window, not that they spent much time at home, the pub was their home where all the cash was spent, the woman got on as best they could.

One of the things that clearly played on Mams mind, as with most of her generation, was the subject of Insurance, they had to know the funeral would be seen off without embarrassment.!

She paid into a so called, Penny Policy for forty or more years and when eventually cashed in it realised the princely sum of £ 80, plus a few coppers. However she need not have worried we, Brenda, Susan and I, ensured she got the going away she would have wished, with the desired funeral tea at the Greystead's Hotel on Dalston road, a place she had attended often over the years, being, apparently, a great favourite with the departed. We then Interned her ashes with her much loved first grandson, Brenda's eldest son Anthony , who was lost tragically some years earlier. Brenda then had Mam's name added to Anthony's head stone, some thing she would have been very happy about, and loved the company of her first born grandson.

Dad's ashes had been scattered in the January garden, as per his wishes, probably united with many of his old army buddies, who shared similar desires.

I have made it clear that this is not for me, my ashes are to go into the river Eden at the Memorial suspension bridge, site of my many early adventures, then they would be carried down to the Solway and eventually out to sea making their way around the world on one last great journey. My last act of pollution to be added to my carbon footprint, the woes of the planet made worse by a dead twit.

23   FOUR JOES.

There were four Joes in our family when I was boy, my dad was called Philip William Joseph, and sometimes got called Joe, as well as Bill or Phil depending on just who he was with at the time.
I also had a no less than three uncle Joes. Joe Gallefor one of my mothers brothers lived in a brand new council house on Pennine Way in Harraby with my auntie Chrisy, I liked to go there because I felt quite posh. They had a brand new upstairs bathroom and toilet, everything smelt new and fresh, then one day I asked to use the loo and somehow managed to break their nice new low level flush, all I did was tug on the flipping handle and all hell broke loose, I was not Mr Popular for a while I can tell you. Still we got over it.. eventually.
Uncle Joe was in the navy during the war and was demobbed wounded. My dad claimed that Joe was always a bit clumsy and after a drink had fell into the hold cracking his skull, so never actually saw active service at all. But I really do not know, a lot of old soldiers seemed to hold grudges of one kind or another. Any one who stayed at home and did not serve in any of the armed services were all subjected to some degree of suspicion of cowardice or worse, profiteering or chasing serving soldiers wives, which I have no doubt occurred, no names, no pack drill.
My remaining two other uncle Joes, what there actual relationship to me was I have no idea but were always referred to as Uncle Joe, well these were real characters, though some would not be so generous in their description as they were also undeniable rouges it has to be said.
The tale I am about to tell was related to me time and time again by my dad to his great pleasure, normally after a drink or two, but to be fair received some credence by other family sources at a later date.

In the mid fifties these two Joes, having some how survived their national service, which had been slightly longer than most due to time served in the glass house, were finally given their discharge. As per normal practise they were supplied with the obligatory demob suit, a train ticket home and some discharge pay.
Upon arrival back in their home town of Carlisle they immediately sort out their old favourite haunts and proceeded to spend.
They were soon intoxicated and the money disappearing even quicker through the generous purchase of drinks for all and sundry. It was the law in those times for pubs to call time and close at ten o'clock, Carlisle pubs being still state Managed, but our boys knew the score that by going to the railway station and purchasing a two penny platform ticket they could carry on drinking to their hearts content in the passenger refreshment rooms, which were licensed to serve drink virtually all night. It was not too long however before the money all dried up. What to do !
Putting their heads together they came up with a remedy for this sad conundrum by sauntering along to the back door of the nearby branch of Burtons the tailors and with skills learned elsewhere were quickly inside. Discarding the despised demob suits they spent a happy hour or so trying on shoes, shirts and of course the most expensive smartest suits in store. The till was deprived of its contents along with the managers petty cash box and before they knew it back they were in the refreshment room enjoying a cool glass of blue bass.
Not long after that a further decision was taken, to take off to London, the big smoke. Having purchased one way tickets they boarded the midnight express train to glory. The journey soon passed, alcohol induced sleep killed the time, they awoke to the sound of the ticket collector calling
" Euston station, Euston station, all passengers must disembark."

They collected together their few belongings and made their way drowsily along the platform toward the ticket barrier, where to their great surprise they were immediately grabbed by the collar by a pair of burly Metropolitan police officers. They soon found themselves in the local nick where they were charged with the burglary of the Carlisle Branch of Burtons tailors. Mystified they enquired into how they had been caught so easily and so far from the scene of the crime. It turned out they had aroused the suspicion of the ticket office staff by the tags still attached to one Joes coat, but what clinched it was the fact they had been so busy trying on new suits that they had left their Army Identification cards in their demob suits. Well it did not take a genius to work out the rest so that was the end of another adventure for the two Joes.

Years later I used to meet up with these two occasionally in Carlisle Pubs always buying them a drink in return for one of their imaginary stories, what a pair, both gone to explain themselves to the higher authority now, how I would love to have been a fly on that wall.

I did have another uncle or at least yet another man who got referred to as my uncle, not a Gallefor this time, but someone who was regarded as the most vain man in Carlisle by many. Convinced he was an Adonis he would wash his face in milk and wear the best of clothes while his children went to school on a breakfast of dry bread, assuming there was some bread. He was one of a type who not only did not work but held on to the family allowance book as his midweek drinking fund, not an unusual practice then as the man was regarded as the head of the family and trusted to do right by them, not all held this trust as sacred. A system now changed for the better. He went on to live to a ripe old age without changing so extending his misery for as long as he could. Still attracting the

ladies well into old age. I would love to name and shame him but he still has family in the City who I would not want to hurt, lets face it we all love our Mams and Dads no matter what and, no one forgives quicker than a child.
Child cruelty is an ongoing, seemingly never ending feature of the human race, I do not suppose it will ever be fully extinguished while children are there to be exploited and abused.

However Harold was away for years abroad with the military so probably was a bit of an innocent victim of all this. A lot of his service was spent with the Junior Leaders regiment stationed in I believe Oswestry, on the English Welsh border north of Shropshire, training young soldiers for leadership within the forces. He clearly had a soft spot for me as we got on like a house on fire, he would chat with me for hours and show me how to do things, like make a fishing rod, how to choose and cut cane. Then when he did leave the Army and open a greengrocers shop on the bottom end of Botchergate, close to King Street the sight of his, and all his brothers and sisters births prior to the family moving to a nicer terraced house on Millholme avenue, just around the corner from the eventual family home on Blackwell Road.
I helped out at weekends and evenings. On Saturday he would take me for lunch at Minn's restaurant, just along from his shop, next to the old Martins Bank whose edifice is still there to be seen, now a charity shop, the name engraved in the sandstone above the main entrance as was. I would feel really posh eating my roast beef dinner followed by some pudding and a cup of tea on a saucer with a shiny teaspoon. The café was situated by the old cattle mart from where it drew its main cliental, both have long since gone . Minn's is now an Alzheimer's charity shop and the cattle mart a pay and stay car park. Nothing new there then.
I loved working there but regretfully Harold was not cut out to be a

Greengrocer, plus of course it was already a dying trade with the first of the new supermarkets making their appearance, Presto's on Portland Place, now English Gate plaza car park (Yes, Another.) and Bi-Right on Lowther street, swallowed up by the Lanes shopping centre,
Harold's shop was eventually closed, I was gutted, but have some wonderful memorise. One of the things that always comes to mind when I think of Uncle Harold is the huge mug he used to drink his tea from. He loved his brew and was hardly ever without his mug of tea. That mug was only ever washed on the outside, you were not allowed to clean the inside which was the colour of dark teak. Harold insisted this spoiled the flavour and stopped the tea from lining your stomach, protecting it from a plethora of ills. I still love strong tea, non of that milky namby pamby stuff, yuck.

Years later when Harold's wife passed away he returned to the uniformed life as a Chelsea Pensioner, he looked just great in his brightly coloured uniform and cocked hat, often returning home to strut his stuff in Carlisle City centre where he was most admired by all, especially the old girls. Never one to hide his light under a bushel, he flirted and strutted like a Cockerel, just as boldly impressive. He loved playing Bingo and was a regular at the old Lonsdale Cinema building. You could hear him shout BINGO !, all over Carlisle. I have said it before, but I will never forget my good old uncle Harold. He has been gone a good while now but I often think of him still, what a character.
Coincidentally my wife Renee's Granddad and Grandmother, Alfred and Mary Rennison, also owned for many years a Green Grocery business on Victoria Viaduct, near where Tesco's

supermarket now stands, growing a lot of their own produce on a site near Mossband, on the Gretna road, close by Renee's family home. They lived above the shop before retiring in old age to a flat in Margaret Creighton gardens, where Alfred eventually passed away, his trade on his death certificate was given as a fruiterer. Again, coincidentally, Margaret Creighton gardens was where my mother also ended her days in a pensioners bungalow.

If the name Rennison rings a bell it could be because Renee's great uncle Richard Rennison, a name shared by her elder brother, was for many years the resident priest at the Blacksmiths shop in Gretna Green, where it is believed he married in excess of five thousand runaway couples. WOW, Claim to fame or what !
Renee lived her early life at Mossband in a cottage with no electric or gas, cooking was done on an open stove or on a primus stove. light came from oil lamps.
Her Dad Wilfred Buntin grew all the families fruit and vegetables, kept hens, bees, shot pigeons, ferreted for rabbits, hares, Etc, fishing the Esk for salmon and trout, collecting mushrooms on the marsh, they never went short of anything, living far better than most of us Townies.

24   CAMP BOTCHERBY.

On a Saturday my pals and I would hang around the Butchers and the Bakers, in Wood Street because in them days there was no refrigeration to speak off, and because no one was allowed to open on a Sunday any food likely to go off before opening on the following Monday, such has potted meats, or cakes with fresh cream or butter cream filling had to be discarded. The ploy was to stand near the back door bins looking like starved waives, tears in eyes through hunger, we had no scruples, you could guarantee some one would weaken, so we would be given what was going rather throw it in the bin. Feasting like kings until we were either stuffed or sick, which ever came first. What we could not stuff down our throats we took home for the others, I was always a greedy little sod so sometimes nothing would be left to take home, but I of course suffered no conscience. My belly was my guide and mentor who never failed me.
Part of the land in between the camp and Wood street used to be the old clay pits, perfect for use as a military training area complete with firing range and an old long abandoned Sherman tank. Fantastic place for training would be warriors and heroes,
we used this spot for playing Jap's and Commandos. Taking turns to be goodies and baddie's, storming the tank and incinerating the occupants with our flamethrowers and grenades. No prisoners were taken and no mercy shown, vicious we were and no mistake.
When bored with all this slaughter and mayhem, we would search the gun range for spent cartridges, along with the remains of pulverised lead, which were then either brightly polished up and displayed in many a boys bedroom with the lead often ending up as weights for fishing line or melted down to be fashioned into various forms by dads and granddads, no doubt bringing happy and not so happy memories.

The area was later a motor bike scrambling track, the noise and smoke, along with the dare devil antics of the riders brought huge excitement to us young boys, and we would try to emulate them with our push bikes, much slower of course but no less adventuresome. Many a bike came to a sad end due to the punishment received, mountain bikes being a thing for the future. The camp long gone now of course as many others over the county and country. The land is given over to an Industrial estate with its variety of small factory units, retail warehouses, agricultural activities, and banks, etc. The small area of married quarters, mainly officer class, extended by new builds of council housing covering the remainder of our once fantasy land.

Just across the road where once were green fields bordering Jonnie Bulldogs Lonning, leading to the river Eden, we find Tesco's superstore with its extensive car park next door to a Toby restaurant. Every where you go today looks just like the last place, all with same superstores, burger restaurants and building societies. One time Towns and Cities had their own character immediately identifiable as such, not so now. You could be dropped off at virtually any place in the U K and would not know where, due to the similarity. And do not get me started on our Industrial heritance, or more like it what Industry.

Thank god no more do we require legions of troops to defend our shores. Though the threat now replaced, possibly even more deadly, by the internal and international problem of terrorism. Many a good lad will not be coming home to his family, nothing much has changed other than the scale of their loss, which offers no comfort to the bereaved.

I lived in Botcherby for the first nineteen years of my life, except for the one year I worked for John Reed of Moss side and the five nights spread over each fortnight spent in London due to the shift pattern I worked on British Rail Dining Cars.

The only memories I have of life there are happy ones. Other than my step brother Eric throwing darts at me, then later telling me to run as fast as I could away from him or he would shoot me with his air gun, so I ran, but he still shot me the sod, hurt like shit ! He did have a violent streak, later getting a life sentence for the murder of his wife, Elizabeth and the attempted murder of his brother in law. Yes, I had a great childhood full of joyous memories, there were bad times but not sufficient to dampen my enthusiasm. We did sometimes did get involved in gang fights, and I can remember clobbering a lad with half a building brick one time, but his head must have been harder than the brick because it bounced off, he seemed to take no harm, just carried on thumping me.

These encounters were usually hand bags at dawn jobs where I do not remember anyone being really hurt, that is except for a girl who lived on our street, who will remain nameless for fear of retaliation. We were all terrified of her, she could beat up any of the boys including most of those older and bigger than her. One day she came after me for some perceived insult and in my sheer panic I threw a huge cobble at her, my fear must have improved my aim, because it hit her smack in the eye which immediately swelled up like a balloon and stopped her in her tracks. She went off to the Infirmary. I got belted off my mother for throwing stones at girls. Girl ! she was not a girl she was an Amazon. Needless to say I avoided her like the plague for weeks, until someone told me that she was in fact avoiding me, clearly she did not want cobbled again, how ever I still took no chances and kept well out off her way. This same nameless Girl as she got older sometimes hung around with my sister Brenda and I recall an incident when they were both coming home along Melbourne Park pathway which was boarded on each side, as I explained earlier, as they made their way along they were approached by a bloke who pulled down his trouser zip and whipped out his knob, asking them if they would like some. Poor man, I doubt if he ever used his knob again after our Brenda's Mate had finished with him. She kicked his balls so far up into his throat, and not just once, I doubt if he ever found them again. The last they saw of him he was laying whimpering on the ground in the fetal position crying for his mammy. He was never seen again, probably off singing soprano in some choir somewhere I expect.

HARRABY SEC MOD.

First School Magazine 1957

The school opened its doors in September 1956, I was twelve years and five months old.

The Staff was made up of :-

Headmaster.   Mr W Urwin.
Deputy Headmaster. Mr G (Geordie) Boak, Maths teacher.

Mr H Addison. English.   Miss J Dixon. Housecraft.
MR H (Harry.) Baines, Woodwork.
Mr G Johnston. PT (and part time torturer. Wall bars ,bloody wall bars)   Mr Shimmin. English.
Miss F Irving. PT.   Miss M Lakeman. Art.
Mr D I Nixon. Science. (and explosives expert.)
Miss L Lawson. Needlework.   Miss Main. Music/Religion.
Mr J C Omerod. English. (My saviour.)
Mr M B (Paddy.) Priestman. History/Maths. (A dead shot with a blackboard eraser, so duck.)
Mr T Thackery. Geography.   Mrs A Marston. Library/English.

School sec, Mrs Beckett. (No relation, lucky for her. Left after 12 months, maybe something I said.)

Caretaker. Mr E Graham.

Ground's man Mr F Armstrong. (1958)

Staff Late Joiners.

1958.

Miss F Byers.. Biology.
Mrs Fowler.. English.
Miss Shackleton..English.

1959.

Mr J Moses.. Maths and English.
Mr C J Armstrong.. Tech Drawing.
Mr R J Macnish.. Woodwork.
Mr T B Graham.. Rural Science.
Mr J J Coyle.. Maths.
Miss E Wallace.. Maths.
Miss A Moore.. Geography and Music.
Mrs E McLean.. School Sec.

1960.

Miss Thompson.. Maths.
Mr Wills.. Art.
Mrs Dickens.. P E.
Mr Malkin.. Geography.
Miss Jelpke.. Art.
Miss Cubby.. P E.
Miss Faulder.. English.
Mr Breckenfield.. Science and Maths.
Mr Masterton.. Science and Maths.
Mr Murray.. Maths.

1960 Contd.

Mr Simmonds.. Commercial.
Mr Robinson.. History and Geography.
Mr Cartmel.. Woodwork.
Miss Campbell.. English.
Mrs Chesney.. English and History.
Mr Cain.. Dancing.
Mrs Dand.. English and Maths.
Mrs Roberts.. English and Maths.
Mrs Prouse.. English.
Mrs Bostock.. House craft.
Mrs Williams.. Needlework.

Other school staff, cleaners, dinner ladies, Etc..all essential to the smooth operation of the school day.

Mrs Tinnion, Mrs Parkins, Mrs Robertshaw, Mrs graham, Mrs Mason, Mrs Amos, Mrs Kerr, Mrs Bell, Mrs Dockerty, Mrs Rutherford. Mrs Little, Mrs Jones, Mrs Graham, Mrs Campbell, Mrs Davidson. Mrs Plenderleith.

(If I have missed you out..Sorry.)

Original School Governors.

Chairman. Alderman   K Payne. J.P.
 Deputy   Councillor B Day
            Alderman Mrs M E Thompson.
            Councillor J Keenan.
                 "   T L MacDonald. M.A. B.sc.
                 "   Mrs J Martin. (The Mayor.)
                 "   R Graham J.P.
                 "   Mrs S E Perkins. J.P.
            Mrs A.M.A Fraser. MBE.

School Roll September 1956

Head boy
Peter Thompson

Fourth Year Boys.

William Atkinson. Thomas Boyd. Ian Charlton.
Geoffrey Graham. Alan Hunt. Derek Meyler-Warlow.
James Edmondson. David Elliot. Donald Gordon.
William Nicholson. Edward Phinn. William Potts.
Gordon Heap. Joseph Slater. Robert Trotter. David Riddle.
Ian Robson. James Wilson. Leonard Turnbull.
Dennis Cook. Ian Douglas. Richard Johnston. Trevor Smythe.
Kenneth Davidson.

Third Year Boys.

James Bankcroft. Bryce Beeson. Alan Blythe. James Bradley.
Ian Calvert. Roger Doggart. Frederick Gill. Geoffrey Green.
Peter Green. Alan Cunningham. Charles Curry. Geoffrey Denwood.
Ian Dockerty. Colin Hetherington. Ronald Grieves. Brian Irving.
Alfred Henderson. Robert Lawson. Maurice Hutton.
Randolph Lichtblau. Derek Napier. Michael Smith. Norman Myres.
James Proudfoot. Walker Wilson. Harold Winskill.
Peter Thompson. John Statter. Malcolm Brown. James Crooks.
Richard Devine. Malcolm Brough. Thomas Briggs.
Richard Dennis. John Atkinson. John Howe.

Second Year Boys.

John Lapping. William Adams. James Potts. Michael Bulman.
Michael Burbage. Ivor Charters. Peter Gill. Brian Kenny.
Stephen Little. Michael McCall. Michael Metcalf. Dennis Riddle.
Michael Thompson. Arnold Tickell. John Underwood. John Watt.
Terence Beckett. Thomas Bell. Ian Boyd. Ronald Brown.
John Cowen. Leonard Cummings. John Dalzell. Kenneth Gray.
Malcolm Heaton. Richard Howe. Alexander Johnstone.
Joseph Malloy. Donald McCluskey. Peter Middleton.
Geoffrey Moses. Kenneth Proud. Trevor Simpson. Alan Taylor.
John Trotter. William Wilson. John Wetherill.

First Year Boys

Ian Bell. Paul Doggart. Ronald Elliot. Peter Farish.
Victor Kirkpatrick. Thomas Kirk. David Terry. Paul Vevers.
Gerald Broad. Alan Burns. Stanley Clerk. Alan Cookson.
Geoffrey Davidson. Roger Devine. David Johnston.
Ashley Kendall. David Lawson. Rodney Long. Dennis McCloud.
Barry Moscrop. David Reeves. Gordon Roberts. John Ruddick.
John Scott. Derek Skinner. Douglas Tuffin. Jeffrey Ward.
James Alford. Anthony Charlton. Henry Coulston.
Leslie Davidson. William Fiddler. David Jefferies.
Harry Kirkbride. Michael Morley. John Nicholson.
Robert Reay. Malcolm Robinson. Alan Smith. Michael Telfer.

Head Girl
Pat Gardener.

Fourth Year Girls.

Irene Corkindale. Patricia Gardener. Edna Haughan. Sylvia Hind.
Joan Lavery. Frances Norris. Shirley Rodgers. Pauline Styth.
Gloria Wardrope. Theresa Bell. Violet Maule. Heather Aiston.
Maureen Collins. Yvonne Henderson. Sandra Jeffrey.
Janet McCormick. Ann Millar. Mary Nicholson. Joan Stacey.

Third Year Girls.

Denise Garnett. Anne Hodgson. Irene John. Grace Lahey.
Barbara Lowry. Doris McCloud. Kathleen Oldcorn.
Eileen Peascod. Olive Scott. Doreen Stringer. Ruth Harrison.
Patricia Batey. Irene Buddy. Emily Dickie. Audrey Glencross.
Isobel Graham. Frances Kerr. Anne Martin. Margaret Mathers.
Pamela Monk. Jean McCluskey. Rita Reay. Sylvia Robison.
Norma Statter.

Second Year Girls.

Sandra Beck. Violet Bowman. Christine Brown. Helen Cartwright.
Pauline Clarke. Maureen Dixon. Patricia Ellis. Mavis Fiddler.
Joyce Hunter. Arline Little. Glennis McClounie. Sheelagh Noble.
Sandra Rigby. Diane Wardrope. Wendy Armstrong.
Priscilla Clarke. Irene Douglas. Valerie Fletcher. Patricia Freakes.
Patricia Hetherington. Doreen Hodgson. Ann McFarlane.
Doreen Maddison. Dorothy Reid. Jean Smith. Gail Sowerby.
Margaret Stevenson. Winifred Hall. Olwen McCloud.
Kathleen Nugent. Ada Potts. Dorothy Smith. Margaret Spedding.
Ann Verow. Olive West..

First Year Girls.

Margaret Arnott. Eileen Brown. Mildred Cant. Janice Elliot.
Sandra Graham. Margaret Hardy. Jean Mathers. Eileen Peters.
Eleanor Smith. Majorie Storey. Barbara Toft. Audrey Beeson.
Marion Brown. Brenda Burgess. Annie Gibson. Ann Lavery.
Vivienne Routledge. Marina Beaty. Sheila Clark. Sylvia Dodds.
June Emmerson. Helen Ferguson. Patricia Graham. Joan Kenny.
Patricia Dixon. * Margaret Murray. * Elizabeth Heap. *Beryl
Cameron. * Jean Anderson. Kathleen Dawson.

* late comers.

Arrivals September 1957.

Boys

Godfrey Barnes, Alan Bennet, Geoffrey Dixon, William Edgar, Frederick Farish, Arthur Main, Peter Martin, Raymond McClounie, Edward McSephney, John Rome, David Snowling, Alan Wardle, Kenneth Alan, Brian Loder, Alan Airey, John Akitt, Moray Armstrong, Christopher Bamburgh, Geoffery Bell, Lawrence Boak, Garth Gardener, Ian Grant, Terence Sainty, Richard Slee, Thomas Smith, John Styth, Edward Teenan, Brain Turner, Alan Beattie, Kenneth Gilder, Roy Hemmingway, Donald Hoggarth, Leslie Kerr, Michael Little, Peter Pearson, Tony Proud, Norman Raine, James Robinson, Robert Rowlands, John Stalker, William Strickland, Edward Watson, Robert Tennant, John Borrowdaile, Keith Bulman, Brian Crooks, Charles Dunkely, Colin Fearn, Terry Hall, Derek Harrison, Bernard Howlett, John Mason, Joseph McAvoy, Stuart McCluskey, Denis McNiel, John Moore, Alan Nixon, Peter Robinson, Stephen Alan, Michael Tickell.

Arrivals September 1957.

Girls.

Joyce Baxter, Enid Couling, Barbara Gibson, Ann Ireland, Julia Irving, Patricia Jackson, Maureen Moscrop, Margaret Parker, Barbara Snowdon, Judith Young, Jane Hodgson, Linda Arnison, Joan Bennett, Kathleen Bulman, Ada Coniston, Anne Gill, Kathleen Ferguson, Kathleen Fiddler, Sheila Gillespie, Barbara Harris, Janet Hawley, Joan Hetherington, Lynda Beck, Jennifer Ivison, Marilyn Thomlinson, Susanne Amos, Joan Atkinson, Joan Beattie, Cynthia Briggs, Paula Densley, Gloria Harding, Pamela Hodgson, Margaret Hulse, Valerie Laycock, Elaine McCormack, Marjorie Potts, Anne Rendall, Sheila Stringer, Irene Thomas, June Wolstencroft, Jennifer Armstrong, Jean Arthur, Anne Cameron, Marilyn Carrick, June Dawson, Carol Finlayson, Hilary Green, Patricia Kennedy, Shirley Wright, Brenda Mounsey, Rita Nicholson, Linda Potts, Yvonne Ross, Jacqueline Shaw, Lucy Young.

Arrivals September 1958

Boys

Peter Helme, Barry Notman, John Percival, Stephen Winter, John Green, Peter Watson, Michael Brown, David Blain, Phillip Potter, John Millican, Graham Bayne, Colin Ashbridge, John Tyler, Michael Finlayson, Thomas Laughlin, Ronald Heaton, Donald Bryston, Eric Ingham, Geoffrey Gordon, Michael Butcher, David Moscrop, Thomas Nicholson, Thomas Robson, Alan Kerr, Brian Redpath, Edwin Statter, Brian Irving, Leslie Geurts, Peter Lawson, Barry Wilson, Alan Glover, Malcolm Lord, Alan Wilson, Thomas Race, John Graham, James Maddison, Michael Glover, David Ridley, David Tinnion, Brian Alford, John Cook, Henry Ramsbottom, Alan Ramshay, John Wakefield, Ian Bell, Brian Carleton, David Kirkwood, Ivor Cornforth, James Christie, Michael Clark, Richard Johnston, Gerald Ward, Brian Dobie, James Wharton, David Lockward, Graham Brown, Barrie Hickie, Ian Landsborough, Paul Wheatley, Michael Norris, Alec Trotter, Finlay Stirling, Norman Foster, George Pattinson, Alan Hall Micheal Davidson, Brian Irving, Alan Hewson, Howard Watson, Norman Mark, Alec Proudfoot, James Baker, John Collins, Lawrence Forster, Ernest Lightholm, Edward Harrison, Richard Proud foot, Ian Elliott, William Bulman, John Parker, Dennis Snelgar, Robert Cook, Barry Dunn, Kenneth McCluskey, Andrew Walters, Robert Brown, Barry Proud, David Manning, James Mitchell, George Perey, Ronald Stubbs, John Tuffin.

174

Arrivals September 1958

Girls

Joan Davidson, Carol Ferguson, Heather Martin, Kathleen Bird, Susan Bragg, Joan Musgrave, Elizabeth Fiddler, Beatrix Barnes, Carol Pennington, Jacqueline Taylor, Christine Harper, Jill Shaw, Clara Taylor, Denise Robertson, Carol Coote, Mary Stevens, Patricia Atkinson, Diane Sewell, Hazel Kenny, Sylvia Swindon, Joan Scott, Pauline Harvey, Irene Holt, Sandra Sisson, Linda Bell, Joyce Hetherington, Margaret Wardrope, Maureen Underwood, Sandra Watts, Brenda Hodgson, Fiona Robertson, Ann Kelly, Elaine Raine, Margaret Fielder, Jacqueline Roberts, Joan Morris, Eleanor Brown, Sandra Beazley, Margaret Dockery, Jane Reay, Jennifer Henderson, Susan Howarth, Gwendoline Richmond, Francis Hayhurst, Anne McClaren, Patricia Sawyers, Betty Page, Patricia Laybourne, Esther Clark, Patricia Sheerer, Lyn Roberts, Norma Gilhespy, Barbara Fenney, Brenda Atkinson, Joan Harkness, Jessie Gebbie, Linda Kenyon, Doreen Martin, Una Graham, Linda Pattinson, Sheila Gent, Eileen Donald, Hilda Murray, Jennifer McGuire, Ann Jordan, Allison Pryce, Elizabeth Reed, Dorothy Thompson, Patricia Telford, Elizabeth McCloud, Patricia Graham, Pat Cowton, Carol Hitchen, Joan Carruthers, Susan Tweddle, Patricia Harris, Patricia Lawler.

Arrivals September 1959.

Boys

Stephen Adams, David Appleton, William Armstrong, Derek Ashbridge, Malcolm Atkinson, Robert Barr, Philip Bayne, Edward Bell, Geoffrey Bell, William Black, Peter Boothman, Alan Bray, Ian Brown, Philip Bulman, Robert Cameron, Stuart Cannon, Ian Carr, Terence Carr, Grenville Clarke, David Collins, Michael Conley, Ronald Coulter, William Crooks, Colin Dodds, Michael Dowell, Michael Dunglingson, Geoffery Gallon, David Graham, James Graham, Roland Graham, Eric Green, Norman Harkness, Michael Hartwell, Brian Hawkins, Leonard Hayton, Alan Hodgson, Harold Hogarth, Geoffrey Hounslow, John Jackson, Stanley Jackson, John Kerr, Michael Killen, Dennis Kirkwood, Dennis Lightfoot, Colin Lister, Harold Longford, Stephen McClusky, Jeffery McGlynn, John McHard, Stewart McKay, Ian Mcleod, John McNiel, James Mathers, Roy Miskelly, David Morris, Malcolm Morris, Donald Musgrave, Robert Nanson, John Nunn, Thomas Pattinson, William Pirie, Frederick Reay, Charles Reed, John Riley, Stephen Rock, Henry Ruddick, David Rutherford, Donald Scott, Peter Scott, Michael Slee, Christopher Small, Leslie Smith, Michael Smith, Raymond Story, Brian Taylor, Frederick Taylor, John Telford, Raymond Thompson, John Thompson, John Trotter, Allan Turner, Eric Underwood, John Wallace, Edwin Whalley, Clifton White, Joseph White, Ian Wilson, John Wilson, Peter Wilson, Paul Worby, Brian Wren.

Arrivals September 1959

Girls.

Patricia Armstrong, Rishma Baksh, Eillen Barker, Joan Batey, Christine Beattie, Angela Beckley, Doreen Bell, Lorraine Bell, Mavis Blaylock, Sonia Blyth, Helen Boak, Enid Bowman, Christine Brophy, Lillian Brown, Shirley Brown, Joan Bushby, Christine Caird, Joan Carrick, Patricia Casson, Susan Church, Muriel Clarke, Margaret Clifford, Phyllis Cook, Joan Cromie, Sheila Cuthbertson, Sandra Dewhurst, Ann Dixon, Patricia Dixon, Shirley Easterbrook, Lynda Eden, Jean Ellis, Lorraine Fisher, Eileen Franks, Kathleen Giddings, Maureen Glendinning, Brenda Graham, Pauline Grears, Marilyn Grogan, Edwina Harris, Linda Hogg, Patricia Humphreys, Susan Hunter, Patricia Irving, Brenda Johnstone, Christine Johnstone, Judith Jackson, Sandra Keelier, Anita little, Judith Little, Pauline Little, Linda McCue, Patricia cIntyre, Jennifer McMurray, Beryl McNichol, Susan Maltby, Janet May, Ann Moses, Joan Mulvey, Kathleen Norris, Mary Purdham, Barbara Rayson, Ann Reay, Joan Robertshaw, Jennifer Sainty, Olive Skelton, Caroline Skowronak, Elizabeth Smith, Jennifer Smith, Babara Sowerby, Janet Statter, Margaret Story, Muriel Story, Joan Teenan, Alma Tiffen, Joan Thompson, Yvonne Vipond, Jennifer Wakefield, Averil Wallace, Elaine Wallace, Carole Wannop, Sandra Waugh, Ann Wheatley, Elizabeth Wilson, Janis Wilson, Linda Wilson, Ann Winder.

Arrivals September 1960

Boys.

Ian kellet, Malcolm Aitken, Allan Brown, Dennis Vallely, Barry Bulman, Alex Mitchell, Barry Middleton, David Elliott, Derek Kenny, Harvey Monoghan, Laurence Sedman, Graham Ridley, Alan Maxwell, Peter Scott, Philip Graham, Raymond Beck, Eric Martles, Ian Bankcroft, Robert Cook, Kenneth Fitzpatrick, Joseph Smith, David Ferguson, Michael Hurst, Christopher Carpenter, Edward Claugue, Ian Bulman, Peter Duncan, Peter Cookson, John Hunton, George McVitie, Dennis Bulman, Christopher Nicholson, John Moran, Geoffrey Shepherd, Barry Bunting, John Jamieson, Paul Ferguson, Peter Mulholland, David Arnot, Raymond Lowe, Clifford Densley, Derek Fenn, James Glencross, Jim Rose, Alwyn Dunn, Gerald Gardener, Michael Ward, Keith Fiddler, James Smith, Leonard Langhorne, John Bell, Trevor Redpath, Kenneth Shackley, Terence Walsh, Richard Irving, Frank Brown, David Pearson, Michael Strickland, David Graham, Thomas Davidson, Dennis Patterson, David Tiffin, David Macintosh, Eric Coulson, Alan Dawson, Colin Wallace, Leslie Gray, Michael Winder, Michael Collin, Michael Reay, Alan Butcher, Leslie McMurdo, David Davidson, George Blackburn, Colin Smith, Michael Beattie, Geoffrey Crooks, John Kirkwood, Stephen Potter, Kenneth Thompson, George Bowyer, Alan Tebay Alan Little, Malcolm Stephen, Richard McCluskey, Ralph Maddison, Michael Bewley, Ian Tiffen, Joseph Smith, Kenneth Lowry, Robert Trotter, Kenneth Williamson, Edward Murtagh, Barry Trickett, Bryn Pattinson, Robert Taylor, Robert Henderson, Ronald Brewis , Ian Ferry, Freddie Thompson, Bobbie Telford, Malcolm Smith, Ivor Armstrong, Keith Lonsborough, Barry Fern.

Arrivals September 1960

Girls.

Mary Ingram, Kathleen Fisher, Jean Faughey, Joan Armstrong, Elizabeth Mills, Gillian Forsyth, June Hyland, Erica Horseman, Joan Belcher, Linda Robinson, Patricia Higgins, Margaret Macleod, Brenda Muir, Margaret Bowman, Felicity Iverson, Mary Bisland, Kathleen Dowling, Diane Charters, June Dodd, Barbara Hardisty, Joan Kendal, Patricia Warwick, June Moore, Irene Raven, Ann Stirling, Olwen Tickner, Christine Stokoe, Hazel Beattie, Glynis McGough, Angela Turnbull, Angela Porter, Lillian Lord, Joan Pennington, Carole Riddle, Ann Moncrieff, Vivienne Smith, Dorothy Byers, Maureen Ullyart, Jean Sowerby, Patricia Clarke, Jean Woodburn, Sandra Cass, Joan Kennedy, Norah Scaife, Margaret Jolly, Doreen Davidson, Carol Taylor, Pamela Alford, Anne Summers, Linda Hayton, Margaret Robinson, Jennifer Cannon, Dorothy Richardson, Jean Kendal, Joan Dixon, Heather Ballantyne, Gwendolyn Swindon, Sandra Lawler, Linda Hodgson, Jean Woolley, Eileen Cairns, Susan Clifford, Ann Whalley, Elizabeth Watson, June Mckay, Barbara Bell, Linda McMorrine, Joan Grears, Patricia Leighton, Maureen Armstrong, Ruth Graham, Hilary Blythe, Christine Little, Joyce Hogarth, Kathleen Brown, Jean Yarker, Christine Ruddick, Olwen Tuck, Elsie Vance, Edna Gill, June Wannop, Pauline Kerr, Linda Armstrong, Ann Elliott, Linda Rayson, Iris Scott, Margaret Ellis, Christine Bryan, Jennifer Graham, Catherine Roberts, Olive Beard, Margaret Stacey, Cecilia Moffat, Ann Black, Muriel Bell, Joan Proud, Julia Cameron, Carol McKinley, Sandra Atkinson.

House Captains.
(Not all at the same time, Inc Athletics.)

Blue. Ann Miller, Olive Scott, Peter Thompson. Ian Charlton. Gloria Wardrope, Pauline Clark, Ian Boyd,

Green. Violet Maule, James Bradley, Kathleen Oldcorn. David Elliott. Thomas Boyd, Teresa Bell. Arthur Boyd. Glennis McCloune, Peter Middleton, William Adams, Peter Green, Terence Beckett.

Red. Eileen Skinner. Gordon Heap, Derek Warlow, Donald Gordon, Joan Lavery. James Wilson, Helen Cartwright, John Lapping,

Yellow. Pat Gardener. Richard Johnston, Leonard Turnbull, William Atkinson, Robert Trotter. Stephen Little, Alfred Henderson,

Prefects 1955 -1960.
Boys

Peter Thompson, (Head boy.) Bill Adams, Brian Armstrong, Ian Boyd, Noel Cimino, (Senior boy.) Lesley Heyes, John Lapping, Joseph Malloy, Stephen Little, Ronald Elliott, Peter Farish, Harry Kirkbride, Dennis Mcleod. Michael Metcalfe, John Underwood, Michael Burbage, Peter Middleton, Alan Cunningham, James Bancroft, Alan Blythe, Alan Cousins, Colin Hetherington, Maurice Hutton, Malcolm Brough, Robert Lawson, Roger Doggart, Randolph Lichtblau, Allan Slater, Michael Smith, Thomas Briggs, James Crooks, Peter Green, James Proudfoot,

Girls

Pat Gardener, (Head Prefect.) Margot Sellers, Pauline Clark, Priscilla Clark, Pat Ellis, Doreen Hodgson, Glennis McClounie, Jean Smith. Sandra Beck, Maureen Dickson, Janice Elliott, Pat Ellis, Mavis Fiddler, Ann McFarlane, Sheelagh Noble, Eileen Peters, Margaret Pirie, Marlorie Story, Anne Hodgson, Grace Lahey, Barbara Lowry, Olive Scott, Ruth Harrison, Eileen skinner, Jean McCluskey, Sylvia Robinson, Norma Statter, Denise Garnett, Irene John, Doris Macleod, Kathleen Oldcorn, Emily Dickie, Eileen Peascod.

1958. Advice given to parents on School wear, about fifty percent turned up in Uniform, some in every day clothes, some just did not turn up at all…

The School Uniform

Although parents are not compelled to buy Uniforms for their children, we hope they are sufficiently interested and cooperative to provide it.

Navy blue has been chosen :~
1. So that parents may obtain the best bargain in town.
2. Because children coming from Inglewood may already have the blue uniform.
The attractive badges are bought in bulk by the School and sold at 6/- each. (Cost price.)

Girls- Outdoor Uniform.

Navy blue blazer with badge.
Navy blue gym tunic with badge.
Girls in third year or above may wear navy blue four-gored skirt.
Winter term-navy blue cardigan.
Navy blue raincoat or overcoat.
Navy blue beret-optional.
Shoes with rubber or composition soles.

Boys- Outdoor Uniform.

Navy blue blazer with badge.
Grey flannels.
Navy blue raincoat or overcoat.
Navy blue cap- optional.
Shoes with rubber or composition sloes to protect the floors.
(PLEASE no steel tips or hobnails.)

Trainers had yet to be invented and black leather shoes were the order of the day, few if any wore jeans, most wore hand me downs from big brothers or cousins. Those turning up in brand new blazers etc, stood out like a sore thumb and were severely harassed.

Harraby Old Students Association.

(Formed 1958.)
President. Headmaster.   Chairman. Colin Hetherington.
Treasurer. Maurice Hutton. Secretary. Teresa Bell.

Executive Committee.
All officers and Gloria Wardrope. Edward Phinn.
Janet McCormick. Alan Cousins. Arthur Boyd.
Olive Scott. Kathleen Oldcorn.

After leaving St Johns I went to the above Harraby Secondary Modern School. Everything there was brand new and we were among its first pupils. The desks the chairs the books, everything but everything smelt and felt fabulous. No ink stained desks with carved names of long gone rebels rousers, no half chewed pencil stubs or text books with pages continually falling out. Everything was clean and tidy, it was amazing. Even most of the teachers were new, most of then being really good and enthusiastic, keen to give their time to those who most wanted or needed it which was a first.. My mentor, as I mentioned earlier, was a man called Mr Omerod, he ultimately turned me around educationally. Never a clever boy or scholastic, I however improved dramatically under his Tutelage . He gave me my love of books, I still have to this day, once hooked I could not let go. The town library became my second home, getting through literally a book a day, such as the William series, Robinson Crusoe, Treasure Island, Biggles and of course comics such as the Eagle, Heroes Alf Tupper, Dan Dare, then later Mad magazine which I loved though my Dad thought I was mad to actually buy it. I also developed a great love of true adventure, Scot of the artic, Sir Edmund Hilary, Stanley and Livingston. I trekked every trail and climbed every mountain, sailed the seven seas and crossed the Sahara with white turbaned, black robed, camel riding Tuareg's.

Among many other things I have to be grateful to him for, Mr Omerod arranged for me to be entered in the annual Carlisle Arts Festival. Taking place in the ballroom of the City's premier hotel, the Crown and Mitre, which had entertained no less a personage then Her Majesty the Queen Elizabeth, not to mention later on the Beatles, no less, buts that another story.

CARLISLE & DISTRICT
MVSICAL AND FESTIVAL
BEETHOVEN
HANDEL
HAYDN
BACH
MVSIC IS
A FAIR AND
GLORIOVS
GIFT FROM GOD
CERTIFICATE OF MERIT
AWARDED TO
FOR
CLASS
CONDUCTOR
FESTIVAL
ADJUDICATOR

As I mentioned earlier John Wetherill and I performed a piece from " Waiting for Godo." by my namesake Samuel Beckett, no relation that I am aware of and definitely no inheritance of talent. I absolutely loved the attention, and must have done ok because we won first prize. I was totally gob smacked, never having won any thing before, my prestige at school soared.
The next school day during assembly we were both put up on the stage in the main hall receiving a great cheer, it was wonderful, or as they say today, just awesome man, Innit !
Upon leaving Harraby Sec Mod in 1959 this was recorded in the School Magazine as my greatest achievement during my scholastic life. Unfortunately I missed out on sitting the Northern Counties School Certificate due to a burst Appendix. Spending two weeks in the City General Hospital being spoilt by the nurses, and almost three months convalescing. Not that I expected to do particularly well but wanted to try for my parents sake. (and mine of course.)

The Y H A trips were without doubt the highlight of the year, I did two trips, years 57 /58. It was huge fun, could be tough, though well worth it, the copy of the school magazine for 1957, given to me by Dot Lichtblau records Wednesday had been marked down for the climbing Scafell Pike, but many turned back to the valley during a rainstorm in Grains Ghyll, about midday. Several however took advantage of a temporary clearance of the mist to make an ascent of the mountain from Sty Head, following a zig zag course spotted from Great Gable the day before. The recent rain had cleared the air and the lower temperature made climbing pleasant for practically the only time during the week. Heaton's Party, (Beckett, Moses, Thackray and Boak.) climbed quickly, running into renewed mist by Lingmell, (At 2.600 feet.) reaching the summit shortly after three

o'clock. We met two other walkers who were plainly lost in the mist, we continued with them over Great End as far as Angle Tarn, near the entrance to Langdale. Returning to Sty Head to pick up jettisoned gear, we were forced to navigate by compass through the mist, but were able to pick up our haversacks on the Wasdale side of Sty Head shortly after 5.30. By this time Beckett had run out of steam and his rucksack, etc, was made over to other members of the party, but even so we reached Longthwaite in time for a large supper."
(NB, I do not remember " running out of steam," Oh' the shame of it.)
 My best pal Geoff Moses also got a mention, not that he will thank me for reminding him.
" Buttermere Hostel is laid out more on the lines of a Hotel - less freedom - a more formal atmosphere. But the great advantage was the splitting up of the male element into three bedrooms instead of one, thus restricting the nocturnal menace of Moses to six or seven victims instead of eighteen….3.30 a.m was no time to be awakened by bale full cries of..Denise..Denise !!!"
(Geoff and Denise were married several years later.)

Among the other staff who stick in my memory was Mr Thackray, the geography teacher who took us on the trips to the Lake District to see real landscapes, now that really was awesome. We stayed at the Y H A hostels, absolutely loved it, lashings of ginger beer and Kendal mint cake, just like the Famous Five in my Library book. Unfortunately as I recall Mr Thackray had a short fuse so was an easy target for the wind up merchants who would often have the poor man turning bright red, asking questions like , "where are the contour lines sir ?" Or "why are the lakes not all bright blue ?"

He would look as though he was about to explode but would calm down just as quickly. He made Geography one of my favourite lessons along with English. Mr Thackray left Harraby a year or so after I did to take up the position of Head of the Geography Dep't at Stokesley Grammar School in the North Riding.

Mr Johnston, the gym teacher was definitely not, nowhere near, my favourite, he brings to mind a drill sergeant I encountered some years later known in the Regiment as the "Screaming skull." Mr Johnston however clearly knew his job producing formidable athletes, such as Peter Thompson who went on to play for Preston, Liverpool and England. The great Bill Shankly described Peter as one of the greatest footballers he had ever seen, what a compliment that was.

The never to be forgotten, the formidable Geordie Boak was deputy head Master, he could stop a rampant thug at twenty paces with a single look. Everyone recalls the time Geordie decided to take a stand against the influx of fashion in the form of long hair, bringing in to school the local hairdresser to trim those with barnet's not to his liking, whether they liked it or not.

In all my time at Harraby Sec I never saw him bested. I believe him to have been a tank commander in the second world war, his left shoulder was severely disfigured due to his being wounded in action, or at least that is what we were told, he neither confirmed or denied it to the best of my knowledge.

Once again in the lakes while staying at Borrowdale Hostel I think it was, I and three others shared a room with Mr Boak, which in itself was quite scarry enough, but worse was his habit of stripping naked before showering and bed, we had never experienced such action, common of course to the changing room later, and would die of embarrassment, but Geordie was a mans man, we loved to fear him.

Another late comer to the teaching staff was Mrs Sergeant, who to her great credit again encouraged me to study, she was married to a bloke who spent a long time in the Army becoming at one time a Sergeant. Really, he was Sergeant Sergeant, no joke.

Mrs Main a passionate teacher of music and Religious knowledge was convinced that we were all desperate to learn how to play the recorder, an instrument that was a mystery to all but the talented few. She did persevere and one or two pupils did display musical ability, one pianist, I think it was Majorie Storey, going on to great things. Miss Main passed away on the 13th of August, just as this page was being written, she will be well remembered as conductor and member of Carlisle Carliol Choir.

Paddy Priestman the maths teacher, terrified me, he could throw a blackboard rubber like an Exocet missile, never known to miss his target, but often just to ensure his message got through, a wooden ruler over the back of the head did the trick. I can still feel my ear stinging. He did not knock any sense into me though I doubt he cared.
The headmaster was a chap called Mr Urwin from Leeds I believe, he always appeared to be firm but fair as they say, except for the time a certain young lady, for want of a better description, broke her ankle somehow on the playing field, why I shall never know but she blamed Geoff and I. As I recall we were not even on the field but no good, we had been found guilty and were duly give six of the best on each hand, Ouch. It will always be the case when it comes to believing someone, a pretty face wins every time, justice, what justice, don't get me going on that one.
The school was divided into four houses, Green, Blue, Red and Yellow. Mr Omerod headed Green House and eventually gave me the role of House Captain briefly, just before I left School, I was

"My photo cut from the Cumberland News by my Mam, a lot of effort but unplaced this time."

gob smacked but loved it all the same. For a short while I also held the position of Athletics Captain, A more miscast role would be hard to find. Although I did excel at putting the shot and throwing the discus, something to do with my rotund build. On the 1958 sports day I came runner up to my friend Randolph Lichtblau in both discus and shot. The next year, Randolph having left School to take up a career in Office machine Technology, then an infant industry, I won both events, but still did not beat Randolph's 91 foot 9 inches discus record, nor do I know if anyone else has since..

My picture appeared in the Cumberland News one sports day when competing again in the shot put, my belly was hanging over my shorts and tongue over my chin with all the effort. My mother though I looked cute and bought a copy of the photo at the Cumberland News offices on Lowther street, I still have it, well moments of glory do not come around too often do they. However running or field sports were not my forte, leaving me gasping in the rear, leave all that to the skinny kids.

Regretfully Harraby Secondary Modern, now known as North Cumbria Technical College is due to be bulldozed in September two thousand and ten to make way for affordable housing. (Still standing 2011.)

The staff and pupils will then decamp to the part new build, partly refurbished Richard Rose academy on the grounds of the ex Saint Aidans School, near the town centre, close to Bitts Park. It should have superb new educational and sports facilities, including a swimming pool and all weather football pitch stroke athletics field. Some of my Grandchildren will be in attendance to benefit from all the modern facilities, in a bright and airy environment.

Andrew, a lovely boy who wants to be a Chef, Rachel, his sister, future undecided, Bethany who shows talent, with ambition as an artist and musician, and football mad Jack. No doubt my wonderful Great Grandson Bailey will eventually attend also. The other four Grandsons, Kyle, now a dad himself, Paul a Graduate of Northampton University, Callum and Matthew also both looking to attend Uni.

Proud of them all.

26   HOLY MOSES SUPPOSES.

My best friend and for many others too, at school was Geoff Moses, a really great bloke, we had some wonderful adventures roaming and camping in the countryside, hitch hiking around northern England and Scotland. Geoff was always up for anything and seemed to have no fear, always smiling and never malicious, everyone liked Geoff and he liked everyone in return. Always a bit of a hippy was our Geoff and always had one of those little plastic Japanese radios fixed to his belt blaring away. How I remember that radio.
one day we were crossing striding Edge on Helvellyn in the lake district, a notoriously dangerous spot for the unwary. There was about a foot or so of snow on the ground and it was very icy, really dodgy, suddenly Geoff lost his footing and with a shout disappeared over the edge, my heart froze as I heard the music from that damn radio slowly getting fainter as he tumbled away down the slope. In a panic I scrambled down the mountainside after him, terrified of what I was going to find, my feet slithered from under me, I feared I was about to suffer the same fate. Grabbing an outcrop of snow free dark rock, I stopped, arm muscles straining to hold fast, looking around me disorientate, slowly I heard it nearby, that bloody music. Lifting myself to see, focusing hard in the dim light, there in the falling gloom I saw him, thrashing about in a bank of drifted snow.
" Help me, Help me." He cried out. I rushed forward forgetting momentarily the treacherous condition's, fearing the worst, my breast thumping, what do I tell his mother, how are we going to get down this bloody mountain. " Help me." he repeated, his beard white with frost." Help me." he implored.
" I cannot find my radio."

We never did find that flaming radio, but no fear, the next time we met up another Japanese contraption was on his belt, worse luck, what a man.

On another occasion when Geoff and I were about thirteen years old we had been out and about somewhere and upon returning decided to visit our local chippy on Florida Mount, a grand name for a rundown short terrace of shops, for our supper of a bag of chips, which was about all we could afford really. So parking our pushbikes against the wall in we went.

It was a Friday night so the Chippy was quite busy with the pubs chucking out and people returning home from the flicks and such. The Chippy in those days was more than just a carry out, more like a social gathering with lots of chatter and gossip, and of course the obligatory alcohol induced singing and merriment, all enclosed in a mist of steam from the fish fryers, which sizzled their accompaniment. Having eventually emerged grasping our pokes of chips we quickly noticed Geoff's pushbike was missing, looking around we saw a man obviously the worse for drink slowly disappearing down the nearby hill on the aforementioned pushbike. We took off in chase and fairly quickly caught up with the thief as the drink impaired his coordination, he could not get his feet to stay on the pedals and was constantly having to adjust his balance. However catching up with him was one thing, getting him off the pushbike was another. He told us, between gasping for beer raddled breath, that he lived on the other side of Carlisle and had missed his last bus, so needed to get back to his home where we could collect the pushbike tomorrow. No amount of argument on our part was going to persuade him, he was determined to go on his way. We were frantically trying to work out what to do next, when out of the darkness came a familiar voice,

" and what is going on here then.?, like a phantom out of the

gloom appeared Sergeant Carleton of the Carlisle Constabulary, his pace stick held horizontally under his elbow.
All three of us started to talk at once, " Quiet.!" shouted the policeman. " You boy" he said pointing at Geoff, " explain."
Geoff told of our plight and the stolen pushbike. Sgt Carleton then gave our friend the opportunity to explain his side in the proceedings, listening with great patience while he did so, with many intervals for rasping beer laden burps.
Eventually Sgt Carleton made his decision and taking our drunken friend by the collar invited him to accompany the said Sgt down a nearby dark lonning, leading to the local Nunnery. A short while later we heard a distinct "Twhack".
The policeman soon reappeared and told us to get ourselves off home and not to cause any more bother. We took no persuading and off we went to tell all who would listen of our adventure.

The nearest I got to quenching my thirst for adventure was when we went hitch hiking, Geoff and I, around Northern England and Scotland. We certainly saw some sights and soon learned how to get by when things got tough, as they often did not turn out quite as planned and with little or no cash, improvisation and a desire to know what lay around the next corner or over the next hill, kept us going. We spent many a night together shivering in our tiny two man tent purchased from the local Army and Navy Surplus store, along with various mess tins, sleeping bags, ground sheets and a primus stove, this was eventually replaced with a French made Gaz stove, much more convenient, none of which cost more than a few shillings and were often of dubious quality, but we got more than the value out of them over the years. I even took to writing evaluation reports on some of the gear, Ie, rucksacks, groundsheets, boots, etc. I would imagine we were off on a polar expedition or traversing some mighty desert where our very lives depended on the reliability of our gear. Talk about a dreamer.

Geoff was extremely resilient and would never give up, no matter what, which meant we struggled on through all weathers, Ice, Snow. Hail , you name it, we walked it, like the Mountie's we always got there, eventually.

I am sure our families sometimes wondered if we were all there and if we had somehow been mixed up with the Romany's who would occasionally camp at the bottom of Botcherby Avenue. Of course as the great man said, " the joy was in the journey not the arrival." We saw many things which would otherwise have been denied to us, and loved every minute.

On the way home from sandy bay at the bottom of Botcherby avenue was a small piece of land that was fenced off with barbed wire and guarded by a huge dog of the Heinz fifty seven variety, with teeth to match. This place has now gone of course, home to a block of council flats for elderly and single folk. But then all there was were a few hens pecking at the dry ground, nothing of any apparent value at all. So there seemed to be no real reason for such great security. Our inquisitive nature was aroused and had to be satisfied. So one day on our return from a hard day at Norman street juniors my mate Geoff Moses, being much braver than me, took it upon himself to investigate. We carefully surveyed the scene, no one seemed to be around, all was quite. Geoff easily vaulted the five barred gate avoiding the rusty barbed wire along the top, moving swiftly over to where the hens were pecking away quite content. Nothing appeared unusual and after a cursory survey Geoff, satisfied there was no mystery to be revealed turned to head back, that was when we heard it, the low menacing growl of something large and mean moving fast and bent on trouble, with Moses as the beneficiary.

Geoff, no mean mover when it became necessary, raced for the gate, the dog, which had appeared from nowhere, making ground on him with every stride, not hesitating Geoff took off in a dive clearing the top bar of the gate, unfortunately at that same moment the dog clamped its jaws around his upper thigh and the velocity off his own movement drew the aforementioned thigh through the jaws of the hound from hell, literally splitting him from buttock to knee. The dog, jaws red with blood, looked quite pleased with himself, after all he was just doing his job, which he had done very well, to good effect. It took poor Geoff some time to recover from that experience but it never stopped him from seeking out adventure when ever the opportunity arose. What a gadgee.

♪

27   DANCE HALL DAYS.

A few years later Geoff, our other best mate Randolph Lichtblau and I got into a rare old fight, not a common activity for us, but what a battle it was. We had decided to go to the County Ballroom on the corner of Botchergate and Station Square, down town where a local group, destined for fame, called Rue and the Rockets were to make their debut. The place was packed in anticipation, the Rockets reputation went before them even though few had actually heard them play. The stage curtains opened to the rousing instrumental March of the Gladiators, possibly an omen of things to come. The band quickly became an established part of the local scene, eventually touring the country far and wide, they were an excellent group creating a following which lasted for generations and still playing to this day.
Unfortunately also in the ballroom that night was a lad I had a run in with some years earlier when he had upset my sister Brenda.
I had caused him sever embarrassment in a local youth club called the Kings, in Globe Lane, long since demolished. When I confronted him for what I perceived was an insult to my sister, I then beat him in the ensuing scrap despite his being at least two years older than me. He clearly had not forgotten this incident and was looking for me bent on revenge. Absorbed in the bands performance I was totally unaware of his presence until he pushed me to one side and, with several of his cronies backing him up told me to get myself and my gang out of the Ballroom or else. Geoff and I looked at each other with a smile as our gang consisted of us two, Randolph, and a girl who knew him and had attached her

self to us for company. She was carrying an umbrella which to her credit she later put to good use on our rivals, I still have no idea who she was.

Within a few seconds it all kicked off, my adversary attempted to take advantage of the fact that I had my back to him trying to take me by surprise, alas for him a girl screamed causing me to turn just in time to administer a perfect, at least in my opinion, upper cut to the jaw, more likely a lucky punch. He went out like a light and dropped to the floor like sack of potatoes. Two to me.

He must have had some thing though because he had at least six girls kneeling around him fussing over him. But true to form he took no further part in the following affray.

All hell proceeded to take loose, poor Geoff took the brunt of it on our side and quickly had several bodies on top of him trying to knock his block off. The place turned into a riot, everybody seemed to be thumping everyone else, what a carry on.

I administered several well aimed kick's to the lads on Geoff, no time for fair play, and he eventually regained his feet, just as well or he was hospital fodder, as it was he was almost minus an ear which some bloke had tried to rip off, then swelled up like a huge beetroot.

The bouncers on the door, made up of relations of the lads in the band, with others from a travelling family we knew, and of course the legendary Sailor, pitched in on what appeared to be our side, probably because we were so outnumbered, and the tide began to turn in our favour. The enemy were quickly routed, but it was not entirely fair because we got thrown out anyway for not being regulars. However we were all in one piece except for Geoff's ear and his bloody nose, poor lad. Several of the other blokes were sporting cuts from the girl with the umbrella, plus a few nose bleeds and bruises.

Me being the jammy one came out unmarked, in fact I do not think anyone actually clobbered me, who said life was fair.
After our experience at the County we changed our allegiance to the Cameo Ballroom half way down Botchergate, compered by Rodney Warr and featuring the resident band of Cliff Eland, with local groups such as the Danube's filling in.
Andy Park from nearby Rockcliffe was the up and coming agent for managing and booking local talent, with an extensive stable of groups and singers, providing local groups seeking stardom.
 We had been going there for a few months, doing the usual nipping out from nine till ten for a drink, having adopted the Cumberland Inn as our new watering hole. The fact it was also the nearest may have affected our judgement, returning to the Cameo two or three pints to the good did wonders for your confidence when it came to asking girls to dance, though regretfully it did not necessarily improve your success rate. One evening having returned to the dance my mate Randolph asked me to help him split up a couple of girls, the one he fancied having refused his advances so in we steamed, lo and behold it worked, he waltzed off with his future wife, tall elegant brunette called Dorothy and I with mine, though of course we were not aware of this eventual outcome at the time. In fact due to my lack of tolerance to alcohol, when I awoke next morning much to my shame, I struggled to put a face to the girl I had taken home the night before and it was only when Randolph called for me later that morning saying to hurry and get dressed as we had a date to take two girls to Silloth in his dads car that things started to clear up. Anyway to cut a long story short, the girl turned out to be a gorgeous young lady called Renee Buntin, who on our second meeting I fell madly in love with and still am, fifty years later.
Renee, it turned out lived in the village of Cargo, to the northwest of the City, a road I was to get to know well having no transport of

my own, I would regularly walk there and back from Botcherby Avenue, about five miles. Occasionally I would strike lucky and get a lift off my uncle Kenneth Rivers who worked for British Rail at Kingmoor Marshalling yard, he drove the shuttle bus to the rail yard and if he came upon me would give me a lift. Kenneth was married to my auntie Pat, though she was not my auntie really, more my cousin, it seems every women who was older than me became Auntie, don't ask. Pat contracted T B, a deadly and common ailment then, and spent ten months in Blencathra Sanatorium, near Keswick, but made a full recovery thank God. More About Blencathra in The Life boys.

We courted for two years or so, I must have walked a thousand miles. One night sitting in her living room, her dad Wilf was cleaning his shotgun, leaning over to talk to me, he pointed the barrel of his shotgun and said,

" I am not bloody daft son, no one walks all this way for nothing." then clicking the gun shut continued, " I am bloody well watching you boy," Gulp !!

He was right of course, but I decided to settle for the loan of her bike, a much safer option, plus it saved my poor feet.

Renee was born on the 23rd of April, Saint Georges Day, which she shares with William Shakespear, who was not only born on this day in 1564 but also died on Saint Georges day 1616. Another notable death on this day, in 1850 was Lakeland poet William Wordsworth, she was nothing if not in good company.

We continued to patronise the Cameo having some great nights dancing to some great bands together, Randolph, Geoff, Renee, Dorothy and I. Happy days. Other spots that got a rare visit were the Queens Hall and the Gretna Hall each seemed to have its turn in popularity whilst retaining a hard core following.

Poor Randolph was taken with Leukaemia, living with the affliction for many years, refusing to give it ground, eventually surrendering on the 10th August 2009. He is most sadly missed by all who knew him. He now lays in Hayton Village Cemetery, a lovely peaceful place to end up.

Geoff was a non swearing teetotaller , his idea of bad language was to call someone a beast, amazing when you think of the time and place of his upbringing. Everyone respected him.

It was just as well he did not take a drink considering the number of times he dragged me home off my head with the booze.

My alcohol tolerance level as I have already stated always was very low, so at least it did not cost me much to get bladdered, nothing changed there then, not a good claim to fame I admit.

Rather than face my parents however he was inclined to dump me in our garden shed, where I would eventually wake up with part of a lawnmower or such stuck in my solar plexus. It did nothing for my hangover I can tell you.

Geoff had a brother called Morris Hutton, who many will remember, he was so much more mature than both of us and always the sensible one so that I always thought he was a lot older than he actually was.

You can be very cruel when you are young and I used to tell him that he must have been born forty years old, or maybe I was just that bit thicker. He was actually a very nice lad. He went on to become a well known and respected professional musician. Our paths rarely crossed in later life but he was always very nice to me despite my having annoyed him by constantly playing on his drum kit when he was not there and sneaking off with his collection of Frank Sinatra records, who he idolised. Morris was another who went long before he should have, his passing came as quite a shock to all who knew him. A fit, cycle riding trim bloke, his passing was most unexpected. You can be sure if you end up in heaven there will always be plenty of good music with Morris there. Sadly missed by his lovely wife Pat.

Among Morris's friends was Colin Hetherington, he too always seemed much older than the rest of the mob as well, probably he was, he added to his popularity by gaining a licence to drive Buses. He would drive the coach on outings to Blackpool and such. He must have put up with a lot of aggro from us dingbats, but seemed to take it all in good part. He now runs his own very esteemed holiday coaching company. Still going to Blackpool though, among other fun destinations.

The first real live band I remember watching was the Four Dollars in the Kings Hall youth club. To me another place of wonderment, the music played by the Four Dollars all inspiring. Later I moved on. Those were the days of the Market Hall dances with all the top sixties groups, from the Who to The Swinging Blue Jeans, Freddy and The Dreamers, The Barron Knights, The Searches, The Hollies among numerous other national and locally acclaimed bands. There seemed to be a sequence when groups would visit the Market Hall one week and be at number one on Top of the Pops the next. We all loved the place and it was packed to the gunnels week on week. It cost two shillings to get in and like the other dance halls had a pass out policy between nine and ten o'clock because they were licensed only to sell soft drinks, this allowed us to pop out to the Bluebell on Castle Street or the Kings Head on Fisher Street for a pint or two, often resulting in quarrels breaking out and sometimes all out battles. Mainly because we were all one pint wonders and could not hold our drink. It was here at the Market Hall that I experienced my second time of being forcefully ejected, it was not even my fault, honest.

For some reason I can no longer recall a lad walked up to me, put his face up to mine and said, " My name is Killer," well I nearly collapsed in hysterics, several other people close by burst into laughter as well which only acted to provoke our friend Killer even further. Lurching forward he took a swing at me with a great looping haymaker, I ducked and he fell on his backside, within seconds two bouncers appeared. Thinking I was responsible for Killer being on the deck, they immediately threw me out, no chance to explain, I was out and Killer stayed in, no justice.

The best of it was I met this bloke again the following week when we were both stone cold sober and got on like a house on fire, he could not apologise enough for getting me chucked out. Still we had some great nights in the Market hall, which was not all daftness, it being responsible for many couples getting together, ending up hitched, still together to this day.

We, Geoff, Randolph and I, on two occasions travelled to Maryport Dance Hall, don't ask me why, must have been the grass growing greener over the hill syndrome or something. The one advantage Maryport Ballroom had over Carlisle was they had a little café in the dance hall which sold tea, coffee and chips, so we tucked in, we were always hungry.

At the next table sat a small weedy looking fella, looked like he had not eaten for a week. He stared longingly at our chips, practically drooling he was. Eventually I could stand it no more, taking pity I asked him if he would like a plate of chips, his face lit up in acceptance and no sooner were the chips in front of him than they were devoured. Any way it transpired he was a member of that nights band who we had never heard of, so jokingly we got him to autograph the plate and as the evening drew on thought no more about it. That was until the following week watching Top of the Pops on BBC One there he was, the same little scrawny lad we had fed in Maryport, Freddie Garrity, with his band, Freddy and the Dreamers. I looked for that plate everywhere, I think mother must have washed it !

The Argyll Cinema in what we then referred to as new Harraby, because most of it was still being constructed, opened when I was around twelve years old, circa 1956.

In order to get there you had to walk down Durranhill Road and cross the old railway bridge which was unlit and quite scary. You then had to pass through an area of old trees with no pathway to the new estate of Harraby East. The Cinema was sited opposite the shopping precinct, all brand new and pristine. It seemed to have a habit of showing Horror films, like "the Roc", a fabled man eating prehistoric bird, or "Frankenstein," man made monster. This would cause the return journey home to take about a quarter of the time it took to get there in the first place. Later it would be a Bingo hall, which to my shame I attended with my Mam, later still the "Cosmo Ballroom" attaining a level of success in the hands of Les Leighton never to be locally equalled, so attracting top bands of the day, not least being the mighty Pink Floyd along with solo performers of note.The building was also a Rollerama, then a pub called the Jailhouse, more like dungeon, dark and dingy.

The only pub left in Harraby now is the Arroyo along from Harraby Sec Mod school, which is soon to be flattened to make way for a new Infants/Junior School. I can not believe our school will be no more.

28   CAMP SITE PASSION, AKA DREAM ON.

Randolph and I finally persuaded our the girlfriends, later wives, to join us on a camping trip to the Lakeland Idyll of Keswick.
We arrived the day prior to our tryst to set up camp and let our imaginations rampage through our ever hopefull brains, lust filled we bashed on with gusto, well you know what they say about the male brain being carried low down.
We of course brought two tents, each just large enough for a couple to share body heat and comfort one another through the cold spring night. God loves a trier I always say, I always say and always try, not a great success rate though unfortunately.
When all was complete we were feeling rather famished and turned to the campers favourite culinary delight, baked beans. Of course being well experienced in the outdoor life we had left the tin opener behind, so Randolph set to opening the cans with his trusty bowie type knife, something halfway between a machete and a small sword. God knows where he got it, if he were caught with it today he would be locked up in Durham Prison.
It was at this point in the proceedings a busy little yellow and black beast buzzed into our lives, taking turns to circle around Randolph's head then mine. We were well aware of this little horrors stinging capacity and did not wish to confirm it, so set too trying to clobber the blighter. Yeah, I know, you can see what's coming next and you are right. Swinging my left arm in the general direction of our tormentor my fingers came into sudden and painful contact with Randolph's lethal weapon arriving from the opposite direction. A stunned silence reigned for the next few seconds. My arm still up in the air was the centre of both our attentions. At first there was no blood, just four amazingly white strips of exposed bone, the skin of my fingers being neatly pushed back were hanging from the

fingertips, the joints pale pink in comparison to the bone. It was like looking at one of those skeletons used by medical students, even the sinews were there to see. Then that bitter sweet sensation of panic took us over, as it does.

Wrapping my now somewhat painful hand in a towel we jumped aboard Randolph's jalopy and raced across the campsite back onto the Carlisle road and the nearby Cottage Hospital.

An hour, and twenty or so stitches later we were back.

Several times over the next few hours we peeled back the copious bandaging to check once more that my digits were in fact still there, which of course they always were, generating nervous laughter, relief disguised by bravado.

That night we shared a tent for the company but got little sleep, my fingers ached and the ground felt harder and more uncomfortable than usual. Randolph said the camp site was built on an old rubbish tip and we were convinced we could hear rats running along, brushing against the low tent walls, probably just the wind, but our imagination would not have it, we were camped in a rat invested hole.

The sun rose early thank God and all thoughts of rats went with the shadows, the girls were coming and we had more to look forward to.

That night I tried every trick in the book to gain sympathy and comfort of the nuptial kind but might as well not have bothered , the sleeping bag stayed firmly zipped up and boy proof.

"Mike and kids take on the big one."

29   SMILES ON THE GOLDEN MILE.

Blackpool, the mere word brings memories flooding to mind. Blackpool trips were a great highlight of the year as they were for numerous other communities in the north of England and beyond. We never had much spends but pockets full of expectation.
The excitement started as soon as the morning broke over the day. Quickly dressing in our Sunday best we joined with friends and neighbours making our way to the coach at the end of the street for the adventurous trip over distant Shap Fell to the Fylde Coast, home to Blackpool, the Tower, completed in nineteen eighty four and the pleasure beach, magic !
In the early days we would be hurried along by our Mam's and Aunties eager to visit the Tower ballroom and be entertained by the mighty Wurlitzer organ, played by celebrity musician of the day Reginald Dixon. The dance floor would be packed to overflowing by dedicated ballroom dance fanatics, swirling in a flurry of sequins and taffeta, weaving in and out, often with instant changes of direction to avoid calamitous encounters with like minded charging dervishes.
Pie and peas would be devoured in Woolworth's cafeteria or fish and chips eaten en route along the prom for fear of missing

something. Whatever, they always seemed to taste like nectar of the gods to us kids. One thing that really sticks in my mind is the public bogs just along from the Tower, they were underground and ponged something rotten. What seemed to a six year old lad ,was a never ending line of white cracked and unreachable huge urinals, with an equally long line of men, all heads bowed concentrating on not peeing on their shoes. Dad had to lift me up to pee. Opposite were another long line of brown cubicles with great polished brass locks on the doors. To gain entry for a number two you had to put a penny in the slot. Using these for the very first time I read a legend written on the wall next to the pot, it said.
" Here I sit broken hearted,
Spent my penny and only farted."
Yep, a penny was a penny in those days, you could get a fair bit for one penny, even a shit.
Much time was taken in the selecting of bars of Blackpool rock to take back home as compensation for those not fortunate enough to have made the trip. Novelty items of confection such as plates of bacon and eggs , or babies sugar dummies were always a favourite as they still appear to be today.
After, the obligatory donkey ride along the beach, provided of course that the tide was far enough out. The boys playing the parts of cowboys or knights of the realm, being threatened with instant retribution by the donkey man if they did not behave. Whilst the girls with their dresses tucked into knickers squealed with false terror. The donkeys had clearly seen and heard it all a thousand times before, the expression on those sad faces fixed downward, and the gait never changing an iota.
A stroll along the promenade with its happy encounters of fellow travellers and pals from school, who despite only having parted a few hours ago were treated like long lost cousins with tales of high adventure and daring do.

Dad would make his way along the golden mile from pub to pub with his mates, eventually appearing on the beach to catch some sun with his large white hankie knotted at each corner providing a sun hat to protect his bald spot.

Its very strange looking back, with the exception of the very young, few wore swimming costumes and no bikinis or bare bellies. Most of the women would not even remove their woolie cardigans or even in the case of the older ones even their top coats. Flat caps and tweed jackets being the order of the day for the older men, with the younger chaps daring to roll up their sleeves, a far cry from the accepted virtually nudity of today's trippers.

Kiss me quick hats were as daring as it got, even then ladies risked being judged as harlots, or worse.

The girls in bright summer dresses with their hair piled up in amazing beehive styles, kept in place by lashings of hairspray. The occasional poser in her sun glasses promenading along attracting wolf whistle's and calls of derision from the Teddy boys in their velvet collard, almost knee length bright drape jackets of blue, red or even yellow and skin tight drainpipe trousers with two inch turn ups above thick crepe brothel creepers with brightly coloured laces. The day was a pageant of colour and delight. The Ted's, would chat up the girls convinced, like Peacocks, that they were irresistible, if not then the lass must be a lesbian, or a slag who had seen more cock than the town hall bogs, its not too difficult to be a dickhead when you really try.

To the very young it was a fantasy land full of magic and mystery they never wanted to leave behind. For the older ones it was an escape from workaday drudgery however fleeting, whilst the teenagers imagined staying in this paradise. Working on the Pleasure Beach, day after day of joy, chasing girls, riding like daredevils on the waltzer's, living the dream. Rock and roll will never die.

Blackpool Pleasure beach was the creation of one William G Bean in 1896, before passing into the more than capable hands of the Thompson family in the 1930's to the present day.
The Big Dipper of the fifties and sixties pales into insignificance compared to the Pepsi Max Big One and others such as the Infusion and Revolution. The park is a futuristic paradise, a pleasure dome of the twenty first century. Technology abounds, exciting the senses and thrilling the soul. For the kids or less adventurous many entertainments are available, no one need not have a great time, from getting soaking wet in Valhalla, to the more gentle Eddie Stobart Truck Convoy, or Tetley tea cups.
The many eating places, Hot dogs, Wraps, Pizzas or traditional fish and chips, keep the energy levels at a working pace, the day flies by in a flash of pure adrenalin.
The cleanliness of the Pleasure palace will impress visitors, despite the thousands of thrill seekers the one thing the place lacks is litter, a credit to the housekeeping team.
The days of the Penny Arcade have also moved on, you can still do a two new penny game, with lots to persuade you to part with your lolly, though a pound a go is more the call now. The one thing that remains constant is the fact that in the long run you will not win.
So as long as you accept you are only here for a good time, taking care not to overdo things, you will leave happy, looking forward to the next time. If however you are broke, there is always the beach with its donkeys to admire, a paddle costs nowt, as long as you avoid the tampons and such, however, just to avoid litigation, the beach is much better now after all the inward investment in Blackpool Resort ! It looks brilliant.

Should you ever decide to pass further down the coast to Southport, I thoroughly recommend a stroll or Tram ride to the end of the Modern Pier, there you will definitely find a penny arcade, a real penny arcade were you have to use real old style pennies, sterling, however where you once got 144 pennies to the pound you now only get ten. The memory bank overloads as you see working machines from the forties, fifties and some even earlier. The Graveyard, spooky, the Guillotine, blood and gore, a football game with opposing teams wearing red and blue jumpers knitted by their Mums, what the butler saw, extremely tame by our standards but a real shocker at one time. (some of the women looked a bit like my old Gran.) One arm bandits like the Big Cherry, get three in a row win four pence, and of course the Fortune Teller advising how to find your sweetheart, the Mystical Madam Zasha sitting smiling in her glass case waiting for some coin action.

I paid my well worn penny and this is what she told me.

" I have been keeping an eye on you ever since you came in here, the way you attract so many admiring glances. Its a good job I'm not the jealous type ! Are my legs shapely?, you bet !
Just get me out of here and together we'll light up the town. "

Well, real life was never like that, well not for me any way. Always the gooseberry, the odd one of three or five, either that or trying with all my might to avoid the spotty sister. That's the problem with having a good looking lad as your pal, he pulled the bird, you pulled the ugly duckling. You would be walking five yards ahead of your so called pal and his dreamboat, with your head down, hands jammed tightly in your jacket pockets, pretending to be so cool, while the poor nightmare of a chick walked five yards behind. God we were cruel to one another.

The return home could provide as much fun as the rest of the day.

There would be the coach driver pacing up and down, cursing the late comers. Then setting off along the Golden Mile for a final look at all the razzamatazz we were leaving behind.

Our hearts sinking slowly to our stomachs, passing the Tower with its five hundred and twenty feet rising majestically above us, its many delights of Circus, Ballroom, Theatre and at one time even its own Zoo.

Madam Tussaud's with all the waxwork stars smiling, frozen in time, the odd one actually looking like who it was supposed to be, but not too many. The modern Madam Tussauds is a world away in quality. The ever flashing lights of the penny arcades calling to us to hurry back and spend our measly coppers. " Roll up and play, the machines seem to say."

The pavement would be packed with all those lucky enough to be down for the week or some, a dirty weekend.

The coach would no sooner clear the City limits when the call would go up from some of the men in urgent need to empty bursting bladders of Blackpool ale and, mothers whose charges needed to throw up the candy floss and ice cream churning in their already travel sick tummies. Oh, the happy times we had.

Soon, however the singing would start, all the old favourites, Roll out the barrel, Sally, the pride of our alley, Sing as you go, Let the world go by, everyone knew all the words, lungs bursting, all wanting to be heard. Then the young bucks would take over, with modern songs, like Rock around the clock, Good golly Miss Molly, poor imitations of Little Richard, Jerry Lee and the King, Elvis. Lifelong friendships being sworn and cemented in an alcholic fume laden tears of solemnity.

Young boys and girls claiming the back seats. Passions being fanned by mysterious desires, causing lots of giggling and red faces, innocent young love, often lasting a lifetime being nurtured if not altogether understood.

Before the advent of the mighty M6 motorway cutting sharply through the Lakeland Fells, shortening journey times dramatically, the bus would drag itself slowly and wearily to the summit of Shap, stopping briefly midway at the famous, excitingly named Jungle Café, a truck stop much frequented by tough hard driving men, nursing their heavy laden charges over the steep mountain pass to far destinations both north and south. The cowboys of the English north. Refuelling both physically and mechanically, refreshing souls and machines before the long drag down through the bottle necks of Milnthorpe and Penrith town, then on to the mighty border City of Carlisle and home. Many a runaway six wheeler sped out of control down the steep fell road,
brakes having gave out under the stress, coming to a sudden shattering halt destroying dry stone walls of centuries standing. Finally we would arrive home, most tired out, children now quiet in deep slumber on Mam or Dads safe shoulder.
The rest of us still happy with the buzz of plans to return to the fabulous Fylde coast, scene of our days pleasure still fresh in our minds. Stories for the telling, to be exaggerated time over, raising jealous bile in the throats of those unable to go with us, raising determination to be on that coach next time for sure.

30   THE LIFE BOYS.

Talking about Justice ! when I was about nine years old I joined the Life Boys, the junior version of the Boys Brigade. We had a great time in the Life Boys, almost all of the other members were either in my class at school or came from the immediate area, so everyone knew each other which made bonding and friendship forming that much simpler. We wore a simple uniform which consisted of a navy blue polo necked knitted jumper a metallised gold badge featuring an anchor and rope design, set off with a sailors hat, which bore the legend, "Life Boys." on the ribbon in gold print. We would meet weekly in a hall near St Johns Church where we got up to all kinds of activities, marching drill, learning to tie knots as all good sailor boys should , semaphore, (signalling using flags) plus lots of goodness knows what else.

Each year the Company went camping to St Johns in the Vale near, the village of Threlkeld just outside Keswick, in the Lake District, where we slept in bell tents, feet to pole, twelve boys to a tent. All except the Captain who was of quite some age, or at least looked pretty ancient to us young lads, he slept in a large double ridge tent which contained a huge brass bed with two feather mattresses, these just about filled the tent leaving room for little else. Of the twelve boys in each bell tent one was a senior with responsibility for our general well being, good house keeping etc. Ours unfortunately felt it his duty to send us off to sleep each night with a grisly tale of the horrible happenings on dark windy nights on Blencathras scary summit.

There was the one about a lost Roman legion who had set off to cross the fell on a dark foggy night before disappearing into the grey Lakeland mist never to be seen again, some times the locals would tell you when the moon was full the desperate band could

be seen wandering still on the dark fell top looking for salvation. But, most nights, if you listened carefully you could hear their screams of terror as they trudged endlessly onward to who knows where.
Well, I could definitely hear them, they were passing right by our tent. I would be bursting for a pee but held on till dawn.
The other tale I recall was of a young boys brigade lad of about my age, who also had to get up in the night because he wanted a pee as well but could not wait, pushing aside the canvas he slowly crept from his tent never to return, only to be found later, on the mountain top tied to a make shift cross with rusty barbed wire, his throat slit from ear to ear. No matter how many times they took down his tragic body the next day it would be back up on the lonely hilltop, wrapped in its coils of rusty barbed wire, fresh blood seeping from his throat.

You might guess, but this, my first camp, did not go at all well, being a townie the darkness of the countryside took me by surprise, no street lights to see your way, only moon and starlight.
On the very first night I found myself bursting for a pee and not wanting to venture into the darkness alone cajoled another lad to accompany me to the tented chemical latrines way down the other end of camp. We had just started to relieve ourselves when the tent door was threw open and there stood the old Captain.
" We do not allow boys to cross swords in this camp." he bellowed. We had no idea what that meant but knew we were in bother. The next day as a punishment, my friend of course having duly sobbed for mercy, then grassed me up as the instigator. All the rest of the company went off on some visit or other, I was left on sentry duty with instructions to take good care of the camp. It did not unduly worry me as I always enjoyed my own company and got on with whatever there was to do.

However I was pleasantly surprised when a pal of mine from school turned up at the camp, his name was Harry Aitken and it turned out he was with another troop of Life Boys camped further along the road. He told me that he had some free time and knowing where I was decided to pay a visit. Of course I was quite pleased with this and took him for a quick tour of the camp before adjourning to the marquee for illicit pop and biscuits. We chatted for what seemed quite a while before he said that he had better get back to his own camp for some reason or other. Escorting him to the gate we made our farewells, he thanked me for the biscuits then went on his way. I stood and watched him disappear over the brow waving enthusiastically then returned to our bell tent to read a comic and relax. Eventually the rest of the company returned from the outing. I had barely got to asking my mates where they had been when the voice of the Captain boomed out once more.
" Beckett ! ".
" Yes Sir." I stammered . " Come here boy." he yelled. I swiftly ran to him fearful of what I had done now.
" Mr Beckett." he asked me. " Can you notice anything different about the camp since we left this morning ?",
quickly looking around I replied . " No Sir.".
" Really", he said, looking quite grim. " Then tell me boy, what is that flying from our flag pole ?"
Fluttering in the breeze at the top of the flag pole was a brightly coloured pair of very large old ladies bloomers. Just as bad, where all the troop pennants on the bell tents had been there was now displayed, smaller if not less bright coloured pairs of knickers.
I was doomed, I washed dishes and cleaned up for the rest of the week, the Captain never missing an opportunity to show his dislike of me. I was an outcast, a leper, barely anyone spoke to me. I just wanted to go home. I remember you Harry Aitken, I remember you.

To put the icing on the cake when we eventually arrived back in Carlisle we were dropped off at the Church hall, I asked if I could enter as I was once more bursting for a pee. I do not know if it was just that the Captain did not like me or if he was a genuine miserable old sod, this man, so he claimed, took pride in being a Christian, but he refused to let me pee, some Christian. I ran to the nearest bus stop hoping to get home before disaster struck but my luck was not having it. As I stood there waiting for the big red number thirty to arrive, the warm flow of fresh pee flowed down my leg. The only good thing was no one else was there to witness my final humiliating disgrace.

A few months later I realised that I was just not cut out to be a Life Boy, so threw in my hat and saught pastures new. I joined the Air Cadets, that lasted about a year, no more than that, though I loved the blue serge uniform, I felt really smart in that even if it was a size too small for my rotund form. I even enjoyed the drilling, we would occasionally get to go to the firing range with our point22 rifles, which were easy to fire due to their lack of recoil, that was brilliant. We also got to stand guard of honour for the duke of Edinburgh when he flew out of Kirkbride air Field, he was very nice, down to earth, told us how smart we all were, then shook all of our hands.
Yeah, Phil the Greek is all right.
We even went to Newcastle to see the Air Force planes, some lucky lads got a flight in a Chipmonk trainer, not me, though I did enjoy the day. I do not recall why I left the Air Cadets, but that's me.

31   TALENT SHOW TIME.

 The owner of the local corner shop, opposite Florida Mount, a certain Mr Diamond……(At least I think that was his name, if not blame Geoff Moses who seems to know everyone and said this was his name, so its not my fault if I have it wrong. Sorry Mr Diamond or whatever your name was just in case.). I always believed him to be a French Canadian and to the best of my knowledge only had the one daughter who I seemed to recall was quite spoilt, a situation from which we all benefited because each year on her birthday Mr Er…Diamond ! would hire out Botcherby Hall, a timber framed structure next to Grice's Croft, long since disappeared. This was a completely unheard of extravagance and he gave a huge party to which every kid in the area was invited. The place would be packed. We would all get a fizzy drink plus a sandwich, sausage rolls and cakes. It was brilliant altogether. Mr Diamond would do his level best to entertain us with his jokes, party games and an old wind up record player. Then there would be a talent contest of sorts, Mr Diamond being the only judge whose word was final. The first year of this occasion no one wanted to show themselves up so volunteers were in short supply. After much unsuccessful cajoling he pulled me, being the closest, onto the stage and told me to sing a song. Everyone was shouting and carrying on, some encouraging, some not so much. Always having been a bit of a show off anyway I soon warmed to the task, bursting into a rendition of "Alexander's Ragtime Band ." As usual I soon got carried away and started dancing about the stage doing my Al Jolson impression, I loved it being the centre of attraction, after that one or two were encouraged to perform, some so shy you could hardly hear them, others like me determined to be heard. Needless to say I was adjudged the winner, only right and proper, though I do not remember what or if a prize was awarded,

probably a bar of chocolate or some such.
The next year I was determined to be more organised and along with my pal Alan Wilson, Whacker Wilson's son, contrived a puppet show. Alan's dad was a great bloke who always reminded me of a comic character well known at the time called Whacker Wilson, so that's what he got. Whenever he appeared the local kids would all shout, Hiya Whacker, I think he liked it, at least he always laughed. Anyway he helped us fashion a puppet theatre from what I seem to remember was an old radiogram type thing, it looked good anyway. We either made or begged the puppets, and rehearsed relentlessly so as to be as near perfect as we could. Needless to say we stole the show once more to rapturous applause, for which we were awarded a box of chocolates no less, wow .

I remember we had a dog once, I say once because it did not seem to be about all that long. It was one of your common or garden light beige coloured variety of mongrel, with a long upturned tail, which it wagged incessantly.
Unfortunately the offending tail would get on Mams nerves something rotten, constantly knocking things over and just generally getting in her way. That is until the day some council workmen arrived outside our house, I cannot recall just what they were doing there, but it involved the obligatory hole in the road, with a little tent like structure over it.
After a while Mam made them a cup of tea, as you do and one of the workmen commented on the dog. Well, of course the subject of the offending wagging tail came up in conversation and the workman in question claimed to have the solution to Mams problem. It involved the use of one of dads old razor blades !.
The dog was taken into the tent, quite happily, tail wagging madly, tongue licking all within reach.

Shortly a loud yelp was heard, followed by the dogs painful cries. The workman put the howling wretch of an animal into our front garden. No more wagging its tail, but running in circles trying to lick the absent protrusion, finding only a bloody stump on its rear end. Poor sod, or should that be dog ?
I cannot remember what happened to the dog, or even its name, but he disappeared shortly after, I assume to a new home, or more likely the animal refuge. We were not a family of pet keepers.
It seemed that people believed animals were immune to pain and inflicted all kinds of cruelty upon them, not always intentionally, just through ignorance I suppose. Dogs still have their tails docked today but hopefully a little more thoughtfully and usually by a Vet.

On another occasion my step brother Eric brought home a hedgehog he had come across. I remember it seemed a really big one and crawling with fleas. When Mam came home from work she spotted the flea ridding animal, immediately picking it up in its cardboard box she took it to the outside toilet, flushing it down the pot. As I said, ours was not an animal friendly house.
I dread to think what the R S P C A would have had to say in this politically correct world we now inhabit.
We did eventually get a budgie, complete with cage and stand, but next doors cat came to visit and Joey became lunch.
I expect all these childhood animal traumas had its effect , as we have never had a real pet. We did once offer to look after our granddaughters hamster and still had it a year later, actually being reluctant to let it go home. Renee had become quite attached to it, well there you go.
Renee has a great dislike to cats and dogs who, strangely, are always attracted to her. If we visited anyone you could guarantee within minutes of her sitting down the household pet would be curling up on her lap. Weird !!

32   GRANDMA'S MANGLE

It was often a struggle for me when a small boy, to make her out in the billowing white steam of the wash house, my Mam, with her Mam, also called Sarah, and elder sister, auntie Annie.
The seemingly vast round boiler, fired by a single huge gas ring, bubbling with soap suds like a veritable volcano.
Glistening white of the bed sheets, blindingly bright in the spring sunshine dazzling my infant eyes, hanging out to dry on the clothes line, itself tied from the corner drain pipe to the old apple tree, which groaned when the wind caught the freshly laundered bed linen like a great spinnaker on an ocean going yacht. Straining the line and causing my heart to thump in dread fear for the dear old tree, it's trunk blackened from the many years of exposure to the smoke of dozens of chimneys burning the remnants of it's carbonated ancestors.
Grandma, her cheeks glowing red from the heat of the boiler, veins standing proud on her forehead, pummelling the wash with her three legged pommel horse. Mam straining to turn the wheel of the old cast iron mangle, already as old itself as my Grandma, who to a small lad like looked old enough for sure. Auntie Annie, her hair

rolled into buns like coils of rope on each side of her head, feeding the greedy brute with boiling hot white linen, forcing out the remaining water in order to dry all the more quickly while the weather held and the fresh morning breeze did its job. Good drying days were a bounty sent by the Lord , said Grandma, not to be taken lightly or ignored, but accepted with Gods good grace and treasured…

The council house on Blackwell Road was the family home and, had been for some years, everyone congregated here, aunts, uncles and lots of cousins, plus other people of some mystery, whose relationships I never did fathom out, but who seemed to be a very part of the family. Day and night it seemed a steady flow of folk meandered in and out. Strangely, I recall they all seemed to have heavily nicotine fingers, even the women, through smoking their Woodbine cigarettes, as was the custom of the day. Several were more than not the worse for drink, again an apparently acceptable state of affairs.
I expect that to ," live for the day " really meant something to those with not a great deal to look forward to. Most of the men folk had no work, and again most with the intention of not looking for it either. They never seemed short of the price of a pint though, clearly there were other ways of gaining a little cash, if all else failed the family allowance book was confiscated to underwrite the slacken of the thirst.

It was much bigger than our house, Grandmas, with a toilet and separate bath room upstairs. Three spacious bedrooms and a front parlour. The main living room was larger still with a great roaring fire, the kitchen was twice the size of Botcherby Avenue, though the gardens were much the same, except along with the apple tree was a plum tree, and a sad old pear which had seen better days.

Quite a few folk had fruit trees in their gardens then, not so many now. The grass was kept down, as much by the trampling feet of hoards of kids as anything else. We may have been poor but we could breed.

We kids were not encouraged to enter the parlour, which as well as been reserved for privileged visitors, ie the priest or doctor, etc, was the birthing and dying room.

I was born in there as were many, Gallefors, Becketts and Allens amongst others. My grandma died in there as did many relatives, taken by age, or tuberculosis, many common ailments now treatable and recovery taken for granted.

I remembered Grandma in the dying room, raised up on a bank of pillows. With the bed already being higher than me she looked to be almost touching the ceiling. Waiting there for the angels to collect her, she had great faith and never doubted where she was going . She went to glory on the 5th of May 1958, at sixty years old, surviving Grandad by only five years.

When she was gone, the bed returned to its place in the front bedroom, the parlour back to normal, ready for the next new soul coming into the world or some other poor soul departing it.

I do not have great memory of my Grandma and Grandad, being as I was still very young when they were taken. What I do most vividly recall of Grandad is the white silken scarf he always wore tied in a knot around his neck, flat cap to one side of his head. He reminded me so very much of Pa in the Broons family of Sunday Post fame, as he was so much smaller and thinner than grandma.

I do believe he died a dreadful death, by drinking battery acid, passing on the 4th of July 1953. wheather this was by some kind of terrible accident or deliberate I do not know for sure, but it just seems such a strange sort of accident, one which I know my dad doubted. But then I was not in his shoes so cannot really be in a position to Judge, " let him without sin throw the first stone."

My auntie Elsie, who had married a New Zealander, a soldier over to fight for his Queen, was whisked of to the land of the long white cloud, expecting some sort of sun drenched idyll only to discover that her new home was little more than a shack on a wind blown hillside where the weather just about mirrored the Cumberland fells with its wind and rain she had left behind. Sad to say she contracted Tuberculosis coming home to die in the parlour of her Blackwell road home. I suppose all those parlour windows along the road held there own share of happiness and grief at one time or another.

My auntie Annie was a character, born 19th March 1908, my dad reckoned she had the last rites spoken over by the priest more than any other ten people. I have no doubt she suffered ill health poor women but blimey she apparently knew how to milk it. She was always gifted at crochet and made hundreds of fabulous doily's and children's dresses and the like, but always handed them over to whom she had decided to grace with the words. " Its not very good I know, but you can always use it for a dishcloth." false modesty I suppose, but God help you if she was to discover anyone actually using her gift for any other purpose than that intended.
Crochet work, was a kind of handiwork much practised by ladies to produce a pattern of connected stitches by means of a crochet needle, being a hooked affair requiring a deft hand. The end result to my eye was similar to knitting but much more intricate.
Auntie Annie worked for a good few seasons in hotels on the Isle of Mann. It may not seem all that far away now, but then it was another world giving Annie an air of adventure, staying away for months on end, hard for me to imagine as a young boy, but she must have been something of a free spirit. Anyway by the time I got to know her she was middle aged with a grown up daughter,

who was actually my cousin but was always referred to as auntie Betty. Betty was to marry Derek Gate, a painter and decorator. Derek was very popular, especially when homes needed his skill and talent. They moved into auntie Anne's house at 20 Ridley road, eventually giving birth to Brenda, Derek and Steven. A lovely family, always a ready smile and very welcoming. Later on I stayed with auntie Annie and uncle Brian, her baby brother as everyone called him, despite his being at least thirty years old then. Apparently Brian was by far the youngest of Grannies tribe and she, along with everyone else doted on him. So when Granny was on her death bed she swore Annie to care for him, which she did to the ninth degree until her time was up on the 27th of October 1982. I stayed a couple of times when mam and dad went on holiday and was well looked after, well spoilt really, could do no wrong. I was a bit concerned at first but soon fitted in and was disappointed when the time came to go home to Botcherby.

I had two girl cousins who I was very fond of, the first being Lal Sally, opposed to big Sally who was my Mam, and lal Irene opposed to big Irene being my auntie, mam's sister.
Sally and Irene were Allans, my other three cousins who I hung around with occasionally, Tony, who died young, God bless him, Lorraine and Paul were all Braithwaites. Auntie Irene having married a Royal navy sailor man called John, who my dad approved of greatly, they got on famously. Dad said uncle John, a Petty Officer, was a war hero, not like the Gallefor's, who as you know, he did not have much time for.
John and Irene worked for years at the Rose and Crown pub on Upperby Road before being given their own pub, The Greyhound at Brugh By Sands. Despite their hard work the Grey Hound was not best supported and eventually they had to give it up.

John continued to work in one or two pubs in the City, finally ending up at the Wrestlers Arms on Currock road, just a couple of doors from his own front door, whilst Irene got fixed up at the RAF 14 maintenance unit where she stayed until made redundant several years later.

Irene had what was referred to as a little drink problem by my mam who loved her dearly, as all who knew her did. She died as a result and was sorely missed.

Mam used to tell me when Auntie Irene had visitors, by which I really mean family, she would serve tea in fine china cups, and while everyone else would sup their Darjeeling or whatever she would have cup of Vodka, but always stayed refined with her pinkie held at the correct angle. No one had a bad word to say of her and not so many can claim that.

John died at a grand old age, and never ceased to smile.

They were both very proud of their children, Paul went on to work at the local branch of Marks and Spencer, always regarded as a prestige job. While Lorraine became a district nurse, another well respected position. Tony, up to his sudden death from heart failure, was well known due to his being a local football Referee.

Cousin Sally died as a result of an accidental overdose of painkillers, a cry for help they said, she was still only quite young, another tragedy, being very popular with all she knew. While my cousin Irene is still on the go, married to Dennis, again, always smiling, always cheerful despite having her share of setbacks like everyone else in life.

33   LIFES DARKEST DAY.

By far and away the worst day of our lives was the twenty ninth of June two thousand and four. I was working in the offices of Rentokil Initial in their Chorley branch, doing my normal "planning days" work, getting my appointments for the next week or so sorted and following up queries and resolving outstanding issues, when a telephone call was put through to me. It took me a short while to realise the voice on the other end was in fact my daughter Karen, she mumbled something about her brother Philip then seemed to break down, saying something about I will let the policeman tell you. There was some talk at the other end of the telephone then a mans voice came on identifying himself as constable someone or other, I never did get his name. He started to speak but clearly was having some difficulty. I thought he said that our son Philip had been found dead in his police car, nothing he said after that made any sense to me. I assumed the worst, Philip our eldest son, an armed response Police Officer, must have been involved in a drugs raid or some such and had been murdered.
I went in to a sort of daze simply acknowledging the officer but at the same time not been sure of what I had heard or indeed what to do. I was devastated.
After a while I tried to pull myself together, not very successfully, having great difficulty trying to explain through my uncontrollable tears to those around me my desperate predicament. Eventually understanding dawned. Norman Rossington, a work colleague arranged to drive me as far as the turnoff for Morecambe on the M6 where I was collected by a Cumbria Constabulary traffic division Sergeant who took me the rest of the way home to Carlisle. I was still far from sure just what had occurred.
When I entered my home my wife Renee, daughter Karen and

granddaughter Rachel started to try to explain, but even they were unsure of the exact details of the tragedy that was unfolding.

The following is what occurred, as I later understood it.

" On the 29/06/2004 Philip James Beckett, an armed response officer with the Cumbria Constabulary reported for duty as usual. Arriving at Ulverston Police station, prior to his six o'clock start, he went through the normal procedures, including checking his E-mails, where he discovered that his request for a transfer to his home town of Carlisle had been approved and a job was there waiting for him. He then sent out jocular e-mails to those persons who had sponsored him in a recent charity Golf tournament to pay up.
Those present in Ulverston Police station that dreadful morning, detected nothing strange in Philips manner, everything appearing normal, nothing to draw attention or suspicion….however..

At approximately five fifty five am, Philip went to his police vehicle with the declared intent of preparing it for the coming days duty. A short while later a muffed shot was heard by Philip's partner, who upon investigation discovered Philips body slumped in the police car. The gun safe was open, all four handguns having been removed, all had been unloaded except one which Philip had used to shoot himself through the head. He had even taken the precaution of using the gun safe door as a barrier to prevent the spent round travelling any further, so not harming anyone else in the vicinity.
Despite an investigation conducted by the Welsh Police Constabulary lasting almost two years, no reason was forthcoming to explain Philips actions that day. Health and safety issues were raised and new guidelines put in place. Too late…

Now, over six years later we are no wiser to understanding what really occurred that bright summers morning.

We went down to Philips home in Barrow that same afternoon and stayed overnight in a local B and B. We were allowed to see his forlorn body through a glass viewing window but could not touch or say a proper goodbye to our boy, a truly painful experience.

Philip James Beckett
27/05/1967 to 29/06/2007.
" Proud to serve."

The funeral was a dramatic and devastating affair attracting several hundred mourners to pay their last respects to a brave and gallant Police Officer with more than seventeen years service.

I always believed, and Philip insisted that he was more than happy in the police, always talking of his job with such passion, so when he visited two days before his death and told me he had had enough of the force I did not think it such a drastic statement.
In retrospect he did appear down, but not to the degree to cause me concern, everyone as bad days at work, God knows.
However my guilt will haunt me all my days. I clearly did not pick up the signals he was sending, was I even listening.
His last words as I recall were.
" I do not know what I am doing here."
God forgive me for I cannot.

The year 2010 saw newspaper reports regarding bullying in Philips old unit, an issue which I raised with the Cumbria police force.
An officer from the police complaints dep't, or its modern equivalent did visit me, partly to reassure me that there was no connection between the two occurrences ? But after hearing me out did promise to get back to me after further enquires, that was several months ago now with no further contact yet!!.

34   BIRTHDAY BALLON.

We bought a fortieth birthday balloon, you know the type, filled with helium, we the took it to the end of the pier. There, having tied a fortieth birthday card to it inscribed with our pent up feelings, stained with yet more tears, pointless exercise really but so soul comforting. We then released it into a bright blue sky, watching fascinated we saw it climb a height, moving this way and that as is was caught by the breeze.
Soon it became a speck up in the distant cloudless sky when, taken by a high wind , it turned to head rapidly back over our heads, traversing the town of Scarborough, heading west as though making its way back to Carlisle and home, Philips home.
Later we returned to our holiday caravan having previously bought a large plain sponge cake, which our grandchildren, Bethany and Jack set too, decorating it with icing, smarties, jelly tots and maltesers, it looked wonderful. Our son Michael took photos for the album with us all smiling, then we blew out the candles and sang happy birthday to Philip. The kids, both large and small loved it. He would have laughed to see us being so silly, but happy at the same time sharing our joy celebrating his fortieth birthday.

Our hearts were bursting with sadness, but Renee and I could not cry in front of the children, they do not understand, thank God. So you save your tears for the night, then the next and the next, your broken heart never mends but is just stored away to be brought out and dusted down when next needs must, Christmas, Mothers day, Birthdays, Anniversaries or just any day without reason, they creep up on you, leaving you feeling guilty for letting him slip from your mind. Still life goes on, Philip would be the first to say get over it. Life is for living not grieving. If only it were that simple.

35   BECKFOOT PARADISE.

On summer days we would all decamp to Beckefoot, a tiny hamlet by the sea on the west coast of Cumbria near to Silloth on Solway. While Renee attended to Michael who was still a toddler at this time, Karen, Philip and I would head off to search for sand lizards and such. Sand lizards seemed to thrive at Beckfoot and once you got your eye in they where not to difficult to catch.
At this time the area and beach around Beckfoot was very popular and could get quite crowded, with car parking a problem, but yet all those people sat on their blankets etc, totally unaware of the abundant wildlife that surrounded them.
On one occasion we caught two particularly large examples of sand lizard, which we were loath to release, therefore decided to take them home as pets. Probably quite illegally.
We would spend several hours a day hunting spiders in the hedgerow to keep our pets well fed. It seemed to be very successful as the wee beasties grew and thrived. We were well pleased with our efforts.
Then one day Philip approached our little friends with a suitable selection of spiders, but what he saw was not two fat lizards but two slimmed down mammy lizards with about twenty or more little replica lizards, all as hungry as mum.
Keeping this extended family fed proved too much, even for our dedicated band of collectors. So once more a decision was taken, this time to release them back to where they had come from, the grassy sand dunes of the Solway coast. We still went to Beckfoot, still looked for sand lizards. That was until someone discovered an unexploded mortar shell on the beach, probably from Eskmeals ranges where I was posted for two happy years, further down the coast near to Sellafield, then another was found, then another.

Subsequently that stretch of beach was closed for years after. No matter how hard we looked we never did find another happy hunting ground like the paradise of Beckfoot.

The seaside village of Allonby just along from Beckfoot has got to be the strangest Solway resort, with virtually nothing there other than a less than average beach, a small kids play area and a couple of hotel/pubs. The single ice cream kiosk has a queue extending halfway down the road bringing a huge smile to Tony Twentyman's face, a lovely man whom I met when we were stony broke teenagers fifty years ago in the Cameo ballroom on Botchergate. The fact he had a fabulous flash car did not influence our friendship in any way shape or form, the fact we could get free meals from his friends café, now that definitely had a influence, yes sir. The car was simply his compensation for a life time in Allonby. Ok, so there is a couple of half decent caravan parks, and the Cumbria coastal way passes through the town, but that does not justify the hundreds if not thousands of people who flock there every time the sun bursts through. Ok yes, wind and kite surfers love it due to the ever present coastal wind, and its good for dog walking, but give me a break what's the attraction. The beach is covered in huge pebbles that break your toes and the water is freezing.   Right, so just me then !.

This attraction for Allonby is nothing new, the Victorians and Edwardians loved it as well building several wonderful Villas but you have to seek them out. There is a colonised building on the back street which apparently held a heated swimming pool for the less adventurous, amazing.

The Quaker industrialist Joseph Pease contributed to the construction of a reading room, there is even a small Quaker cemetery. Now that is something I can understand, God botherers looking for seclusion landing in Allonby, but what are the other couple of thousand there for ?.

36   THE DAY I MET MELVYN BRAGG.

It seemed a good idea at the time, a day out at Silloth.
Silloth a Victorian one time must visit holiday town, on the northwest coast of England, bordering the Solway Firth. Now a fall to sleep backwater reserved for day trips on lazy summer days when you cannot be bothered venturing further a field.
In my youth it was a different story, the population of about three thousand trebled in glorious summers with sand dunes and beaches to rival any, we thought we were in heaven.
We were not the only ones to appreciate Silloth's beaches, no lesser a figure than L S Lowry was a lover of the region regularly walking the beautiful sands whilst visiting his friend Geoffrey Bennett manager of the Cleator moor branch of the Westminster Bank. A yet more famous artist, Turner, no less, was most impressed with the sun sets and seascapes which are believed to have been featured in his work. Coincidentally, Lowry's friend Geoffrey Bennett was the vicar of Rockcliffe parish when Renee and I were wed at the church there, he would have officiated but was taken ill and had to cancel, regretfully he died not long after.

My abiding memory of Silloth was one of glorious summer sun, fabulous sand dunes inciting adventure, But not today, today the sun decided to stay tucked up warm beneath its duvet of grey cloud, destined for rain. The wind from the Solway fair cut us in half causing us to abandon our short visit to the local market and car boot sale on what was at one time a Military Airfield used to train both British, Canadian and American pilots flying Hudson bombers. So many ended up in the Solway it became known as Hudson Bay. So instead we headed for the amusement arcade on Silloth green, with its twinkling lights calling the scattering of visitors to come part with their hard earned cash in the one armed robbing machines. Again, when I visited as a boy the green was a hive of activity with donkey rides, Punch and Judy shows, ice cream and candy floss vendors, no longer a viable activity. The green was bare except for the wind blown decoration of crisp packets and old fish and chip wrappers.

This was not a problem for my youngest son Michael and his kids, Bethany and Jack who loved these spots, quite happy to stay and pour in the pennies, I can only assume they get this Gambling bug from my parents who loved a flutter, especially the Gee Gee's.

I am however far too mean to spend my money so frivolously so soon departed stating my intention to brave the elements and take a stroll along the sea front. Upon opening the door facing the sea I almost lost my resolve as the gusting wind attempted to throw me off my feet, but I rallied and headed down the slippery grass slope to the promenade already occupied by a brave few wrapped in winter coats and thick multi coloured woollen scarves.

The grey, almost black sea was being whipped up in white topped waves with tinges of green reflecting the white of the clouds, looking for all the world like Vincent Van Gogh's seascape at Saintes Maries. Of the few daring souls about, my attention was quickly brought to a figure strolling vigorously along the pathway, a spring in his step. Who could that be I wondered. Not one of the common herd, looked different somehow.

Talking about celebrities, I met Melvyn Bragg today, that's right, Lord Bragg of Wigton, and what a nice man, really nice and down to earth, not a pompous bone in his body, chatted away to me as though he had known me all his life.

I told how I admired his writing and envied the talent and creative skill he imbibed, of course I had to say something really stupid, cannot believe this, " I own several of your books, all from the charity shop though as I cannot afford new prices."

What a prat, a right Rodney, God if I had a brain I would be dangerous. He replied graciously how pleased he was that his work was still circulating. Clearly life had taught him how to deal with ardent admirers and the odd lunatic. Shortly after that he went on his way, his hair blowing in the wind, probably wondering which nutter would accost him next.

Any way a couple of days later we went to visit our friend Janet Queen, the gardener and writer / broadcaster. She was most impressed and suggested I send Melvyn a copy of my book, Rainbows End, but I must do so soon while he would still remember me, she said. I was not too sure, but succumbed to the lure of acquiring a famous friend and posted it off with a short letter via his agent whose address I got when I Googled him that night, I was stunned to read that Melvin is seventy years old, he did not look anything like that, life is so unfair.

When I first saw him walking along the sea front, even from a distance it was clear this was someone special, in his camel hair type coat with its dark velvet collar and scarf worn in that chic manner of the confident natty dresser, shoes polished to reflect the odd bright cloud. Not wanting to lose this opportunity I hailed like a long lost friend.

" Hello there, How are you ?.

" I am very well ." he replied moving toward me.

We talked as old friends for a few minutes until my gaffe caused my initial brashness to subside and I brought the conversation to an end as casually as I could, a little despondent because I knew we may never meet again.

My book, as I like to refer to it, is actually a recording of my grief at losing my eldest son Philip to suicide, I cried copiously through painful remorse as any parent would, but writing was my way of dealing with my feelings which I struggled to cope with, however I gained no release from the guilt I felt and still feel to this day, and probably will to the grave.

Any way I did not expect to hear from him any day soon, if at all, so was thrilled when just a few days later the postman knocked me up out of bed with a parcel. I could not look at it straight away as I had left my specs by the bed so just dropped it on the kitchen unit while I opened the blinds and returned upstairs to dress.

When I came back down complete with specs I saw the returns postal address as the BBC Television Centre London.

I quickly tore open the parcel to reveal a book and a further envelope marked, The House of Lords. Nervous with anticipation I opened the letter to find a handwritten note from Melvyn.

Now, I have got to be honest and say that hand writing was without doubt the worst I have ever seen, no joking, it took Renee and I at least an hour to decipher it, we decided it was a form of shorthand Melvyn had developed with his writing, but it was most definitely worth the effort. It basically said,

" I have received your book Rainbows End and read several of the poems which moved me deeply. I lost my first wife to suicide about forty years ago and it is the most terrible thing. I managed much later to write a fictionalised account of the life we led called, "Remember Me." He then continued to wish me well when closing the letter."

The book was signed and dedicated to his friend Terence, a nice touch I thought. What a nice bloke, he has definitely made me a fan for life. I have just started to read the book and am sure I will enjoy it immensely, I will conclude this episode a little later.

So I now have two fellow Authors as friends, Melvyn and Janet, brilliant, never thought it would happen, and both have found my poems worthwhile, well whatever next!!..

Carlisle and surrounding areas seem to produce its fair share of writers, Margaret Foster from Raffles no less, definitely one of my favourite writers, wonderful story teller, her first success, " Charlie Girl " becoming a most wonderful movie. Her husband from over the river Hunter Davies, well I recall his first book, "Here we go round the Mulberry Bush " loosely based, I believe on his pursuit of the lovely Margaret, which also became a major British film.
If you visit the independent book shop next to the Crown and Mitre Hotel, Bookends, you will find a surfeit of local authors covering all aspects of the County and its multitude of Characters. Everything from surviving on a fell side farm to manufacturing Chocolate biscuits. Other notable Carlisle citizens include, Poet Bernard Barton, Artist Samuel Bough, Musician William Best and Historian Mandell Creighton.

My first published article of sorts was a piece printed in the school magazine on our forms visit to Carlisle Castle. Encouraged by my then mentor Mr Omererod, I wrote about Kinmount Willie and the dungeons, the Norman Keep, and the surrender to Bonny Prince Charlie, gaining Carlisle the shame of being named the traitor City by the notorious Duke of Cumberland, the butcher of the Scots.
At that time of our schools visit Carlisle Castle held one of the best collections of ancient armour and weapons in the country which I believe were seconded to the Tower of London no less, to improve the attractiveness to the burgeoning tourist trade. Needless to say I was very proud of my efforts, which did wonders for my self esteem, having been such a slow starter and failing miserably in my eleven plus exam. I had never expected to pass like my sister Brenda had and gone on to the Margaret Sewell high school, mam and dad were rightly very proud of her. I was in awe of her achievement.

Among the successful candidates at Norman Street were Christopher Boyd, well known in Insurance circles, Peter Batey, whose dad had a lemonade factory, making him very popular, and another lad called Thirwell.

Later I wrote several children's stories which were published in Twinkle Magazine, aimed at girls of around seven or eight. Each week I had to produce as near as possible unique story involving Princesses, Knights on white stallions and all manner of hobgoblins, etc. unbelievably difficult, for which I was paid the princely sum of Four pounds a page. The Illustrators working to my descriptions were paid ten times that amount, life's a bitch sometimes, true !!.
This is not something I usually boast about too often it being so girly. Since then virtually no success at all, still God loves a trier, or so my Mam said !.

In September two thousand and three Renee and I were sitting, well lounging really, on Maspalomas beach in Grand Canaria, well known for its fantastic sand dunes reminiscent of the great Sahara desert, where most of the sand was blown from in the first place by tropical storms and such. It was pure bliss. Most of the folk there were of the naturist persuasion, with it all hanging out, so not wanting to be the odd ones out we participated. You get a remarkable sense of freedom when you discard your clothes, especially when caressed by lovely sunshine, cooled comfortably by caressing Atlantic winds, but of course the sand gets everywhere and yes I do mean everywhere, cracks and creases, no hiding place. Bliss, total bliss.
As I lay there, with the sun blazing down warming my cockles, I became aware of just how lucky I really was, turning to Renee I said.

" We really, really have been so lucky, we have not had a bad life, our kids are all grown up and off our hands, two happily married sons and one daughter fairly happily divorced, eight lovely grandchildren", smiling contentedly I continued. " Our kids have never got into drugs, been to jail, or even been in trouble of any real meaning. Not like some of our friends, sons dead from overdoses, others in and out of nick for one thing or another, daughters with a tribe of waifs and no idea who their dads are. Yeah, we have been really lucky that way."
I picked up the factor twenty and gave my nether regions a going over, you cannot be too careful with those delicate little areas. Fate was clearly lending an ear for that was the last time you would hear me say anything like that, I can tell you.

The following January, new years day in fact, Michael arrived at our door, not full of the new year spirit, but full of distress, he had just been told by his wife she did not want to be with him anymore as she had a new love in her life, what kind of person does that to someone at that time? He did what he felt was the right thing by her and the kids he adored and moved out, with the promise she would not move in her new man without telling him first, needless to say this did not happen, his feeling's clearly not counting for much and the cuckoo was in at the first opportunity like a rat up a drainpipe. Michael was completely distraught for months, But, however give him his due he has made every effort to get on with his life, having bought himself a new home he has the kids every weekend which he loves and looks forward to immensely. He is the very model of everything a good father should be, putting the welfare and happiness of his children above all else and they in return love him for it.

We have been on holiday with him several times due to his concerns over something happening to him, and the kids being on their own. Fate of course proved him right when he went off to haven with the kids, we followed on next day only to find him laid up with food poisoning from eating shellfish of some kind bought from a sea front stall. He was really very poorly having had the camp doctor attend to him. He lost three days from his holiday but we all had a great time, so that's all right then. life's a bitch.

37   I HAD A DREAM.

I had a dream of going to Paris to write a novel, smoking French fags, getting legless on cheap vin rouge in some spiders web bound attic in the quarter Montmarte. Strolling the west bank on balmy Autumn days. Mingling with the artists at their easels seeking the inspiration to produce the masterpiece to make their name and enter them in to the Lourve, tourists peering over their shoulders, "They may not be connoisseur's, but they know what they like." Students debating the outrage of the day, plotting rebellion against the traitors in power. Bring back Madam Guillotine.
Paul McCartney and John Lennon had a similar idea, seeking musical inspiration but instead lazed about on the west bank smoking camel shit and eyeing up the birds, eventually heading back to the "pool" starving and non the wiser.
Good old Les Dawson too had dreams of authorship, living in Paris until poverty also drove him home to Lancashire and fame of a totally different sort.. At least they give it a go where as I only got to Paris as a day tripper with my ticket to ride, well a weekend really, staying at the local Ibis hotel in the Picasso district a good twenty to thirty minute metro ride from Paris proper. I loved travelling the Metro because of all the characters on board, buskers jumping on and off at each stop, doing their two minute attempt at performing before rattling their plastic cup of coins in everyone's face seeking donations accepting the odd Centime. Some, not many were really entertaining whilst others were just high on drink or other strange substances. There always seemed to be a surfeit of Chinese looking girls who stared worryingly at Renee's finger's loaded as they were with rings, souvenirs of various anniversaries. I kept having visions of ringless bloody stumps.

Two days was just not anywhere near long enough for even a cursory visit to the French capital, we saw virtually nothing. By the time we had done the Tower, Notre Dame, the river boat tour, and all the other obvious things, we missed the Louvre , originally a Palace becoming a museum in the late century,(Must go back), and other great centres of art and culture. I had turned into tourist without realising the metamorphosis.

Because we had very little actual cash we virtually survived on Macdonald's milkshakes, quite nourishing really and wonderfully cool in the beautiful sunshine of gay Paree !.

The reputation of French cuisine was totally wasted on us barbarians, though we did have a very nice Chinese! on our first night, though I do not have a clue what else we ate, should be ashamed really.

We came close to death crossing the road to the Arc De Triumph, along with several other idiots who, like we, did not see the signs for the underpass. How the tarmac was not awash with fresh blood escapes me. We did a couple of pavement cafes, enjoyed the sartorial elegance but begrudged the price for a tiny teacup of black sludge and a caramel biscuit. The waiters were clearly aware of our lack of sophistication, putting on their best scowls to show it. The only tip they got was to look both ways before crossing the road. But, after all that I would go back tomorrow, I loved it, the history, the splendour of the buildings, the colour, just marvellous. It is easy to see the attraction of its exuberance.

We sought refuge in a small park to rest our feet. With glorious sunshine beating down upon us we sat by what seemed an aluminium statue of Ex President Pompidour , all shiny in the light of day. We lay on the grass soaking up the rays when we were rudely poked in the ribs with a big baton by a Gendarme and told to move on.

" You must not sit on the grass." he scowled.
I thought only Carlisle Parkies were little Hitlers. People would tell me the French were a miserable lot and I would take it with a pinch of salt, because I really believe all people are ok once you take the time to get to know them a little, but dear me, some folk seem hell bent on putting me to the test. We called into a Tabac to buy a stamp for our obligatory postcard home and you would have thought were trying to steal his wallet, surly does not do it.
After all we must go back some day. But with a little more time and cash. Having read " A year in Provence" more than once, plus Peter Mayles follow up tomes, the south of that country sounds wonderful.

38   EASTER AND HERE COMES THE TALLYMAN.

It is Easter time again bringing with it memories of lovely warm spring days, when mam would put herself into hock so as to dress us up in our finery, not to be dressed for Easter was almost sinful. This came courtesy of Mr Frame, aka the tally man, who lived in a nice three bed semi on Warwick Road. Yet another man dad could not stand.

Credit drapery to give it its real name was a common source of ready cash in the fifties and sixties and beyond. You would be giving what was essentially a short term loan, enough to cover any out of the ordinary needs, like dressing the kids for Easter, or Christmas presents, which would then be repaid weekly to the tally man, so named because he kept a tally of what was owed. As the loan reduced the Tally man would bring with him certain items to tempt mam into renewing her debt, ie, bed linen, a shirt for dad, shoes for us kids. Mr Frame was the devil tempting mam's innocents.

Everyone dressed for Easter, nice new clothes, short trouser suits with shirts still bearing the crease marks from where they had been neatly folded in the boxes they came in, pinned down as though it was feared they may escape, smart tie, worn not without protest at being strangled, all spick and span. I loved the smell of the new clothes, made me feel special. The girls in bright new flowery dresses, with bows and ribbons. Some with Easter bonnets, all feathers and beads. We were fortunate in that we got to keep our new clothes, but for some they were in the pawn shop window by the next week.

We would call on all the neighbours who would tell us how lovely we all looked and then give us a treat, paste egg and a orange, or if we were really lucky some chocolate and three pence or even sixpence for the fair.

All the relatives had to be visited which meant the long trek to Currock and Grandmas house, then around to various aunts and uncles spread out over Upperby and the brand new estate of Harraby, no car, no bus all on foot. It meant a long day but I seem to recall the sun always shone down on us, so we all enjoyed it, returning home laden with goodies and a pocket full of coppers to go to Slater's fun fair on Easter Monday .
That night we would all sleep like logs to awake bright and early Monday, driving mam mad with our constant question. " Is it time to go to the fairground yet mam"?, we must have drove her to the edge of dementia.
A better mother there never was, always putting herself last, working all hours, scrimping and saving to give her children the best she could. She never let us down, nor spent a harsh word. Mam left us broken hearted on the 6th January 1995 at 76 years of age, having been born on the 16th of April 1919.

The fair was an amazing place for us naïve gullible kids, loud brash bright modern music, all the current hits blaring out, hundreds of flashing, mesmerising, multicoloured lights raising our euphoria to a crescendo. Barkers urging us all on to hurry up and spend our cash. As though we needed encouragement.
" Three darts for a penny, could be your lucky day, one bulls eye wins the prize, come on and win a goldfish", and boy did we want to win a goldfish.
God know how many of those poor goldfish survived to see the next day or even the journey home in their tiny plastic bags gripped tight in small sweaty hands, swinging to and fro. Those that did survive the trek must have been in a daze for weeks after.
On the Dodgems, the Carousel, and Waltzer's among many others, we were spoilt for choice, terrified and thrilled at the same time, some parting with the contents of their stomachs, ice cream, candy

floss, roasted nuts, all the stuff we hardly ever saw for the rest of the year and feasted on when opportunity arrived.

The day would pass in a whirl of excitement and wonder, never wanting to end, laughter and tears in succession, followed by the joy of new delights, we were in heaven. The crowd buzzed along on a wave of expectation, young girls and boys eyeing each other, fancy taking fancy, many a romance exploded into life only to die tragically in the grey light of dawn when dad found out and put an end to it. You are far too young for that sort of thing my girl, so that's that !!. Others not so lucky, feeling the painful result of a nights passion when nine months later motherhood dawned and not even knowing the fathers name, then a real disaster for a young girl and her family, shameful disgrace. Some like acorns grew and went on to lasting relationships, even marriage and kids of their own to take to the fair one fine April day.

Then before we knew it we were back to being broke again.

All our precious wealth spent in the rash moment of pure pleasure. The walk home was always an anticlimax compared to the high excitement of the day. Everyone talking at once of the thrills and disappointments experienced, but all desperate for next year and Easter time to call again, it was brilliant.

Summer days spent beneath blue bell skies.

At least it was for us kids, mother was still paying the tally man six months later, settling up just in time to start the debt again to pay for Christmas.

One thing you can say for our mam she never let us down, working permanent nights at the Railway station refreshment rooms, provided for holidays, birthdays and all the other annual events that made up for a happy life for us kids.

With mam working for British Rail she was entitled to some free rail travel and once took a trip to London for a day with some of her work mates. Whilst there she visited Petticoat Lane, a renown London street market, on the go since Tudor times and formerly known as Middlesex Street, which is forever associated with the activities of the legend of Jack the Ripper. Petticoat Lane was somewhere she had always wanted to go so an ambition was achieved. I can still see the presents she brought back for us, despite probably having little spare cash for herself. It was a fountain pen and propelling pencil set in a holding case. It was far too grand for a little dunce like me, but I loved and cherished it for years, until it disappeared as usual into the mists of time. I remain convinced in the existence of black holes which swallow up our relics of times past, another of life's mysteries.

Also around this time I attended an exhibition in the covered market hall, I remember it for two reasons , one was a television showing coloured pictures, long before such became commonplace, and the other was a little dark haired man with a big grin sitting at a small green baize table doing card tricks and offering for sale similar packs of trick cards, sharing his amazing magic knowledge, at a price all could afford whilst claiming,
" You will like this, but not a lot." you are right it was the one and only Paul Daniels, still awaiting fame to catch him up. But of the charming Debbie McGee there was no sign.

39   MORE SUPER HEROES.

We all need heroes from time to time, well I certainly do.
My first hero was Jesus Christ. Far from being a religious nut, in fact having very little faith at all, I still do not doubt the existence of Jesus of Nazareth, but as a man, not a Devine being or son of some God or other. A man with a real mission to improve the lot of his fellow Jews. For despite what we are supposed to accept the fact is Jesus was a Jew and did not wish to be anything else but a good Jew. Christianity was the invention of others who followed him, though not all with any Divine intent.
Next on my list of heroes comes Dr Ernesto "Che" Guevara. who I discovered while serving with the Kings Own Royal Border Regiment in British Guiana in South America. The first peoples freedom fighter of the modern age, a true warrior, who having earned his spurs and worldwide fame in the Cuban revolution, spent some time in the government of that land then went on to try to conquer new lands before being murdered by agents of the CIA in Bolivia. My final hero was the late great John Lennon. Lennon undoubtedly had feet of clay along with his psychological problems believed to be tied to the early loss of his mother plus other trauma. Many blamed his marriage to Yoko Ono for his troubles, when she in fact seemed to be his true soul mate, and at least for some time stimulated his creativity. His death at the age of just forty robbed the world of an undoubted talent that would have gone on producing for many years to come. It appears heroes are just not built to last.
Talking of heroes, whilst working for the commercial department at Carlisle United football club I met on a virtual day to day basis two more local heroes. Peter Beardsley and the legend that is Bob Stokoe,

goal keeper and record holder for most league appearances, four hundred and sixty six. The one and only Alan Ross had just left his post with the commercial dep't, so I missed working with him. Everyone knows Peter went on to greatness with Liverpool and England, but not everyone will know he was bought by Carlisle United from Gateshead boys club for little more than the cost of a team strip, what a deal. Peter was undoubtedly one of Carlisle best ever players, along with post war record top scorer Hughie Macalmoyle and England striker Stan Bowles.

The crowed loved Peter and even when Carlisle eventually sold him to Vancouver Whitecaps of all people, for around three quarters of a million pounds part of the deal included his return to Carlisle during that clubs Close season. Say what you like but Stokoe was a shrewd manager.

Bob Stokoe was a legend not only in Carlisle but in Sunderland also where he won the F A cup as underdogs, beating the mighty Leeds as they were then , one nil.

My boss at the club was another legend of sorts the one and only Colin Hutchinson, the commercial manager who introduced the first lottery in the county and made the club a lot of money on the strength of its novelty value.

He had me towing a golden galleon, made of sheet metal by Bendall's engineering, one of the then Chairman's companies, around the county visiting all the local events such as the world renown Grasmere sports, Skelton show , Penrith, and the Cumberland shows, Silloth harness racing among many others, where my wife Renee and I sold thousands of lottery tickets. We did not do so bad either, being paid ten per cent of sales we worked the crowd and made a few bob thank you very much.

I also recruited agents as far away as Morecambe. Plus I sold stadium and programme advertising.

Colin was in the fore front of sport commercialisation, moving on to the likes of Chelsea FC, becoming managing director. He was a clever bloke, but when he first arrived in Carlisle he smoked like the proverbial chimney, sixty or more a day. A visit to his office reduced your eyes to tears with the smoke, you could barley see across the room. Amazingly he stopped without a problem sometime later, probably added years to his life. I liked Colin he was alright.

Since I mentioned Colin I have read in the main stream press of him being described as the voice of reason to Ken Bates gruff bonhomie. Ever the politician our Colin.

Whilst I loved working for the club I could not say the same for some of the people there and soon left them to it. Football is like show business attracting more than its fair share of ego maniacs.

Other jobs I held down, not counting five years military Service included, store detective, dog handler, cook, ring pull can top maker at the Metal box Factory, double glazing salesman, assistant manager in a men's clothing store, contract cleaning manager, and Chemical rep. The last twenty five years or so were spent at Initial Textile Services, with a great bunch of lads including, Phil Fiddler, Terry Turnbull, Alan " Aye Aye" Davidson, Davy "Cat" Graham, "Dangerous" Brian Armstrong and the late Terry Geddes, plus many more fabulous characters. At one point in my life I was changing jobs every couple of months or so. Most sales jobs were based on commission only so you kept changing depending who was paying the highest commission rate. This varied between twenty and twenty five percent, plus various bonuses or inducements. Because of the no sale no pay regime bribery and corruption thrived with many a council employee allegedly accepting the odd brown envelope or gift. Regretfully an awful lot of them became unemployed as more stringent security was introduced, those who escaped prosecution that is.

After the sinking of the oil tanker The Torrey Canyon off the Cornish coast all harbour masters, dock owners etc were obliged to stock a minimum quantity of a chemical Oil Slick Dispersant, (OSD) in case of accidents creating problems for wildlife, tourism and such. This caused a stampede of reps to the doors of the prospective buyers with cash they were obliged to spend.
An old school friend of mine, being more forward and fearless than most walked into the office of a major Government dockyard and putting a brand new colour television in a plain brown cardboard box on the purchasing officers desk, most folk still viewing in black and white, then blatantly asked him what else he wanted and would be supplied that very day in exchange for the relevant order number, which was soon forthcoming. He asked for a stereo system he had seen in a well known high street store and received it a little over an hour later. The resulting commission received amounted to the equivalent of almost a years pay to most people.
He who dares wins, well for a while anyway.
My friend runs his own company now and has done for some years, I often wonder if any of his trusted employees are screwing him over as he did so many others. I did work for him as a sales manager for a while, but ended up having a major fall out that went to court, due to a balls up by his so called lawyer it cost him a packet, but I was not complaining.
I was not really cut out for commission only sales, instead of giving the sob story, i was all too often on the receiving end, just too nice I suppose…

While working for Border Guard dogs I was assigned an Alsatian Bitch called Rusty and we took to each other straight away, she loved me and I her. No one was allowed to come any where near me without she went into an attack mode, snarling and growling, unfortunately she did not a have tooth in her mouth due to some canine calamity, so could do no real harm, but she put up such a show no one dared to put her to the test. The down side for me was that due to her lack of dental care she could not chew her food gulping it down en masse, then shortly after giving out with the most outrageous burps and farts which in an enclosed space like a security cabin were just overpowering, causing me to rapidly vacate leaving her looking sad and mystified as to what was happening.

However she was a great comfort on cold black dark nights wandering around some factory or other where the windblown rustle of an old crisp packet was enough to make you jump out of your skin. We never did catch any thieves or trespassers, but I am not complaining. Once a chicken always a chicken.

Some of the dogs were a bit more difficult to handle and the occasional incident allegedly occurred which I will not go into for fear of litigation. Apart from the poor pay in what was in the main a good job for me having little or no supervision and being left to get on with it, which most of us did quite diligently.

40   ROSE CASTLE DAYS.

Renee and I decided to sell our Carlisle home and use the cash raised by putting a lump sum aside for each of the kids, so as to enjoy life.
A small rented cottage in the country was to be the ideal. So we put our house on the market and set to looking for our Idyll. We had only looked at two properties, the first, a small barn conversion that sounded brilliant but in fact was dreadful.
The second prospect, "Chauffeurs Cottage" was in the grounds of Rose Castle, the Palace of the Bishops of Carlisle for the last six hundred years. Renee immediately fell in love with the cottage and we moved in soon after courtesy of Niece Alison's horse box.
Sixty six Bishops had taken residence here and our front door was only ten or so metres from the entrance to the accommodation of Graham and Mollie Dow's , the then current Lord Bishop and his wife. Wow!!.
They had been in residence for the last nine years and were due to retire the following April, 2009, which they duly did.
We got to know them quite well, though never quite attained buddy status. I wrote a poem about him which was published in the Cumberland news.

Janet Queen was, to my great shame ,unknown to me before our time at Rose castle. Though not to Renee and her sister Dorothy, who, like many in the Borders, were both aware, and in awe of, Janet's local celebrity status through her weekly gardening column in the Cumberland newspaper, Cumbria Magazine and advice sessions on BBC Radio Cumbria. However This was quickly redressed, I became an immediate fan having first come under the spell of her charming welcoming nature. Janet with the sometimes assistance of her husband, the one and only mighty Jim Waugh, himself a great character, looked after the grounds of Rose Castle, and had done for seven years or more. I say the sometimes assistance of Jim because they also own a home in the lovely Italian Tuscan hills, in which Jim spends many months of the year renovating with his skills as a woodsman and talent in masonry. He also keeps the garden there in check from the invasion of weeds and saplings, being so close as it is to the Chestnut coated hills of that region of Italy with its wild boar, still hunted there, not being the least of his problems, often raiding his vegetable garden when food in the forest was scarce. All this was truly worth while when the local wine could be purchased by taking your own bottle to the nearby vineyard and refilling for the equivalence of a few pence. Plus Jim was taken under the arm of several local ladies who ensured he did not starve, providing sustenance in the form of Tuscan fare. He in return became one of the community offering his dexterity with the chain saw and forestry knowledge, a great asset in a land where the chestnut tree provided so much to the local economy. Janet would visit Tuscany at Christmas for several weeks, plus again during the summer months when dining in local restaurants provided welcome fare. Though you could not always be sure just what was to arrive on your table, with on one occasion blackbird's forming the main dish, needless to say Jim could not resist giving it a try, much to

Janet's annoyance.

As I said earlier Sixty six Bishops had made Rose Castle the seat of the Bishops of Carlisle, but the new incumbent, Bishop Harland, whether he had any influence on the decision or not, declined to continue the association on the grounds of economy. No doubt his hand was forced by the church council, but the slight was deeply felt by the Christian community, especially in the surrounding villages who took immense pride in their association with Rose Castle and its history. Having felt the wrath of Scots, Roundheads and Border Reiver's, being burn down several times in the process, even Hitler made his presence felt when the Bishops abandoned the Castle to its fate as a storage depot for the mighty RAF. To be reclaimed after WW11 came to its conclusion.

However, there were always those ready to rebuild and revive, breathing new life into its red sandstone walls.

Janet was a good friend to Renee and I, always available for good gardening advice as well as a chat to put the world to rights.

She was kept busy by always being around to guide and advise visiting groups, such has the many women's institutes and others. Often she would visit such associations in return to give illustrated talks on both horticulture and the history of Rose Castle. Often followed by a suitable rendition on the violin of which Janet was also a great exponent. She published "A Dairy of a Bishop's Garden." in two thousand and nine which was immensely informative and sold well. Comparing as it did with the efforts of the 45th Bishop William Nicholson who in the 1700 hundreds imported many diverse plants from the Royal botanical gardens in Edinburgh, a list of which is included in her book.

The other reason I have for being grateful to Janet was the unfaltering encouragement she gave me to write, reading my efforts always positive and supportive.

We enjoyed our time at Rose Castle , despite the freezing cold

rooms and mouldy walls, which being townies we were not used to. No double glazing being the greatest miss, the oil fired central heating so inefficient as to be worthless. The open fire in the living room was a God send on long cold wintry evenings, though the many holes in our rugs from the sparking logs were not so welcome. One time I banked up the fire for a cosy night in, only to receive our one and only ever telephone call from the Bishop, a mere twenty metres away, who quite calmly and regally informed me that our chimney was on fire, inquiring, were we alright.
He had his three sons and their families staying at the time and all were assembled at the various windows, clearly entertained by the sight of our pyrotechnic chimney pot, The panic over, I went to his door to thank him for the timely warning , but he was then distracted by the sight of our television set which he could see through our kitchen window and was showing a football match, featuring Man City, his team apparently, he quickly withdrew back into his home, calling the family together to watch the match. Some supporter, not even knowing they were playing.
The gardeners cottage next door was much worse, though eventually modernised to an extent, with the addition of a wood burning stove and improved heating system, the difference being amazing. However Janet, though slightly built and thin as a twig, was tough as they come seeming to take no harm, or at least being a Highland Scot would never admit to it. We tidied up our part of the garden which was part of the tenancy deal, slashing and burning the overgrown shrubs and beech hedges. This was the type of gardening that I loved, ripping out eyesores and starting anew. The wild roses adorning the back of the house looked amazing if somewhat bedraggled, however Renee soon worked her magic on them with her secateurs, bringing back some form and encouraging new healthy growth. We must have shifted fifty barrow loads of discarded growth altogether, my knees felt like the

world was ending. The result was well worth it though, the conifers trimmed, shrubs pruned to a more acceptable state and new plants added. The next year it all looked grand, just as it should.
We would be visited several times daily by the two peahens and the ancient peacock, no one knew just how old he actually was , he just seemed to have lasted forever having being found and saved from certain death by Jim and Janet after being struck by a car on a nearby road. Defying his age he still chased the girls with his magnificent show of dazzling tail feathers, however when he caught up them he often appeared not to know what to do next. He caused great amusement, leaping on the back of the peahens with amorous intention, only to fall off the other side landing in a heap looking bemused. Comes to us all I am told.! The poor lad was to be taken by a fox a year or so later when age prevented him from taking to one of the many old trees to safety for the night. Nature will out.

After feeding the peahens the guinea fowl would come clucking along wanting their share. The whereabouts of these ladies was never a mystery, their chatter being heard for some distance, always our favourite of the birds was two toes, always lagging behind due to having lost part of his foot after become entangled in a strawberry net, by the time Janet found him part of his leg was beyond saving and was summarily removed by the local vet.
This did not deter him and he thrived for several more years before succumbing to old age, bless him. He is probably up there in guinea fowl heaven as we speak, clucking his head off, demanding someone feed him.
There were also three geese to be looked after, though they were more pets then anything else. They had to be locked away each night to foil the prowling fox, who did eventually succeed in taken

one of the peahens, caught nesting under a tree in the orchard, a daft place to be for sure, but they are not famous for their brains, poor lass.

Next door to the Castle was Rose Castle Farm, run by Stephen and Helen Hetherington, with there three children, (Now four with the arrival of Adam after our departure), a story book farming family if ever there was one. Their main source of income being their dairy herd of well over one hundred milkers, with the obligatory pony called Chester, or as my great grandson Bailey insisted on calling it Chester Zoo, a one time visit, having clearly being imprinted on his brain. A few chickens roamed the grounds, along with Jess the lovely border collie farm dog, who insisted on sleeping in the byre and smelt like it too. All subsidised by Helens Bed and Breakfast business, with visitors returning year after year to experience the ambience of true country life. The family is absorbed in the local community and church, well respected and loved.

Below the Castle runs the river Caldew, a much frequented riverbank walk in all seasons, mostly regardless of weather. However I did not see much evidence of fishermen along its banks, possibly due to the licence restrictions, though I would have expected it to be quite popular.

Castle bridge straddles the river at this point, an old and revered structure. The view of the Castle from the river bank is well worth seeing, with a cairn erected by the local historical society giving a brief resume of the Castle's colourful history.

The orchard at Rose Castle produced a prodigious amount of fruit, apples, pears, plums and even quince. Regretfully the greater amount of this bounty would lay rotting on the ground. The birds could only account for so much of ripe fruit.
The Bishop, his family and the Castle staff harvested so much, as did the locals such as Renee and I, along with Helen and her family from Castle farm. On the odd occasion some one would arrive and collect windfalls for cider making etc. Janet would brew Damson Gin as well as baking and freezing pies ,etc. I preferred to make crumbles with loads of butter and Demerara sugar, again freezing the excess for treats on cold winter evenings.
The strawberries never lasted long, with the kids, but I did get my share of gooseberries. Some of the bushes not being in the most obvious or accessible places, so the fruit could ripen to its best.
The remains of a long out of use fish pond is situated by the driveway into the Castle grounds, its stock of coarse fish long ago consumed by some distant Bishop or other.
The castle was once virtually self sufficient, with even oranges and a grape vine growing abundantly in a lean to conservatory type building running along the back of both gardeners and chauffeurs cottages, which then were the bakery and laundry, with substantial cellars for storage. There must have been a fleet of gardeners, maids, cooks and cleaners. Rose in its heyday must have been a glorious sight to behold. Some have rallied to its cause, local landowners, politicians ,celebrities, etc. with a friends of Rose Castle web site being established. However the future looks bleak.

Now the future is more uncertain for Rose than it has ever been, almost certain to be sold off probably to some developer to turn into luxury flats, or possibly a Russian billionaire seeking his own chunk of history.
However there is a concerted effort afoot to save Rose Castle for the local community, orchestrated by Jane Hasell-McCosh of Dalemain House and the friends of Rose Castle. I have already gone into the prospects of Rose, so we will have to wait and see just what occurs.

After twelve months with no sign of our house selling due to the credit crunch, we had to admit defeat and move back to Warnell Drive. Still here two years later.
Anybody want to by a nice semi detached ?.

41   WEDDING BELLS OVER EDEN.

Saturday the fourth of April dawned blue and fair.
The church of St Mary's in the English border village of Rockcliffe, built in eighteen forty eight on raised ground overlooking the river Eden which in turn meanders its way slowly along to the Solway Firth, both waters renown for excellent salmon and sea trout. The churchyard boasted the remains of a one thousand year old Norse cross.
The splendid old church with its many stained glass windows illuminating the interior, looked like the ideal spot for a wedding. Which was good seeing as that very thing was about to occur.
The blushing bride was Renee Buntin ,the dashing groom, well that was me. I was three weeks short of my twentieth birthday, Renee just three weeks short of her eighteenth. A virtual child bride, beautiful as a fairytale Princess.
We had been courting over two years by now and always knew we were destined to be together, still are ,over forty seven years on.
We should have taken our vows in front of the then local Vicar, Geoffrey Bennett, best friend and confidante of world famous artist, L S Lowry, but fate stepped in and the reverend Bennett took ill. Shame really, lost a claim to fame there. Give the man his due he did seek us out later to apologise and wish us well. He did not last very much longer poor man.
Apparently he had joined the church after a life in finance, finally becoming manager of the local bank in Cleator Moor, where he was often visited by his close friend Lowry, who not only painted Geoffrey's bank, the Nat West, but many scenes around West Cumberland with whom he appeared to have an affinity, especially the port of Maryport, of which he produced several paintings of

note. Several of these hung in the vicarage in Rockliffe. Wish he had given me one, worth millions now.
Apparently Vicar Geoffrey Bennett also thought himself a bit of an artist and on one occasion when Lowry had left a Sheila Fell landscape painting in his friends care, Bennett decided the scene would be improved by the addition of a few cows in the background and duly painted them in. When the painting eventually was returned to Fell she was not at all amused.

Lowry of course was also a great friend of Sheila Fell who he took under his wing. The young lady from Aspatria found fame as a painter of Cumbrian scenes, in and around her native town. Sadly as with many others of artistic bent she died young. The result of a fall down stairs I believe. But in true artistic manner, the fact no more of her work is forthcoming has done wonders for the value of those she left behind.

Right then.. Back to the wedding of the year in Cargo village.
The day went well, with family and friends attending in numbers and doing us proud all dressed in their finery, ladies in bright floral dresses, topped off with the obligatory flower laden floppy hat.
The lads in their Burton's or John Collier made to measure suits, hankies in top pockets, some with matching ties as were in vogue at that time.
The best man was of course my best mate Geoff Moses, the one and only, who insisted on trying to kid me that the wedding was off and Renee had changed her mined, the first time he tried it my heart did jump, but you cannot have a face like Geoff's and expect to get away with a lie. A non smoker, non drinking, honest as the day is long all round good guy, unless you know different of course. (If so let me know.)
My other best pal, Randolph tried the old, best mans lost the ring

gag, now he could be believable, and made me panic for a minute, what a sod.

True to our luck the wedding photos taken by the man from the Border press Agency on Lonsdale street were lost a short while later in a fire. So we had to scurry around our guests to obtain copy photos taken by them, fortunately Renee's brother Richard and my mate Randolph were keen amateur snappers so we managed a good album full, probably as good as any you could expect.

When Renee did eventually arrive in the church she looked radiant and worth waiting for, in traditional white she looked a picture strolling along the aisle on her fathers arm.

The brides maids were Renee's twin sister Audrey and best friend Dorothy Little, girlfriend off my mate Randolph, eventually also to marry and be together until Randolph's sad demise from Leukaemia forty five years later. He left behind two lovely daughters, Carol and Wendy with grandson Luke.

The third Bridesmaid was my little sister Susan, wearing the same red velvet gown she had worn at my other sister Brenda's wedding two years earlier, she looked lovely and we still have her photo on our wall. The service went off without a hitch, other than me getting cramp when we had to kneel for the blessing, the price being clearly displayed on the label on the soles of my shoes. At least I did not have " help" on them like some lads.

We had the reception at the Coop restaurant on Botchergate, a very nice happy affair. The manager at the Coop, whose name escapes me was a true gent. In those days if you got married before the fourth of Aril you got back the tax you had paid that year, hence so many early April weddings, he agreed to wait until I received my rebate to pay for the do, eventually getting his invoice settled sometime in June. I cannot imagine any caterers agreeing to a deal like that today.

The speeches all went off well, Geoff read his out from notes written for him by his Mam I suspect, causing suitable embarrassment all round of course. I tried to be confident and suave during my speech, thanking both sets of parents for their involvement, (sadly, Renee's mam had died a few years earlier), and help in making it such a grand day, but had no chance, being the subject of all kinds of jokes and innuendo, ducking to avoid the odd bread roll winging my way.
Mine and Renee's dad's made brief appearances quickly moving on to the toast's of sweet sherry. As they say on these occasions, a great time was had by all.

"The Bride"
4th April 1964

"The Bride"
4th April 2011.
Still Beautiful.

Later we had an evening dance in Cargo village hall organised again by Renee's twin sister Audrey and her mates, who did a great job for which we were both very grateful.
A local band kept the party going, with plenty food and drink supplied by guest's at the hall, like many, those days had no liquor licence. However that did not deter anyone from having a ball, you cannot get a better do than a right royal country rave up and rave up we did. We might not have had much cash but we knew how to enjoy ourselves. The hall was an old wooden construction which swayed with the music. I do not think it lasted very long after that. Eventually Renee's dad Wilf, drove us home to our rented rooms at number nine Victoria Road, a lovely house owned by a sweet old lady, who moved out for the night knowing we were not going

away on honeymoon. Most discreet.

Wilf dumped a bag of coal round the back, no doubt nicked from the CAD where he was a stoker, and gave me a ten bob note as a wedding present. Generous to a fault was old Wilf. However to give him his due he was always there when needed with his handyman skills and was not adverse to lending out the odd few bob when you were stuck. He went to the great boiler room in the sky on the 14th May 1982, at the age of 74, being born on the 27th November 1908 the same year as my prior mentioned Auntie Annie.

While I was away in the forces Renee stayed for a while with her big sister, Dorothy Wall, on Mayfield Avenue, it was while she was there that our daughter Karen was born, I do not know who was most excited me or Dorothy. I was given a nice compassionate posting at Carlisle recruiting office so to be home for the birth. Those days Dads were forbidden access to the maternity Hospital except for two hours of visiting a day, by the time Philip arrived just two years later, it had all changed and dads were expected not only to be there but to help out. When second son Michael turned up I virtually delivered him myself, the young Chinese nurse with me was completely panic stricken, before we could do anything he was laying on the bed howling his little lungs out.

It was five years later when we came out of the Army that my parents bought our present from them, a new bed. Considering all we had in the world when we moved into our first council house at ninety five Briar Bank was an old double mattress, a washing machine, a spin dryer and two cots for the kids, the bed was most welcome. The Army supplied all your needs when taking over married quarters, right from the basic furniture such as beds and three piece sweet, down to knives forks and spoons, you wanted for nothing. So when demob came around it was all to buy, or in our case beg steal and borrow.

We were lucky in so much as we qualified quickly for a council house due to our military service which bumped us up the queue quite a bit. We were given a nice semi, 95 Briar Bank, where we lived for several years. With Saint Augustine's Catholic club at the end of the road we were not stuck for entertainment, many a good night spent there, that is until some bloke decided to grope Renee's bum, I was barred for thumping him. For a third time I was unjustly dealt with. Life's not fair, have you noticed that as well ? We moved into our current home thirty six years ago with the declared intention of staying six months then moving into the country, still here still talking of the country, though to be fair we did move to Rose Castle for a year as I said earlier, hoping to sell our property, but that did not work due to the credit crunch so we are right back where we started from.

42   BOTCHERBY REFRESHED.

The red bricked houses from a distance look much the same as they did in the nineteen fifties, except many have since passed into private owner ship via the council sell off schemes allowing tenant's after a certain time to purchase their homes, an option taken up by a good percentage. This and the various housing associations efforts to modernise and upgrade properties, has clearly had the affect of encouraging home owners and tenants alike to show off the pride they have always had in the Estate. Driving along Botcherby Avenue recently I could not help but be struck by excellent improvements put in place there. The community spirit is alive and well just as it always was.

Additions to the area such has Eden park Crescent, built while I was still a lad, and Broad Oaks Grange a later construction are both now well established.

The Community Centre set in the old Schoolhouse at the bottom of Victoria Road has been refurbished to an excellent standard, adding to the sense of well being in the area. The services and activities provided causes the mind to boggle, do you want to learn Italian, or perhaps how to paint in oils, what about keeping fit, with Pilate's, (What's Pilate's ?), While the kids are at the youth club Mam and Dad can get into line dancing or play Bingo. (Now Bingo I understand), wow, I tell you, if you want to try it Botcherby Community Centre probably do it. Give them a call on 01228 596992.

FRESH, (Botcherby Health living Initiative) offer advice and practical help on such modern problems as a Healthy lifestyle, Drink and Drugs awareness, Weight management , I need that one. They offer cookery courses among many other useful life improving activities, their Telephone number, 01228210016. Good luck.

Saint Josephs Nunnery, home to the Little Sisters of the poor, a place of great Spirituality and prayer, became for a number of years a care home for the local elderly, remaining a source of compassion and love. I used to visit as part of my duties with Rentokil Initial and always found the atmosphere so buoyant. Many of the residents knowing me from my Botcherby days, they may have been getting on but were sharp as tacks, reminding me of past misdemeanours, occasioning my face to redden up. Eventually closing I believe due to the huge cost of overheads in maintaining such a large grand old building. The heating bill alone must have been colossal.

The Edifice itself was destroyed by fire, the work of a local arsonist, who having failed to complete the job first time came back to finish it, an act that not only took away a large chunk of Botcherby's character, the building containing many fine features of both religious and architectural importance, but lost him his freedom by getting himself put in jail. Good enough for him too. Again this site is now home to the residential houses of St Joseph's Gardens, with Willow Park covering the orchard, much loved and raided by us lads, all in a lovely setting.

The Premier Inn, Lakeland Gate Hotel and restaurant on Walk Mill field suffered a similar fate before it even got a chance to open its doors to the public. Being of part wood construction it went up like a roman candle, then if that were not bad enough a few years down the line it was a major victim of the floods, along with the newly constructed homes on Walk Mill Crescent. Many of us were amazed to see this estate being built on the old Walk Mill site, which for many years previously would flood every spring causing us lads much joy, building rafts from old bed frames and such to go sailing on the temporary lake it provided.

Feddon's Market Gardens along from the Nunnery are now more new build, called St Josephs Court on Victoria road.

At the bottom of Wood Street remains the beautiful little Church of St Andrew, built circa 1870, where I and all my friends gathered for Sunday School with Father Peppin, who would make all those stories of Jesus and the Apostles come to life, you felt the lord Jesus in your heart, a warm comfy feeling, that left us feeling all guilty for being naughty, but not usually for too long. He spoke so quietly, causing us to creep forward to hear because we did not want to miss a single word. Had it been left to this man the entire world would have been converted, becoming a far better peaceful place.

I keep referring to him as Father Peppin because that's what we all heard, he was such a quite spoken man I have never been sure my memory is not playing a trick on me.

All those names I try to find in the blackness of my mind.

Fr. Richard John Oakley being the current Parish Priest, takes services every Monday at nine o'clock. The church is bounded on each side by what is now Church Farm, formerly the site of the afore mentioned Border Dairy, with the indomitable Mrs Robertson, St Andrews close on the other, also new to Wood street is Brampton Orchard, private houses built on what was Bells farmyard.

Otherwise apart from the modern feel to the place, especially the bottom where the clay pits no longer exist, with the lane to Scotby three field, site of many a lovers tryst, gone.

Grices Croft , now under Sinclair Court, the only reminder of its very existence the old sign on the derelict petrol station next to the bus stop and that looks ready to fall down.
The old Coop building on Durranhill road stands empty, its service to the community as a source of household provisions since 1933 no longer required, having been a car parts whole sale outlet among others it now needs some TLC. Any offers ? Just along the way, Florida stores, one of the few reminders of old botch, still doing business, supplying a service to the folk nearby.
Florida mount, standing on the brow of the hill, keeping Durranhill and Victoria roads apart, is a bit of the original Botcherby, with two or three of the old retail outlets now residential units, it still boasts a Church Charity Op Shop, Bakery, Chungs Chinese take away, with the ever present Post Office on the opposite corner, and a " Simply food and drink " store opposite.

Botcherby will still be here and going strong in another hundred years, some will still be singing its praises, some wishing never to have seen the bloody place. These streets have seen it all, war and peace, joy and tears, families grown and moved on others moved in to start over, the horror of drug dependency, the ecstasy of love found, the despair of love lost. A mini world of its own, saints and sinners side by side, Coronation Street and Enders together have nothing on the Botch…Well I for one loved it.

43   WYWURRY

Still why worry, Wywurry is the name of a small secluded caravan site in north Sussex, not far from Great Yarmouth, perched on the edge of cliffs plummeting down to the North sea. Renee and I intended staying only the one night as it was late and we could not find anywhere else to stay at such short notice.
However as these things have a habit of doing, the peace and serenity captured us and we were still there a week later not wanting to go home . We promised our selves a quick return, now twenty years later we still have that promise to keep. Why is it we do these things, find somewhere wonderful, then shove it to the darkness of our minds and never return. Perhaps we are frightened of not rediscovering the joy once known, fearful of desperate disappointment. They do say you should never go back, I wonder does that apply to the place of your childhood.
But it is still a great name, Wywurry, ah the memory.

Author relaxing in the orchard at Rose Castle.

Author with wife Renee in State Room at Rose.

THE END
(For now.)

Printed in Great Britain
by Amazon.co.uk, Ltd.,
Marston Gate.